NETROOTS
ONLINE PROGRESSIVES AND THE TRANSFORMATION OF AMERICAN POLITICS

MATTHEW R. KERBEL

Paradigm Publishers

Boulder • London

Paradigm Publishers is committed to preserving ancient forests and natural resources. We elected to print this title on 30% post consumer recycled paper, processed chlorine free. As a result, for this printing, we have saved:

4 Trees (40' tall and 6-8" diameter)
1,399 Gallons of Wastewater
3 million BTU's of Total Energy
180 Pounds of Solid Waste
337 Pounds of Greenhouse Gases

Paradigm Publishers made this paper choice because our printer, Thomson-Shore, Inc., is a member of Green Press Initiative, a nonprofit program dedicated to supporting authors, publishers, and suppliers in their efforts to reduce their use of fiber obtained from endangered forests.

For more information, visit www.greenpressinitiative.org

Environmental impact estimates were made using the Environmental Defense Paper Calculator. For more information visit: www.papercalculator.org.

Copyright © 2009 by Paradigm Publishers

Published in the United States by Paradigm Publishers, 3360 Mitchell Lane, Suite E, Boulder, Colorado 80301 USA.

Paradigm Publishers is the trade name of Birkenkamp & Company, LLC, Dean Birkenkamp, President and Publisher.

Library of Congress Cataloging-in-Publication Data

Kerbel, Matthew Robert, 1958–
    Netroots : online progressives and the transformation of American politics
/ Matthew R. Kerbel.
        p. cm. — (Media and power)
    Includes bibliographical references and index.
    ISBN 978-1-59451-494-4 (hardcover : alk. paper) — ISBN 978-1-59451-495-1
(pbk. : alk. paper)
    1. Political participation—Technological innovations—United States. 2. Blogs—Political
aspects—United States. 3. Internet—Political aspects—United States. 4. United States—
Politics and government—2001–
I. Title.
    JK1764.K47 2009
    320.973—dc22

                                                                                2008055633

Printed and bound in the United States of America on acid-free paper that meets the standards of the American National Standard for Permanence of Paper for Printed Library Materials.

Designed and Typeset by Straight Creek Bookmakers.

13 12 11 10 09   1 2 3 4 5

To the countless ordinary people who are idealistic enough to believe and smart enough to know that the only way to salvage democracy is to engage it.

Contents

Boxes and Tables

Preface and Acknowledgments

In 1999, I published a book called *Remote and Controlled* about how television was damaging our national discourse and undermining our collective sense of political well-being. An entertainment medium by nature, television, I contended, was ill-suited to the task of informing us about and engaging us in politics. Television shows are staged events; they're fake. And while politics has always been part spectacle, television emphasizes the show at the expense of everything else. It invites us to passively and uncritically share its obsessive attention to the strategies and tactics of political campaigning, to media events designed to sway our emotions, to the use and manipulation of symbols and images offered up for our amusement. And it hypnotically insists that its pictures and words wash over us as we stare motionless from a comfortable chair, passively absorbing the message that politicians are disingenuous, that they're all alike, that the political system isn't worth our time or effort. No wonder so many people were cynical about the political process during the television age.

When I shared the manuscript with my editor, she told me that all this was fine, but I hadn't ended the book with a solution to the problem. I was at a loss. I told her that I didn't see a solution to the problem, or at least I didn't see a realistic one. Others who had written on this subject and wrestled with similar problems had tried to offer solutions, and while I appreciated their efforts as well-meaning, I simply didn't see how we were going to diminish the pivotal role television played in American life at the end of the millennium. Suggestions about strengthening political parties at the expense of television, developing standards to require journalists to behave more responsibly, or somehow kindling a new participatory spark in a video-addled culture, no matter how thoughtful or creative, were not likely to happen. And I couldn't come up with anything better.

My editor was not convinced. If I wanted people to wade through 50,000 words detailing how bad things are, I couldn't leave them in despair. I had to at least offer a semblance of hope.

So I gave it a shot. In my classroom, I invite my students to look at television as an unnatural entity, as something that slices and chops reality into an edited product that seductively looks like real life but is in fact nothing of the sort. What if, I wondered, others could begin to look at television in this way? They could become knowledgeable consumers of political messages, and that might diminish television's more detrimental effects. Imagine if people started talking back to their televisions! I had no idea how this would come to pass, but I liked the sentiment and believed it to have merit. So that's how I ended my book, with a plea for education. It was the best I could do at the time.

Several years later, I noticed something strange. People on primitive websites were beginning to express their views about politics to no one in particular through something called weblogs. Their numbers were small and the technology was rudimentary, but they were out there and they were behaving in ways that television never inspired people to act. Our political dramas had turned unsettled with the Clinton impeachment and the stalemated 2000 election, then dark and foreboding following the terrorist attacks of 2001 and the subsequent invasions of Afghanistan and Iraq, turning the page on the complacency of the 1990s. And here was this emerging medium giving those with the means to afford a computer and Internet access a way to express outrage or enthusiasm for what was happening in the political world. That hadn't been happening before.

So I began to wonder: Could computers be the antitelevision? Could it be that technology and the way people used it might supply an innovative solution to the dilemma that I was unable to address in a realistic way several years before?

It was difficult to know. All sorts of predictions were being made about what the Internet would produce. It was going to revolutionize the world and change the way we relate to each other. Or it was an overblown fad, a latter-day hula hoop that would have its moment and then inevitably recede into the distance. In truth, no one knew what was going to happen because no one could predict how the technology would evolve. But I couldn't shake the thought of those ordinary people expressing themselves online for no reason other than they wanted to and they could.

I went back to my editor with the idea for what would become this book. At the time—because she couldn't see the future either—she said it was too soon: no one would know what to make of a book about the Internet. And her instincts were correct. In the intervening five years, as the technology continued its steep march up the growth curve, weblogs have moved into the mainstream and a movement has developed among those on the digitally connected left. By 2006, they were claiming their share of success for the strong performance of Democrats in that year's midterm elections, as they pushed to reshape national politics in their image. Had I not waited, I would have missed the start of what could be a profound change in national politics, spearheaded by the emergence of this new technology.

Suddenly, there was a lot to study, and there were a lot of important questions to ask. Why, after lagging behind conservatives in their Internet presence, had progressives emerged as the dominant online force? What are their goals and how effective have they been at achieving them? Are they simply talking to each other, as some would have it, or are they having an influence beyond an insular virtual world? Can we find any clues from history about the likely effects of new technology on political regimes and political power that might provide insight on where Internet politics may lead? Is lasting political change in the cards?

And what of the personal and interpersonal effects of being connected online? As the Internet helps turn ordinary people into activists, it appears to be doing what television could not. People may still be firmly planted in their chairs, but with a keyboard instead of a remote under their fingers their orientation toward politics seems radically different as they engage and seek results rather than self-medicate with moving pictures.

This book attempts to provide an understanding of the loosely affiliated groups that collectively call themselves the progressive netroots: who they are, what they hope to accomplish, what they've done so far, and how likely it is they will succeed in a plan so audacious it would result, if realized, in the transformation of America from a television-focused center-right nation to an Internet-focused center-left nation. Their means and motives are often inaccurately portrayed in the mainstream press, either for a lack of understanding on the part of established journalists or because established journalists are among their targets. They have been portrayed as politically naïve, ineffectual dreamers and inconsequential gadflies, and as zealous lefties out of touch with mainstream thinking. But these characterizations miss their mark and serve to trivialize a group that is steadily gaining in influence. Mainstream actors misrepresent them at their own peril.

What follows, then, is an effort to understand and place in historical context the progressive blogosphere, perhaps the least understood important political elite in American politics today, as well as an attempt to finally write a satisfying conclusion to my previous book about television politics and cynicism. I am privileged to have had Jennifer Knerr as my editor for both projects, as her insights and pitch-perfect instincts, now as in the past, make me a better writer than I could be on my own. I am equally grateful for the editorial guidance of David Paletz, whose work in political communication I have long admired and respected. And I am indebted to the individuals who took the time to review this manuscript prior to its publication.

This is my seventh book project, the seventh time I have permitted impossible deadlines and the ever-present threat of writer's block to interrupt the more subdued rhythms of everyday life. My wife, Adrienne, has been along for the ride on all seven, my daughter, Gabrielle, for five, and their patience, support, love, and understanding are as much a part of this work as anything I contributed.

My two research assistants, Andrew Bausch and Noura Korbage, made developing this book manageable and writing it enjoyable. Joel Bloom, my coauthor on earlier work, helped launch my interest in Internet politics and was an important source of inspiration for this book.

I am particularly grateful to Chris Bowers, whose support and assistance manifested itself in countless ways, from helping me understand the goals of the progressive blogosphere to assisting me in reaching out to other bloggers to providing one of the central analytical frameworks for this book. Chris is a blogger/scholar, an effective practitioner with the heart of an academic who is interested both in building a movement and understanding its effects. I doubt I could have written this book without him.

And I am deeply indebted to and appreciative of the bloggers who took the time to provide me with feedback on their goals and objectives as well as their perceptions of their effectiveness. I thank them all for their contributions and hope I have done justice to their voices. They constitute a new, emerging political class, a twenty-first-century twist on grassroots political elites who have arisen at other times in our history when politics was becoming untethered from mass political opinion. Whether or not you agree with their platform, they are replenishing democratic discourse by providing that element so badly lacking for so long: they care, and they engage. For their system-affirming efforts, this book is dedicated to them.

Matthew R. Kerbel
Wayne, Pennsylvania

1

The Emerging Era of Internet Politics

First, let me say that I really enjoy blogging.... I love linking to smart work by others, something you just can't do in a print column. But the smart stuff is being drowned out by a fierce, bullying, often witless tone of intolerance that has overtaken the left-wing sector of the blogosphere. Anyone who doesn't move in lockstep with the most extreme voices is savaged and ridiculed—especially people like me who often agree with the liberal position but sometimes disagree and are therefore considered traitorously unreliable.

—Joe Klein, Time.com, June 6, 2007

There is a big cohort of passionate, smart, politically savvy activists—people who know how to organize, raise money, communicate and effectively utilize technology and new media—who have come into politics within the last decade who feel like their strategies have been effective but their voices are not being heard. If these voices are ignored by the Democratic establishment, we could lose not only all the resources they bring to the Democratic Party, but could well lose the opening we have for a long-term Democratic majority.

To my friends on the inside: listen—really listen—to what the outsiders are saying. Take the message seriously. Engage in conversation, even if it gets really tough at times. You don't have to agree with everything said, you don't have to march in lockstep. But if you don't engage, in a really serious and thoughtful way, there will be hell to pay as our party breaks apart.

—Mike Lux, Open Left, September 14, 2007

The narrative goes something like this: the liberal wing of the Democratic Party, in the form of immoderate bloggers lacking in political sophistication, threaten sober, long-standing professionals in their own party in a grand battle over the party's ideological direction. If the bloggers win, it will come at the expense of the party's viability because the liberals threaten to push the Democratic Party out of the political mainstream. In this telling of the story, bloggers are characterized as naïve extremists engaged in an ideological struggle with temperate Beltway insiders. They are portrayed as a monolithic lot of young upstarts whose lack of political experience leads them to foolishly demand that experienced pros relinquish the all-important ideological middle ground to an out-of-step liberal agenda.

The problem with this story, though, is that it is fiction. There is a battle raging between Internet activists and establishment Democrats, but it is a battle over power, not ideology. There is no ideological orthodoxy online, with progressive activists and the candidates they promote holding a range of views on the issues of our day. Many in the online progressive movement are savvy and sophisticated. What unites them is a common interest in altering the way politics is done in this country by challenging the Democratic Party elite—officials, consultants, and monied patrons—for the purpose of establishing a progressive majority that would deviate in its philosophical principles from the dominant conservative philosophy of the past two generations *and* Democratic Party regulars who acquiesce to and benefit from that status quo. And the path to *that* objective runs directly through the mainstream media—vehicles like Joe Klein's *Time* magazine—whom they regard as enablers of traditional political arrangements through a flawed but powerful conventional wisdom machine.

Their efforts did not subside after the 2008 election, even as they felt a sense of vindication after years of wandering in the wilderness. Indeed, in the hours following Barack Obama's election, Internet progressives were hard at work trying to define his victory as a progressive mandate in light of mainstream media narratives to the contrary. Despite Obama's sweeping victory, progressive bloggers and online activists still work to overthrow what they regard as a bankrupt political process built around interest group money, high-priced consultants, shrill television ads, and insider journalists trading in conventional wisdom and gossip, and to replace it with a small-*d* democratic system built around small-dollar public contributions, outside-the-Beltway consultants, Internet discourse, and citizen bloggers working to promote a new progressive politics that cannot easily be pigeonholed by the left-right dichotomy of the prevailing political era.

That's a pretty tall order. But they have a new medium to help bring it about. And new media are well suited to power struggles such as this, because they hold the potential to upend traditional methods of communicating, organizing, mobilizing, and engaging citizens—once someone comes along and figures out how to use them. That's the key: to figure out, be it through luck, hard work, or simple trial and error, how to tap the Internet to bring about new political outcomes. History suggests it can take a long time before the mysteries of a new medium are fully revealed. But—through skill and serendipity—progressives have had a head start over conservatives, and they are showing signs of progress.

* * *

In the pages that follow, we will explore a host of interrelated questions about online progressives in order to understand who they are, what they hope to achieve, how well they are doing, and how likely they are to accomplish their goals. Theirs is not the first political movement to try to transform politics, nor are they the first to have access to a new technology to help them in their efforts. What can we learn from history about how other political figures utilized other technological innovations, and what can we learn about how other technological innovations factored into political transformations?

If, like some past transformational figures and movements, progressives are well positioned to use technology to facilitate their ends, what is it about the Internet that dovetails so well with progressive goals and objectives? Why is the left better situated than the right to benefit from online politics? How did a progressive movement emerge online, and how is that movement structured to take full advantage of what the Internet offers activists?

The Internet is still an emerging medium, and many people are either not online or are online but not involved with political websites. In contrast, our society is saturated in television pictures. How, then, can this more limited medium compete with its older and more pervasive cousin? How can progressives credibly challenge the dominance of a political system built around the ten-ton gorilla that is television with websites that get a fraction of the exposure?

It should come as no surprise that progressive activists strongly opposed the Bush administration and its policies. But why are they at odds with offline Democrats who ostensibly are their brethren? If the two groups are in a battle over power, then what is the origin of their dispute, and how is it likely to play out? Likewise, why does the online left express such disdain for mainstream reporters, even those who are self-described liberals? How does the battle between Internet progressives and mainstream journalists factor into their battle with the Democratic Party establishment?

What would it mean for online progressives to realize their objectives? Their self-stated goals are political, journalistic, and social. Politically they aspire to find, support, and elect progressive candidates locally and nationally under the Democratic Party label for the purpose of making the Democratic Party a genuine progressive party and making a newly progressive Democratic Party the majority party nationwide. Journalistically they pose a frontal challenge to the traditional reporting model built on the values of objectivity and balance, asserting that the story lines produced in this fashion undermine progressive objectives while opposing them with the partisan, citizen-driven discussions found on progressive weblogs. Socially they advocate a politics of inclusiveness to replace what they regard as the divisive, alienating politics of the television age, believing that the communities they have built online can serve as a model for a new, less cynical era. How well are they doing as they push each of these objectives? What evidence can we find to demonstrate the effectiveness of this budding progressive movement, and how can that evidence be interpreted?

As we seek answers to these questions, we will come to discover that the progressive movement is well positioned to achieve some of its goals; indeed, when evaluated on its own terms it is already remarkably successful. It sits perched at a moment in history symbolized by Obama's historic victory that, like other transformational moments, invites the possibility of rapid and lasting change, but as in the past whether and how much they succeed depends on how well they understand and can exploit the political situation, their place in it, and the advantages offered by the technology that gives them the upper hand.

Specifically, we will discover the following things:

Technology facilitates political change—eventually. One thing we will find is that technology tends to exist for a while before being brought to bear on consequential political changes. New technology does not guarantee political change. Rather, people first have to figure out how to use it, and that takes time. So it was that inexpensive printing technology emerged long before it was put to effective political use by Andrew Jackson, who consolidated his political base by developing a network of cheap party newspapers to facilitate the construction of the first mass political party. The telegraph was not a new invention when Abraham Lincoln put it to use as a vehicle for strong presidential governance during the Civil War. Commercial radio broadcasts predated Franklin Roosevelt's presidency by a dozen years and three administrations, but FDR was the first president to use radio effectively to shape public opinion. Television factored into every campaign and administration since 1952, but it took a comeback by Richard Nixon in 1968 to demonstrate its full political potential.

So it is with the Internet, which by virtue of its relative newness remains a puzzle to many who use it. Just as the first practitioners of radio regarded it as a wireless telegraph and the first practitioners of television viewed it as radio with pictures, early incarnations of the Internet resembled television with a keyboard. Then came the exhilarating, promising, ultimately unsuccessful efforts of Howard Dean's presidential campaign and, four years later, Barack Obama's state-of-the-art Internet operation. As political actors inevitably unpack the potential of the new medium, the most sophisticated mastery of online politics has emerged on the political left.

The power of the Internet rests with the ability to understand and use its decentralized structure. Early political websites may have resembled television, but the Internet is built around an entirely different architecture. Television is a centralizing medium; a billion people will use it simultaneously to watch the Super Bowl. The Internet works in reverse: take any group of n Internet users and they will access close to n different websites.

This characteristic of decentralization permits all manner of interaction. So a social networking site like Facebook or MySpace permits people to link to a web of friends, who have a web of friends, who have a web of friends, and so forth, with each friendship pair free to exchange comments, pictures, programs, and the like, creating countless possibilities for collaboration. In such an open environment, individuals who engage in a common endeavor—be it stamp collecting or political movement-building—will find their efforts reinforced and even improved by the contributions of others. The more complex the endeavor, the more likely people will gravitate to roles they feel they are particularly capable of fulfilling, and over time the sum total of their efforts will be a robust stamp collection or political movement, or whatever they set out to achieve.

The open source model of development, which we will discuss in Chapter 3, suggests that the Internet, unlike other closed media, is ideally suited to this form of collaboration, and indeed it is the only way to take full advantage of what the Internet has to offer. *Open source* describes how the progressive blogosphere goes about performing its three most important functions: mobilizing for political action, reporting news, and community building. It refers to a process where many minds collaborating freely will produce a more effective product than a few people laboring alone, or put another way, a large group of amateurs can achieve more robust results than a small, isolated group of experts. The key is for people to have access to the project and the freedom to contribute as they wish. In politics, this can be tricky. Traditional politics is about centralized command and control. Internet politics, to be effective, needs to be about access and empowerment.

The left is better situated than the right to take advantage of open source Internet politics. Progressives (as today's liberals prefer to be called) as well as conservatives have weblogs, and initially web traffic on the right far exceeded its counterpart on the left. But in the early years of the twenty-first century this started to change, then change dramatically. The reason has to do with how the two sides, or blogospheres, are structured. The right blogosphere is more vertically organized, meaning that web content tends to reflect and amplify the messaging of companion conservative voices expressed in other media; more important, its high-traffic weblogs generally do not facilitate user interaction. The left blogosphere is more horizontally organized, meaning content tends to encourage a multiplicity of voices and horizontal links to other blogs and affiliated progressive online institutions. The result is a platform for creating an online community that frequently spills over to political action in the physical world. This outcome is as much a product of accident and necessity than design, but by taking advantage of the open source capabilities of the web progressives have positioned themselves to dominate politics during the Internet era.

The progressive blogosphere is neither particularly ideological nor extremist. Contrary to the popular image of bloggers as dirty hippies in pajamas, the Internet left is not populated by pacifist Berkeley dropouts still arguing over the merits of Lyndon Johnson's escalation of the Vietnam War. Although any large, amorphous group will include a range of temperaments and backgrounds, these are serious people—serious enough to spend their time building a political and social movement rather than succumbing to the lure of lighter pursuits. Although most of these bloggers self-identify as progressives, there is no litmus for participation in the progressive blogosphere, and they do not adhere to a fixed agenda. Disputes will arise over the best means to achieve a host of policy and political objectives, over what the Democratic Party should stand for, and over candidate preferences in primary campaigns.

Although antiwar sentiment is pronounced, progressive bloggers will be quick to point out that most Americans share their position—and they'll back up the claim with statistics. It is true that progressive bloggers were ahead of the public opinion curve in their views on Iraq, and they can be loud and sometimes rude in the way they express preferences, which is most likely why they are easily dismissed as being off to the extreme. Although they do vehemently want Democrats to end the Iraq War, even when the war was popular the purpose of the progressive blogosphere was not to demand orthodoxy on any one position but to build a movement aimed at achieving lasting power in the Democratic Party by uniting grassroots progressives in common cause via the Internet. The term *netroots* describes this movement of Internet grassroots activists.

The netroots are an elite movement. We are used to thinking of the media in mass terms, because this is the language of radio and television. But the organization that has developed on the Internet, though open to anyone, formed around a tiny subset of those *n* sites that make up the larger web. Although the exact number of people engaged in progressive politics at any given time is undefined, those who choose to participate are self-selected, self-motivated, self-styled activists, small in comparison to, say, the number of people who attend all major league baseball games in a given summer or the audience for *American Idol.* This sets the netroots apart from mass movements, even though they seek to bring about mass political change.

As an elite, their objective is to effect change from the inside, to challenge or replace prevailing political elites with those who share their values about how the political system should operate. Because their objectives are not ideologically driven, this would entail changing the way politics is conducted more than it would entail implementing a specific agenda, although progressive policies, broadly speaking, are assumed to follow from progressive processes. The netroots elite would rebuild politics in their image to reflect the open source nature of the blogosphere. They seek to build links among candidates, officials, and voters to establish a politics of engagement that would lead to effective representation.

The Internet does not need to penetrate society in order to be a politically influential vehicle. Netroots activists do not have to be large in number to have a large influence; the Internet is their megaphone, and the freedom to collaborate multiplies the force and effect of their individual voices. This enables them to be effective even though the Internet is still a maturing medium that has yet to saturate homes like television. Significantly, it does preclude the participation of those who, for reasons of income or geography, do not have high-speed Internet access, but it does not undermine the ability of those who are connected to press an agenda. Open source politics has created an outlet for new voices to influence the political process that would not have been heard in the days of television politics.

Netroots activists oppose the Democratic establishment as strongly as they opposed the Bush administration. Even in the wake of Obama's election, progressive bloggers regard the mainstream Democratic Party as a bloated, rigid aristocracy wedded to outmoded ways. Although there are exceptions in the form of party officers and officials who understand and engage them (like Howard Dean, the former Democratic National Committee [DNC] chair who gets credit for the broad Democratic gains realized in 2008 by enacting a fifty-state grassroots agenda compatible with netroots objectives), the netroots are highly critical of the means and goals of party regulars they regard as too timid to stand up for core progressive values or too clubby to take on friends. Initially exuberant over the Democrats' return to power after the 2006 congressional election—in which the netroots were highly engaged—optimism quickly turned sour when it became clear that the new Democratic majority was not going to defund the war, pursue impeachment proceedings against President Bush and Vice President Dick Cheney, or use their muscle to enforce subpoenas against administration officials who chose to snub congressional oversight efforts. Although some saw the reason for this as cowardliness, the greater concern was that it was simply strategic, a hard calculation that there was more to gain by letting Bush hang around and alienate more independent voters than by confronting him, galvanizing Republican opposition, and being accused of engaging in a partisan witch-hunt. Similarly, anger and disappointment erupted online following the 2008 election, when prominent Democratic insiders balked at punishing Connecticut senator Joseph Lieberman—a perpetual target of netroots wrath—for his vocal embrace of John McCain's attacks on Barack Obama during the 2008 campaign.

Netroots activists regarded these behaviors as bad politics and bad policy. They felt it played to the worst preexisting belief about Democrats—that they lack conviction—and that the public would rally if only they pressed the advantage against one of the least popular administrations in U.S. history and its apologists. The netroots felt that letting the administration get away with what were viewed as inexcusable abuses of power offered tacit legislative approval of Bush's more egregious actions, and that in the interest of good government the Democrats had no choice but to act forcefully and aggressively. In short the two sides had a disagreement over strategy and tactics, albeit rooted in progressive principles. Netroots activists felt that pursuing good policy would make good politics; established party leaders felt bloggers didn't know what they were talking about.

This specific dispute, important as it was, is emblematic of an even larger disagreement about how to position Democratic candidates with the electorate. Netroots activists are disgusted with party figures who play not to lose (rather than play to win) by engaging a small band of Beltway advisers who urge them to cobble together just enough voters to get by without doing anything to give the opposition the chance to attack them with their favored epithets: liberal, elitist, and out of touch (not insignificantly, Barack Obama's lopsided victory was engineered by consultants based outside Washington, a fact not lost on progressive bloggers). Among the netroots, this is the equivalent of relinquishing progressive values and ideas out of fear of being attacked, a form of surrender. They feel it is the behavior of a broken party operating in a broken system that leaves officials out of touch with the electorate. And they make the case that it is a losing strategy that fails every time a Democrat pretends to be a Republican and ends up on the short end of a 52–48 electoral split.

So they press the establishment to change or else move out of the way so they can implement their own strategy for progressive politics, which they believe will culminate in successful election outcomes and progressive governance. They have no interest in playing it safe. Establishment Democrats want to find just enough Democratic and independent voters to survive; netroots progressives want to create more Democrats. They would do this by challenging everything the establishment knows, by upending a political system built around interest group money, expensive consultants, and television in favor of a collaborative, citizen-centered open source politics funded by small contributions and sustained on the Internet. This is why the two groups are at war.

Netroots activists oppose mainstream journalists as strongly as they opposed the Bush administration and oppose the Democratic establishment. Add insider journalists to the list of people netroots bloggers want to replace—and mark down citizen bloggers as their replacements. Progressive activists accurately see Republicans as better suited to television politics compared to Democrats, with the superior ability to craft, disseminate, and adhere to winning emotional messages and to get reporters to discuss political news on conservative terms. In contrast, progressives are more suited to the Internet, a wide-open medium that thrives on debate and disputes. Their solution is to gradually push television and the reporting apparatus that surrounds it off center stage. This would have the added benefit of silencing pundits who pontificate about personalities and political trivia and call it reporting.

In truth, those inhabiting the progressive blogosphere recognize that they are not going to replace television or mainstream reporters, but they want to challenge their influence nevertheless. They tend to see efforts to be objective—the holy grail of mainstream journalism—as quaintly outdated in a hyperpartisan world, and in any event they regard what passes for balanced coverage to be hopelessly detrimental to the advancement of progressive viewpoints. They see the world portrayed by mainstream journalists as being inhabited by hard-right Republicans and the Democrats who acquiesce to conservatives out of fear, placing the center of the political debate somewhere out in right field. But on the Internet the center-left is the mainstream, and bloggers practicing a new form of journalism are trying to make that the standard.

Netroots activists gauge their effectiveness on how well they influence political outcomes, media narratives, and political engagement. Broadly speaking, the netroots elite is seeking to achieve three outcomes. Principally they want to win elections and govern. This means having an influence on the selection of Democratic candidates; promoting netroots candidates who share the strategic approach to politics heralded in the blogosphere; helping them get elected (along with some non-netroots Democrats, for the purpose of building Democratic majorities); making more elections competitive; and building the progressive Democratic brand from the bottom up in all fifty states. In support of this effort, they seek to influence the way the media talks about politics, challenging and changing mainstream press narratives they believe undermine progressive politics by blatantly or subtly advancing conservative frames. And as a means to their political ends—as well as a reflection of how they experience politics—they wish to build communities virtually and in the physical world: communities of progressives who come together around the sense that a politics that serves the common good can only be produced by collective interests. These are their goals; it is appropriate and meaningful to assess their record of achievement in these terms.

There is evidence that the netroots are making progress toward their political objectives. After several years of laboring to build a grassroots political base, progressive activists can claim a fair amount of progress in the electoral arena. They expanded the congressional playing field in 2006, putting more House seats in play for Democrats than in any cycle in recent memory through recruitment efforts waged online, then repeated the accomplishment in 2008. They spearheaded successful small-dollar fund-raising initiatives before the Obama campaign made the approach mainstream. They have supported a growing number of successful candidates for state and local positions, some of whom are winning elections in deeply red states. They have nurtured a set of netroots congressional candidates who were heavily engaged in online politics through investments in online fundraising, highly interactive campaign websites, and outreach to progressive blogs. Many of the federal candidates receiving netroots attention started the 2006 cycle as underfunded long shots in Republican-leaning districts who were ignored by the national party establishment because the odds of winning weren't good. In the end, quite a few were successfully positioned to take advantage of the Democratic tidal wave of 2006 in no small part because of the netroots support they received early on.

We can find in a number of the 2006 congressional races the seeds of the combined Internet/television campaign approach that would be successfully embraced by the Obama campaign two years later. Through hybrid campaigning (explained fully in Chapter 4), candidates attempt to balance the decentralized advantages of the Internet with traditional top-down campaign approaches, utilizing new media and online campaign techniques to secure their base while reaching less committed voters through television, direct mail, canvassing, and other traditional means. This movement toward blending a decentralized online approach with more established methods is significant, for it suggests candidates like Barack Obama who appreciate the new technology, along with netroots elites, are exploring ways to find the right balance between old and new, between control and decentralization—and achieving success with these efforts. Having a large pool of congressional candidates who started out as long shots made 2006 an appropriate year to engage this experiment—and in many instances the experiment worked.

There is only limited evidence that the netroots are making progress toward influencing mainstream media narratives. Try as they have to change the way political debate is framed in newspapers and on television, progressive blogs remain replete with posts denouncing news messages they believe to be false, misleading, or generally unhelpful to their cause—a sure sign that they have a way to go before their take on events reaches the mainstream. This is not to suggest that they have been entirely ineffectual, although their ability to influence mainstream coverage (at least on the national level) has been uneven and episodic and has required assistance from people and events not of their making. But bloggers operating at the state and local levels report satisfaction with their ability to shape news agendas and feel their influence has been steadily improving. On the blogs, in an ongoing exercise in open source journalism, groups of readers periodically brainstorm over the best way to frame progressive positions, developing and refining messages in the hope that high-profile Democrats will repeat them.

The evidence of netroots community building is strong. After living through decades noted for political cynicism and disengagement, netroots activists have built a web of virtual communities that energize people to take action online and often in the physical world as well. Bloggers are nothing if not passionate, and although their sometimes coarse ways of expressing themselves have earned them a reputation for being rude and disrespectful, from the inside the all-too-familiar rant has the cathartic appeal of having a safe place to unburden oneself with supportive, like-minded friends. If those on the outside don't like what they read, they are welcome to go elsewhere. It's a big Internet with something for everyone.

Those who choose to stay, by their own admission, feel a sense of belonging that suggests the virtual community pays emotional benefits similar to real-world interpersonal engagement. Granted the evidence for this is impressionistic, but it is also widespread. And at times when online associates have had the opportunity to meet in person, by their own report they were supportive and respectful in a way more suggestive of friends reacquainting than strangers meeting for the first time. This points to the progressive blogosphere as a source of social capital for those who invest in online activism, despite the fact that much of the time they are alone in front of a computer screen. The reason for this apparent paradox—people feeling connected to people while physically alone and detached—stems from the enormous sense of purpose generated by political activism. Together the bloggers have an agenda, and they are getting something done in the real world. In the process, the more active among them are bonding with each other across time and distance.

Although it is fair to ask whether virtual communities are the functional equivalent of real communities, it is also not the most interesting question to ask about the netroots. More relevant is the fact that they're talking about community at all. The issue rarely came up during the second half of the twentieth century, which was distinguished by the prominence of television in our political and social lives. During that period, political scientists and sociologists worried about how we were becoming increasingly disconnected from each other as well as from our elected officials. A large body of literature arose to study the detrimental effects of isolation, anomie, cynicism, and disillusionment that characterized that time. So to hear bloggers talk about the connections they feel with one another and the positive sense of what they're doing is as refreshing as it is jarring to those attuned to the "whatever" attitude of a more cynical age. Even when the relationships are virtual, the attitudes bloggers express toward each other and the political system are real, and they're different from what we heard when television dominated our lives and our politics.

Netroots bloggers practice and seek a politics of community facilitated by Internet interactions. On this score, Internet progressives practice what they experience. The notion of community they use to describe their blog relationships also applies to the model of politics they hope to implement. This is not by accident. They view the formation of community as a fundamental progressive tenet, and they regard an unholy reliance on individualism as a root cause of the problems we face. Would we have gone in over our heads in Iraq, they might ask, if we were all required to sacrifice? They are tired of the politics of division, which they perceive to be advantageous to conservatives, and so they seek to unite and conquer.

*   *   *

These points will be addressed in detail in the pages that follow. Chapter 2 looks at four key advances in communication technology—inexpensive printing, the telegraph, radio, and television—and asks how these developments were related to periods of transformational politics. Each technology played an important role in advancing new political coalitions or modes of governing—but not immediately. Technology has not dictated political change during our history, but new means of communicating have always proved irresistible to smart, opportunistic politicians looking for an edge. The trick has been to figure out how to use new technology to its full advantage, a lesson with important implications for Internet progressives—and conservatives, for that matter, who currently lag behind in their approach to Internet politics. The left and right blogospheres are structured differently, in a manner that leaves progressives better positioned to take advantage of the open source potential of the web. I discuss these differences and their ramifications in Chapter 3.

The next three chapters will consider evidence for the effectiveness of the progressive blogosphere on the three sets of assessment criteria they have established for themselves. Chapter 4 discusses their considerable success at achieving political outcomes and influencing the broader political debate. Chapter 5 addresses how well the netroots influence mainstream media narratives and reviews their efforts at promoting open source journalism, which lag behind their political achievements. Chapter 6 discusses the issue of virtual and real-world community building, both defining initiatives of the online left and points of great accomplishment.

We end with an evaluation in Chapter 7 of the promise and challenges of open source politics in the age of Barack Obama. By design, the netroots seek to upend an entrenched elite and transform the political system. They want to move the country in a leftward direction using a communal approach to politics resonant with what they do every day online. This makes them a threat to establishment political figures whose power and livelihoods derive from the traditional way of doing business. With the netroots now too large, vocal, and successful to be ignored, established figures need to figure out how to approach the netroots and the brand of politics they advocate. What they do, and how the progressives respond, will shape the front lines of a battle over the future direction of the Democratic Party and the country. One key social benefit of this battle, independent of how political struggles play out, is that the netroots are at the vanguard of a system-affirming participatory politics the likes of which we did not see during the television age.

Even with Barack Obama in the White House, their success is far from assured. To be sure, Obama's victory was won in no small part by using hybrid campaign approaches honed online over the past several years and by employing messages that resonate with the netroots' call for community. And there is no question that online progressives embrace Obama's victory as their own. But there is a tension between Obama and netroots activists—even among strong netroots supporters—rooted in the campaign's reluctance to fully engage and deploy netroots resources in favor of a more go-it-alone approach that permitted the campaign to maintain control over its daily operations. And Obama's language of postpartisanship grates against the more partisan elements of the progressive agenda, inseparable as it is from the new president's call for a departure from the politics of the past.

Today, with the country undergoing a transition to a new political regime, the direction of our politics is in flux, and the meaning of Obama's victory remains open to interpretation. Netroots activists are heavily engaged in trying to define the 2008 election as an endorsement of a progressive agenda rather than simply a rejection of the Bush years. Powered by a new technology and by a belief in their ability to use that technology to get results, they are attempting to exploit the opportunities they face and transform the political process to reflect their approach and their goals. Such a grandiose effort would have been unthinkable just a few years ago, but given the initial success and growing strength of the netroots, their efforts could herald a transformation of U.S. politics.

* * *

Before proceeding, a brief word on method and approach. Conceptually, *progressive netroots* is a nebulous entity, posing a challenge to the first and fundamental step of any research initiative: defining key terms. Who, exactly, are we talking about here? Anyone can frequent a website. Whereas some people post regularly and comment actively, others come and go, or visit once, or visit frequently but lurk without leaving evidence of their presence. Are all these people part of the progressive netroots? There are numerous progressive websites, many of which link to each other, but when the user moves beyond the most heavily trafficked sites it becomes unclear which and how many sites constitute the netroots universe. Some blogs focus on single issues or state or local concerns; others are small sites that have the feel of personal diaries written for immediate friends and family. And what of the online activist organizations like Moveon.org that are not set up like blogs but are heavily invested in the same activism that occurs on the blogs? They are part of the progressive netroots universe as well.

Solving a dilemma like this requires making some trade-offs and drawing on creative investigating using multiple methodologies. Bloggers may come and go, but they leave behind a body of work. Reviewing a sample of that work can provide clues to the larger phenomenon it represents. The progressive blogosphere is like a cluster of stars in a galaxy, where it is not necessary to examine or even identify all of them to capture the salient tendencies of the system. The key is to choose your examples carefully. In this case, there are obvious choices. By virtue of their traffic and their structure, several national progressive blogs stand out as preeminent: Daily Kos, Crooks and Liars, Eschaton, Fire Dog Lake, America-Blog, MyDD, Talking Points Memo, and Political Wire. All of these are in some fashion *community blogs*—sites that permit user commentary—and each regularly receives more than a million unique visitors per month.

At the same time, the progressive blogosphere is far more than these national sites. Numerous blogs focus on single issues or work toward the same goals as national bloggers on the state or local level. To exclude these would present a distorted view of the blogosphere. Thus a comprehensive accounting would have to include evidence from these bloggers as well. By taking into account high-profile national blogs and a range of subnational blogs, and by employing multiple methods to understand the content of blog posts and the attitudes of those who write them, we can through the preponderance of the evidence begin to address the common characteristics of this far-flung universe.

The methods used here are both qualitative and quantitative and are designed to complement one another in order to assemble an aggregate picture of the netroots. They include a deep reading of blog posts appearing on top national blogs; survey data on the attitudes and opinions of a sample of national and subnational bloggers; an analysis of metrics of political success advocated by top progressive bloggers; and a case study analysis of the largest progressive blog.

A deep reading of the eight most visited progressive blogs (mentioned above) provides an understanding of blog content and process, particularly what bloggers were saying, to whom they were speaking, norms of blog behavior, and patterns of communication both within and among blogs. Accomplishing this required spending time in the weeds of the eight largest virtual communities: examining diaries, reading comment threads, following hyperlinks to other online sources. This exploration proceeded for more than a year prior to the writing of this manuscript, dating back to December 2005, when progressive bloggers were gearing up for the 2006 midterm elections. The intent was to function like a virtual cultural anthropologist engaged in nonparticipant observation and thick description of a community or—in the language of the blogosphere—to lurk. Because blogs are virtual, this approach offered the advantage of being able to observe exchanges among blog participants without influencing them by virtue of not having a physical presence. This made it possible to analyze what people on the various blogs were saying and how they said it in order to develop an understanding of their ideas and ideals, beliefs and goals, means and expectations. A certain degree of generalization is inevitable from this method, but the point is to sketch out central tendencies rather than to represent every variation. Comments about the netroots are therefore meant to capture aggregate characteristics of the blogosphere and should not be assumed to apply to everyone engaged in the netroots at every level.

The blogger survey was designed to garner a range of self-assessments from netroots progressives blogging on predominantly state and local blogs. It asked respondents to assess the effectiveness of the progressive blogosphere in attaining political outcomes, shaping media messages, and community building both in the present and immediate past, as well as to speculate on what they expect the future to bring. The results were particularly useful in shaping the discussion of media framing and community building, which have an impressionistic component best understood through the assessments of those involved. Respondents were also asked to make comparisons to the conservative blogosphere. The survey yielded quantitative data on these items in addition to a wealth of comments, which are sprinkled throughout the book. Those interested in a more detailed discussion of how the survey was developed and administered should consult the appendix.

Seven metrics designed to determine the political effectiveness of netroots activists were derived from a close reading of blog posts and from consultation with a top national blogger heavily engaged in political activism. Ranging from the number of House seats left uncontested by Democrats to the effectiveness of online fund-raising to the success rate of web-endorsed nonfederal candidates, the metrics reflect the objectives of those attempting to bring about political transformation within the Democratic Party and nationally. They are discussed in detail in Chapter 4 and in the appendix.

Finally, the discussion of community building appearing in Chapter 6 is informed by a case study of Daily Kos, by far the largest community weblog in either blogosphere, with five times the number of unique visitors than the closest progressive blog and three times the number of page views than the nearest progressive or conservative blog. The reach and scope of the site, the fact that it was one of the first progressive community blogs, and the presence of features designed to facilitate interaction (like diaries, comment threads, and open threads) make it an ideal prototype of online engagement. A qualitative assessment of Daily Kos posts about the Daily Kos community provides insight to the way affiliated bloggers view their interactions and the environment in which they blog.

These approaches together offer a window into an amorphous movement that is steadily gaining steam—and gaining ground in its efforts to reshape U.S. politics in its image.

2

Technology and Political Change
Slow March to Sudden Burst

I think that we [in the blogosphere] are still in the very early stages of what to expect from online organizing and reinventing the media to a more democratized form. I believe there will be new organizations yet to emerge that will change the face of how all this affects political dynamics.

—Anonymous Blogger

I think we are in the middle of a maturing process. In 2004, I would never have contemplated that I could have an active hand in helping recruit a candidate for the U.S. Senate, or raising funds to turn the Texas legislature to a Democratic majority, or having a ghost of a chance that my ideas on messaging would reach anybody but a random reader. In 2004, I thought I was screaming into a void. In 2006, I realized there were a lot more folks screaming, too, and we started figuring out ways to fix what was broken in our political discourse.

—Texas Blogger

Many a new media innovation began with people screaming into a void. When new technology becomes functional, the natural tendency is to try to figure out what to do with it. Often we simply don't know, at least at first. When it comes to technological advances with the potential to influence politics, every major invention since the emergence of the republic has met with utopian sounding declarations of the coming of a new dawn along with doomsayers predicting the end of humanity. The telegraph, radio, and television were all championed in some quarters as technological solutions to the problems facing a society strained, respectively, by territorial expansion, immigration, and urbanization. Whereas John Dewey imagined the radio would engage people in civic and political pursuits, futurists such as Alvin Toffler believed television would unite the nation in a teledemocracy that would look something like a big, wired New England town meeting.[1] Then again, critics like Walter Lippmann strongly doubted that radio would be an effective vehicle for educating masses of people, and at each turn new technologies raised anxieties about potential rips in the social fabric.[2]

The Internet is no different. There are blog triumphalists whose voices can be heard on the web declaring a new age of cybercommunity, whereas others decry the increasing isolation and fragmentation of society as people sit alone at home and type on computer screens to others who largely agree with them. Then there are those who just think the Internet won't matter much either way. The discussion eerily echoes the fault lines surrounding four earlier technological breakthroughs—inexpensive printing, the telegraph, radio, and television—when each of these innovations was new.

If, in these earlier cases, technology failed to attain the utopian heights of its strongest supporters, it is also the case that each of these technological advances factored into the most important political transformations in our history. But each transformation looked quite different from the high-minded civic expectations of technology's greatest promoters. Radio may not have produced a civic culture, but it did play a role in the development of the welfare state. Instead of television reproducing the New England village green, it enabled a string of politicians to manipulate emotions in the successful pursuit of their agendas. The law of unintended consequences can be greatest when we don't have a clue as to what a new technology will bring about.

One important common thread shared by these four technological innovations is that each played a role in securing a dominant place for a new political regime. In no case was technology the sole cause of political change, nor did technology make political change inevitable. Instead, communications technology and political regimes have grown up together, engaging in something of a parallel evolution.[3] As F. Christopher Arterton writes, "A complicated relationship of social needs, cultural patterns, economic constraints, and technology capacities exists, implying that technologies alone are not highly determinative of their political application."[4] Although it is difficult to imagine the Jackson regime without cheap printing technology, the emergence of Lincoln's Republican Party without the telegraph, FDR's New Deal coalition without radio, and the success of late-twentieth-century conservatism without television, it is possible that each political transformation could have come about from other means, and it is surely the case that a multitude of other factors figured in to their ascendancy.

Another important thread is that each transformation capitalized on an emerging technology that had existed for some time without making a dent in the prevailing political system. In each case, the difference between technology having a role in reshaping the political order and simply being an ineffectual curiosity rested with an individual, group, or party understanding what made the technology different, then employing the technology as no one previously had done to maximize its political benefits. So it is that improvements in printing had been taking place for years before Andrew Jackson molded an inexpensive national consortium of newspapers into the backbone of a mass political organization; that the telegraph had made the unified, instantaneous transmission of news possible long before Abraham Lincoln employed it in an unprecedented message control operation; that radio had been an established fixture in politics well before Franklin Roosevelt put a carefully orchestrated human touch on the first mass medium to enter people's living rooms; and that television had maintained a central presence in national politics for a decade and a half before Richard Nixon used it to create the false illusion that he had reinvented himself. Each of these moments heralded a dramatic change in U.S. politics, and each occurred only when a savvy political leader applied outside-the-box thinking to emerging technologies and figured out how to tap previously undiscovered political advantages.

Printing Technology and the Jacksonian Revolution

The transformation of U.S. politics ushered in by Andrew Jackson in 1828 was as much the product of successful institutional development as technological change, coming as it did before the telegraph and telephone unleashed the first era of mass communication. But it was precipitated by improved printing technology that led to falling printing costs and the consequent explosion of newspaper publishing at a time of growing literacy and expanding suffrage. Printing technology had been growing more efficient and papers had been more widely and easily distributed during the early decades of the nineteenth century, but prior to Jackson these tools were not enlisted in the cause of mass party building. Once they were, America witnessed a revolution in party politics and governance, as Jackson developed a national newspaper network to serve as the core of a political machine that upended a quarter-century-old Virginia presidential dynasty and ushered in the country's first mass-based party regime.

When Jackson first sought the presidency in 1824, a string of three two-term Jeffersonian Republican presidents from Virginia had governed the country since Thomas Jefferson defeated John Adams in the election of 1800. The manner of presidential selection during this period was well established, with successful contenders building the largest base of support in Congress, in part through the promise of cabinet positions to the leaders of their congressional factions. The stepping-stone position in this early patronage system was secretary of state, as four successive presidents of this period—Thomas Jefferson, James Madison, James Monroe, and John Quincy Adams—served in that capacity during an administration prior to their own. It was an elite-based process closed to all but a privileged few with close ties between the executive and legislative branches, and it assured that the president would be selected from among a narrow band of insiders.

Jackson was hardly a member of the club. A military figure with roots in the hardscrabble Tennessee frontier, Old Hickory was in background and temperament different from the members of the ruling elite of the day, and although he had served briefly in the House and Senate, when he first ran for president in

1824 his political base was in the countryside. When that year's multicandidate field failed to produce a majority winner in the Electoral College it was left to the House of Representatives to select the president. Although Jackson had won the most popular and electoral votes, the House went with Adams[5] after House Speaker Henry Clay endorsed him. When Clay was appointed secretary of state (and Adams's heir apparent) in the new administration, Jackson and his followers railed against what they perceived to be a corrupt bargain—a deal by insiders to deny the presidency to the man with the largest democratic following.[6]

Jackson almost immediately began preparing for revenge in the 1828 election. But in order to be successful he recognized that it would be necessary to break the stranglehold on the nominating system imposed by the congressional caucus. A patronage relationship between federal political figures and the printing industry was key to the survival of the caucus system, and Jackson realized that he would have to attack or circumvent it as long as he was not part of it. For the first three decades of the nineteenth century, when U.S. political parties were in their infancy and when outwardly seeking high office was considered unseemly, ambitious national politicians promoted their candidacies through the writings of supportive newspaper editors who in turn were rewarded with government printing business when their patrons were elected. A good portion of this business was supplied by Congress and by executive branch departments through contracts to print legislation and official records.[7] With the locus of this arrangement in the nation's capital (first New York and Philadelphia, then Washington), members of the congressional caucus and department secretaries could keep tight control over the printing contracts that provided the foundation of their rudimentary media organizations. It was a closed system.

In a manner that foreshadowed the contemporary progressive blogosphere, Jackson undermined this arrangement by creating a national network of partisan newspapers to compete with the Washington information monopoly. Several trends worked to facilitate the success of this effort. The early nineteenth century saw expanded suffrage, an explosion in the number of directly elected offices, and rising literacy rates—all of which worked in Jackson's favor as he labored to build the first mass political party. By 1826, twenty-one of twenty-four states had white male suffrage free of property restrictions. Voters rather than state legislators began choosing governors and statewide officials, and whereas in 1800 only two states chose presidential electors through statewide popular voting, by 1832 only South Carolina did not. Political participation increased accordingly. Only 9 percent of eligible voters cast ballots in the 1820 presidential contest. When Jackson made his comeback eight years later, fully 57 percent voted, an unprecedented figure that looks pretty good by today's standards as well.[8]

Still, despite everything Jackson had working for him, he needed a way to organize and rally supporters in this far-flung nation, and newspapers were the available medium. To that end, it was critical to Jackson's success that Americans of that era loved to read. Literacy was widespread and growing. America at that time had a higher literacy rate than any European nation, which created a developing market for printed material, which in turn spurred investment in technology that made printing cheaper and more efficient.[9] And as printing became less expensive, newspapers flourished across the country, penetrating even the most remote areas in what could be regarded as the first U.S. information revolution.[10]

But cheap, effective printing technology began to materialize years before Jackson's victorious 1828 campaign, and improvements in post roads made newspaper delivery relatively quick and reliable years before Jackson emerged on the scene. Annual newspaper circulation was soaring in the decades before Jackson, shooting up from around 5 million in 1790 to almost 80 million in 1830. This is partly because during the early years of the nineteenth century it had already become a relatively easy endeavor to establish new papers in frontier communities using type sent by wagon or barge, and partly because newer presses in cities operated efficiently enough for urban papers to be produced in large quantities, lowering publication costs. And a postal network with greater reach into local communities than anything in Europe multiplied sixfold between 1789 and 1820, permitting unfettered circulation of newspapers in the years before Jackson.[11]

Likewise, party newspapers were hardly a new invention. John Quincy Adams, who would lose to Jackson in 1828, also had editorial support around the country.[12] What made Jackson's efforts revolutionary was his understanding of how to turn a multitude of local newspapers made possible by cheap, efficient printing technology into the basis for a national political party organization. No one had ever used the technology that way before.

Jackson's Democratic Party started by spending thousands of dollars to purchase dozens of existing newspapers and to establish dozens more in cities as far-flung as Richmond, Albany, Cincinnati, Concord (New Hampshire), and Philadelphia and throughout Jackson's home state of Tennessee, as well as in many smaller locales. Although these papers served to bring partisan news to Jackson's supporters nationwide, this was a fairly traditional function of the early-nineteenth-century press. The real strategic genius of Jackson's campaign rested with the technique of *management*—using these papers to coordinate communication among the state party organizations and grassroots officials that formed the backbone of Jackson's national political network.[13] By penetrating the countryside with inexpensive pro-Jackson newspapers and using them to synchronize campaign operations, circulate a unified campaign message, generate excitement, and organize and mobilize voters, Jackson and his supporters built an apparatus capable of performing the core political functions of a first-of-its-kind mass democratic party,[14] and they did it in the absence of a true mass medium of communication.

In this system, newspaper editors doubled as local party officials. They could speak on behalf of the campaign and routinely held formal positions on local or state campaign committees. This gave Jackson an independent outlet for coordinating and spreading the Democratic Party message, an outlet owned and operated by the campaign and facilitated in no small part by postal laws that permitted newspapers to circulate through the mail free of charge. Editors took advantage of the free postage by subscribing to a multitude of papers from across the country and excerpting what other editors were writing, creating something of a crude national political message machine that anticipated the wire services of the next generation while further assisting Jacksonian Democrats in their party-building efforts.[15]

In terms of what they produced and how they worked creatively with the technology at their disposal, what Jacksonian Democrats did with inexpensive printing technology more closely models today's progressive bloggers than any subsequent media-influenced political transformation. This comparison at first glance may seem strange, owing to the fact that the Jacksonian revolution was the least technological of the four discussed here, and because it centered around a technology that had been around in some form for almost 400 years. But consider for a moment the context in which Jackson operated and what he produced. Like today's bloggers, he was an outsider to an elite national power structure, and so like today's bloggers he faced the daunting dilemma of trying to obtain power from the outside. He had at his disposal a recent technological advance (cheap, easily distributed newspapers), which was broadly available to anyone else who wished to use it, like today's Internet. His solution to his political problem rested partly in utilizing that tool differently than anyone else: as the connective tissue for a new political structure, much as progressive bloggers have been experimenting with ways to use the Internet to build a movement strong enough to contest and win elections and influence mass opinion.

Both efforts were built at the grassroots level. Although Jackson's efforts were centralized, in meaningful contrast to the spidery Internet and the decentralized online progressive movement, his use of newspapers functioned like today's blogs to unite disparate supporters, sometimes in remote places, behind a unified political cause. Each political function performed by the Jacksonian Democratic press has been embraced by the progressive Netroots: synchronizing operations, message development and dissemination, generating excitement, organizing and mobilizing voters, and, of course, raising money.

Perhaps most important, Jackson's efforts were aimed at democratizing the electoral process and engaging a broad electorate in a participatory culture, two defining goals of Internet progressives. It's not by chance that Jackson chose to name his party the Democratic Party in contrast to Jefferson's republicanism. On this score, although they might not have embraced Jackson's politics, progressive bloggers in 2006 and 2008 set out to accomplish something close to what he did. The 1828 election ushered in a new, party-based mass political era characterized by widespread participation,[16] echoes of the wave elections of 2006 and 2008. More people were eligible to vote, to be sure, but those who turned out were captivated by a dramatic campaign that engaged them emotionally.[17] In finding a way to circumvent a nominating system stacked against him, Jackson used the limited tools technology could offer him to create the first participatory political system.

The Telegraph and Lincoln's Republican Politics

America began to embrace industrialization during the years between 1828 and Lincoln's election in 1860, and although industrialization's full force would be felt after the Civil War, dramatic changes were already coming into focus during Jackson's time that presaged the emergence of the first age of mass media. Technological innovations that would permit the transmission of information at unprecedented speeds across an ever-expanding country would, during the middle nineteenth century, dramatically alter the way Americans received their news and, eventually, the way political leaders used information to further their ends.

Improvements in printing and transportation professionalized the newspaper trade, putting an end to the days when papers could be established cheaply and quickly by small vendors. By the mid-1840s, the Hoe rotary printing press radically accelerated the speed at which newspapers could be printed, churning out 20,000 pages an hour—twenty times more than less expensive flatbed printing.[18] A vastly improved transportation infrastructure made it possible for newspapers to travel farther and faster, spearheaded by the coming of the railroad (there were forty miles of track in 1830 and 30,000 miles in 1860), steamships, and canals. Paved roads (88,000 miles in 1860, a ninefold increase from 1820) lead to improved stagecoach service, and an explosion in post roads (from 72,000 miles in 1820 to 240,000 miles in 1860) and post offices facilitated swift mail service. The time it took information to travel across vast spaces shrunk accordingly. If someone mailed a newspaper in 1832, chances are it took anywhere from four days to one month to arrive at its destination. That same paper mailed in 1860 traveled across a much larger country in three days or less.[19]

Then there was the telegraph. When Samuel Morse electronically telegraphed the words "What Hath God Wrought?" over an experimental line between Washington and Baltimore in 1844, only futurists could have imagined how the instantaneous transmission of information over great distances would change everyday life. Before the end of the decade, top New York newspapers recognized they could save the cost of having reporters compete for the same news by pooling their resources and sharing news stories via telegraph. The resulting consortium, originally called the Harbor News Association[20] and later the Associated Press, would grow with the telegraph to transform the way information was distributed.[21]

For one thing, the rise of the wire service facilitated the demise of the party press that formed the backbone of the Jackson regime by making it possible for newspapers to thrive without the benefit of party patronage.[22] Commercialism, an inevitable outgrowth of industrialization, fed the rise of the penny press—cheap newspapers that profited from commercial advertising. To the extent that editors sought to boost circulation figures to extract the maximum cost for ads, they came to regard themselves as advocates for business rather than political interests and their readers as consumers rather than partisans.[23] Although commercial considerations did not eliminate partisan advocacy, especially in urban areas where an abundance of newspapers permitted market segmentation,[24] the shift in perspective by publishers to regard readers as consumers marked a watershed in the political role of print news.

The emergence of a large commercial press was accompanied by the rise of a professional press as well. Early in the Jackson era, newspapermen were printers. By midcentury they gradually began to see themselves as reporters and journalists. In the years before the Civil War, as newspapers became businesses, journalists introduced standards and guidelines and began to patrol their work.[25] Reporters began experimenting with new techniques. For instance, the 1858 Lincoln-Douglas debates for the U.S. Senate became national news because reporters for the first time traveled on the campaign trail and published shorthand accounts of the proceedings, staking out a healthy distance from the candidates that marked a shift away from the close candidate-press relationships of the past.[26] The application of professional conduct (and the quality of coverage) was uneven: it wasn't unusual for reporters to publish false information on behalf of public officials in exchange for bribes, or to trade in innuendo.[27] But in the previous era no money would have had to change hands for openly partisan newspapers to print information to benefit political patrons and to undermine the opposition.

The growth and commercialization of newspapers along with the evolution in reporting from trade to profession marked the emergence of something that would look far more familiar to us than the party press. Here we see the origins of modern news marketing and reporting: urban newspapers with large advertising departments and the technology for efficient mass distribution producing a product with broad market appeal and less partisanship that could reach large numbers of people with national wire service news in relatively short order. It was America's first mass medium. And as a mass medium, it had a mass influence on everyday views of politics.[28]

These changes weren't lost on politicians. With the emergence of mass publishing and the demise of newspapers as an arm of the printing trade, presidents could no longer rely on the press for self-promotion.[29] In a symbolic and substantive nod to the extent of this change, the creation of the Government Printing Office in 1860 put an end to the practice of using government printing for patronage. That same year, Abraham Lincoln became the first president not to rely on a newspaper as a propaganda voice.[30]

The partisan political role of the press during the early industrial period evolved into something diametrically opposite to what it had been thirty-two years earlier. By the time of Lincoln's nomination in 1860, the editorial tail—formerly a mouthpiece for candidates and officeholders—was wagging the political dog. Horace Greeley, editor of the nationally distributed *New York Tribune*, decided to flex the muscle that came with his influential media platform to sway the selection of the Republican presidential candidate—and, as kingmaker, assure that the eventual nominee would be indebted to him. Specifically, he worked to block the nomination of William Seward, who came to the Republican convention as the frontrunner. Motivated in part by his personal desire for political influence, in part by his wish to see the Republicans nominate an antislavery candidate he felt could win nationally, Greeley eventually settled on and successfully promoted Lincoln after convincing enough delegates that Seward was, in contemporary parlance, unelectable.[31]

This was a complete reversal of the role reporters and editors played in building a national communication medium for Andrew Jackson, in which candidates could establish newspapers and command partisan support, and it foretold the relationship between reporter and politician that would become normal during the age of rapid market growth and organized urban machine politics that would dominate for the remainder of the century.[32] For the most part, this was a period characterized by colorless presidents. The exception, of course, was Abraham Lincoln, whose administration marked the end of the political dominance of Jackson's Democratic Party and served as the bridge to the Republican politics of the industrial era.

Where Jackson used the technology available to him to organize the decentralized grassroots, Lincoln used the technology of his day to amplify the power of the presidency. His approach, recognizable to anyone familiar with contemporary politics, was top-down: monopolize the flow of information available to the public in order to exercise command over the messages people received. His reason for doing this, of course, was the Civil War.

Other presidents had served during the telegraph era, but none faced anything resembling the challenges posed by southern secession. Lincoln's task was no less than maintaining the nation and his administration of it during a period of unprecedented military mobilization. To this end, he employed technology in a manner his predecessors had not. Just as Jackson took advantage of inexpensive newspaper production technology, Lincoln maneuvered to co-opt the technology of his day: the telegraph and the wire service that had developed around it. His objective was the same as it would be for a long line of Lincoln's successors: to get a favorable message to as many people as possible while denying purveyors of opposing messages an equal opportunity to promote their perspective.[33] In this respect, it's not unreasonable to say Lincoln was the first president to engage in news management—a strategy to control the flow of information, made necessary during an age of centralized communication technology when presidents no longer directly controlled the press.

Lincoln's insight to the political ramifications of the telegraph was that the president could have a monopoly over information provided he exercised a comparable monopoly over the technology of information dissemination. When information is made available in a centralized manner, successful information management means controlling the source. Whereas future presidents would employ less draconian means to this end, Lincoln, through the war powers of the office, took statutory control of the American Telegraph Company, which operated along the East Coast. By 1862, government control of the telegraph extended nationally, permitting the administration tremendous command over news coming from Civil War battlefields.[34]

These wartime measures permitted the administration to curb the content of national military and political information. But to make sure that the news he wanted people to read ended up in print and was reported the way he wished, Lincoln employed an access strategy that would also be emulated by a number of his successors. Recognizing the value of maintaining good relations with top-level Associated Press reporters and the news value of a war president to the new professional class of reporters, Lincoln engaged in what could be regarded as a kind of nineteenth-century attempt at spin control. He cozied up to Associated Press Washington bureau chief Lawrence Gobright, offering him exclusives in the knowledge that they would be favorably reported and telegraphed nationwide to appear prominently in newspapers.[35] Lincoln's monopoly over the telegraph gave him a distinct advantage over his political opponents. Because the opposition press did not have access to its own newswire, the Associated Press story became the official story. Lincoln was able to, in contemporary terms, use technology to control the message.

With the end of the Civil War, Lincoln's assassination, and the tormented successor presidency of Andrew Johnson, the White House's monopolistic control of the wires faded into history, to be revived in the twentieth century around different technologies. For his part, Johnson discovered the bitter fruit of a media strategy poorly employed. In the wake of Lincoln's successful efforts to elevate the newsworthiness of the president, Johnson discovered that he was the recipient of a fair share of press attention, whether or not he preferred it that way. But Johnson faced a hostile political climate and lacked Lincoln's news management skills. The press corps quickly soured on Johnson after briefly giving him the benefit of the doubt. Said *New York Evening Post* editor Charles Nordhoff of President Johnson, "He is really vile, vulgar, coarse, mean, bad in every way, & not least in a kind of low cunning, [which] always defeats itself."[36] That's not the way you want influential editors thinking about you in an era when they, rather than the president, set the agenda.

Whereas inexpensive printing capability made possible the weaving together of a nation, the telegraph and wire services inevitably and inexorably shifted the locus of political reporting to Washington and initiated an era of centralized communication that would continue in various forms throughout the twentieth century. Through the age of radio and the age of television—until today's Internet—mass media would be centralized media, and ambitious politicians would look for ways to control the medium in order to leverage it for political advantage. The combination of mass media technology and an independent or quasi-independent press necessitates media control strategies. Lincoln understood this and knew how to execute a strategy designed to monopolize the flow of information about his administration by utilizing the prevailing technology as no one had before during a moment of extraordinary consequence. During another crisis several generations later, Franklin Roosevelt would do the same with radio, unlocking the political magic of another new technology after his predecessors had tried and failed.

FDR, Radio, and Manufactured Intimacy

Like television and the Internet, radio emerged slowly, went through a long period of germination, then exploded in popularity. In fact, there are more than a few similarities between how radio and the Internet developed, notably the long period between the emergence of the technology and its successful use as a political instrument. Eventually, a president who knew how to unleash the potential of the medium would use radio to forge a lasting political coalition, upend the national political debate, redirect national economic policy, and lead the country through a global war. But all of that was far in the future when Heinrich Hertz first demonstrated, in 1887, that radio waves could transmit signals through the air at the speed of light. And it was hardly imaginable at the turn of the century, when Guglielmo Marconi put Hertz's theoretical discovery to practical use by building the first device capable of transmitting radio signals across the Atlantic Ocean.[37]

Marconi's machine was called a radio telegraphy device: a telegraph without wires. Its purpose was to compete with transatlantic telegraph cables to send messages great distances through the air. Thus radio began its life as a wireless upgrade to an existing technology, and even as transmission of the human voice became feasible during the first decade of the twentieth century, it would have been a stretch to foresee how the wireless would in form and function evolve into something quite different, much like it would have been difficult to imagine that personal computers would one day emerge from their slow, oversized, vacuum-tubed ancestors. So it was with the political potential of the new medium, still more than two decades from being realized. People would first need to understand what made radio different before they could learn how to make it serve political ends.

Radio's emergence was slow, and for a long time it would have been reasonable to think it would never happen. For years, radio was the domain of hobbyists. Amateur radio clubs were a popular pastime during World War I, their enthusiasts regarding themselves as "the advance guard of the radio revolution,"[38] not unlike the early bloggers of the early twenty-first century. But if there was a revolution happening in radio at that time it was located out at sea, where commercial and naval vessels used it to communicate with other ships. And though there was certainly a romantic quality to the new technology, it remained a distant curiosity to most people. Like the Internet during the 1990s, people tried to make money with radio but couldn't quite figure out how. And it's no wonder. In 1921 there were only 50,000 wireless receivers in the United States.[39]

Seemingly out of thin air, everything changed. In 1922 there was a twelvefold increase in the number of domestic radio sets. By the end of that year there would be 556 radio stations, just two years removed from the first commercial (and political) broadcast on KDKA Pittsburgh, of the 1920 Harding-Cox election.[40] As it happened, one of those entrepreneurs looking to make money with the new technology figured out a way to turn a profit with radio by creating public demand for radio receivers. His secret, scorned by skeptics, was to create a buzz by offering the public high-profile programming. Several years later that entrepreneur, David Sarnoff, would help found the NBC radio network.[41]

The tipping point cleared, radio took off. During the boom years of the 1920s, radio sets went from a curiosity to an affordable luxury. By the 1940s they were a necessity. Technology was keeping up with demand. But in these early days there was a radio divide resembling today's digital divide, with radio ownership and stations clustered in wealthy regions just like high-speed Internet access came first to wealthier households.[42] It would take years for this divide to disappear, but it happened. Although radio would not reach full saturation until the early 1940s—much like high-speed broadband will take years to reach ubiquity—in the 1920s radio was drawing the interest and investment money of speculators, many undercapitalized, who wanted to get in on the ground floor. Like many Internet startups of the late 1990s, the great majority of these ventures failed.

Once radio established a beachhead in the American living room, it follows that politicians would want to take advantage of the first mass medium that permitted simultaneous direct transmission of a message to countless numbers of people. Warren Harding, the first president to include radio in his media strategy, was not shy about using the emerging medium to reach out to the public during his brief scandal-plagued administration.[43] But in the early 1920s, radio didn't have the reach to make much of a difference.[44]

Calvin Coolidge spoke on radio an average of once a month and was actually quite good at it. Although less personable than Harding, he had a natural radio voice and spoke in short, accessible sentences that could be easily digested by listeners.[45] He not only knew it, he grasped the advantage radio gave him, saying, "I can't make an engaging, rousing or oratorical speech, but I have a good radio voice, and now I can get my message across to [the public] without acquainting them with my lack of oratorical ability."[46] Listeners seemed to agree: Coolidge was at one point voted fourth in a poll of most-liked radio personalities—ahead of popular humorist Will Rogers. But Coolidge saw radio as a new medium that could serve traditional political purposes rather than as a transformational medium that could create new political opportunities. So his radio appearances took the form of formal addresses and prepared speeches.[47] He succeeded in reaching a lot of people with his voice. But that was all.

If there was ever a president who needed a breakthrough medium to help him out of political trouble, it was Coolidge's successor, Herbert Hoover. Yet Hoover did not find any relief from his problems on radio. Ironically a moving force in early government regulatory decisions about radio when he was commerce secretary during the Coolidge administration, Hoover had limited understanding of radio as a tool of mass communication, and the medium never liked him.[48] Shy and a poor speaker, Hoover was not a natural fit for radio.[49] Although urged by allies to use the microphone to connect with Americans suffering under the burden of the Great Depression, Hoover resisted. He neither understood how to make radio work for him nor had the inclination to figure it out.

This is not to say that the public never heard his voice. By the early 1930s, the radio boom had made broadcasting mainstream. All public figures used it, including many in Hoover's administration, and by the end of his term Hoover had appeared on radio ninety-five times—just nine fewer appearances than Franklin Roosevelt made during his first term.[50] By Hoover's administration, politicians of both major parties had come to see radio as a standard item in their political toolkit, just as by the turn of the twenty-first century it was hard to find a serious public figure or candidate who didn't have a website—even if it was rudimentary and lacked the functionality of political websites of later years. Furthermore, radio had already effected changes in political behavior. In the 1924 campaign, Coolidge's Republican Party—which figured out the political value of radio before the Democrats did—abandoned the century-old practice of presenting long oratorical addresses and barnstorming the country in favor of shorter broadcast speeches. A party memo from that year demonstrated a clear recognition of the style and length of speech that worked best over the air as well as the relatively short attention spans of listeners. It perceptively noted that the language of radio was "not that of the platform orator"[51]—and warned to keep radio addresses to ten minutes or less.

But the very thing that made radio effective was the thing Hoover resisted: he was uninterested in trying to use it to reach out to a vast nation. Although he began addressing the country more frequently as the nation's troubles worsened,[52] radio was never part of his governing or political strategy. During his reelection campaign, he refused to use radio at all. Instead, Hoover saw radio as an intrusion into the work he was elected to do, and he preferred to focus his energy on conferring with Washington elites to combat the Great Depression.[53] Hoover gave no inclination that he understood how radio could be a vehicle to accomplish what he needed to do at that moment in history: mobilize the country behind him. But his successor knew.

Franklin Roosevelt had been using radio for a long time. He was familiar with its nature, and it was kind to him. During the years when Coolidge was establishing himself as a conventional radio personality and Hoover was viewing radio as a distraction to important business, FDR was learning how to persuade people by refining and repeating a simple message and, in the years immediately preceding his presidency, honing his radio skills as governor of New York by giving radio addresses to build public support for legislative initiatives. As early as his stint as assistant secretary of the U.S. Navy during Woodrow Wilson's administration, FDR demonstrated a flair for the dramatic, conducting naval yard inspections with pomp and fanfare to drum up press coverage.[54]

So when FDR reached the Oval Office he knew precisely how to reap the political benefits awaiting the first person to figure out that radio is a medium that could move people—and lots of them. Roosevelt had both the insight and the ability to use radio for his purposes—the combination of knowledge and skill necessary for a political entrepreneur to unlock the secrets of a new technology.

Roosevelt's signature fireside chats were unique because he spoke directly to his radio audience. This no doubt sounds simplistic to generations raised on electronic media, but it was revolutionary in its day. The name for these presentations, originated by CBS News Washington bureau chief Harry Butcher, evokes Roosevelt's informal, direct, personalized way of speaking on radio.[55] The term *fireside chat* suggests an image of the president entering your home, sitting by an open fire, and talking with you. No president in history had ever pretended to do anything of the sort. Presidents were distant figures who spoke in official settings using formal language. Roosevelt addressed his radio listeners as "my friends."

It took a lot of work for FDR to sound spontaneous. These efforts are well documented. Roosevelt paid tremendous attention to his delivery and would practice his radio addresses by staring at a blank wall, trying to visualize the people in the audience. He modulated his voice so that it appeared genuine and real, as if he were talking to rather than at his listener. Although FDR had speechwriters, he always reviewed final drafts to make sure they were written in his voice and to ensure that the phrasing was simple enough to feel natural, his cadences pleasing, the length never so great as to become tiresome. He spoke slowly and used illustrations to underscore his conversational, approachable tone. And he was religious about avoiding overexposure on the airwaves, averaging around twenty-five radio broadcasts annually, only two or three of which were fireside chats.[56] He knew what happened to guests, even virtual ones, when they overstayed their welcome.

Radio broadcasts were employed as part of a larger media strategy that sought the same objectives as every media strategy employed by every astute president who ever served in a mass media regime: control your message, transmit it effectively, and dominate the national agenda. In the language of the television age, Roosevelt's fireside chats were media events—public rituals manufactured by FDR and his advisers to sell the president's agenda by building a bond of trust between public and president.[57] Efforts to build and market FDR's message and personality were coordinated through his press office, with press secretary Stephen T. Early in charge of monitoring the size of the audience and its reaction to Roosevelt's radio appearances.[58] His radio broadcasts were strategically slotted for what we would now call prime time—when he was assured the largest potential audience—and they were reinforced by radio appearances from surrogates like cabinet secretaries and First Lady Eleanor Roosevelt, whose words were carefully drafted to amplify the president's message.[59]

The result was a degree of message coordination and control unparalleled in the history of U.S. politics at that time. FDR's message reached a mass listening audience unadulterated and unfiltered and provided a critical counterweight to newspapers, the medium of previous generations, the largest of which were lined up in opposition to the New Deal. If Roosevelt had been forced to compete on what had been the traditional media playing field of his day, it is hard to imagine that he would have had the same transformational political capacity, with powerful newspaper moguls like William Randolph Hearst free to fashion the public debate through vast print empires.[60] So Roosevelt nurtured the young medium, giving radio reporters a prominent place at his press conferences, appointing commissioners to the newly formed Federal Communications Commission who were generous to radio ownership, and funneling choice information to radio commentators like Walter Winchell and Gabriel Heatter, who in turn spoke supportively of the New Deal.[61] People continued to read newspapers, of course. But FDR had his own media platform from which to operate.

These efforts paid off handsomely. Radio turned the president into a star, perhaps the biggest radio star of his day. His ratings were higher than Jack Benny and Charlie McCarthy. One fireside chat, delivered on September 11, 1941, was heard by almost three-quarters of the U.S. public. Theaters would go vacant as people stayed home or gathered with friends to listen to the president.[62] People would write letters to the White House to tell the president how moved they were by his presence, as though he were a visitor or family friend.[63]

The difference between Roosevelt and his predecessors is that FDR understood that radio exists in the realm of illusion (a recognition that fuels the success of contemporary political talk radio as well). This insight, of course, was common knowledge to radio professionals who, years before Roosevelt came to power, were hiring announcers based on their ability to generate emotional reactions in people by reading them gibberish.[64] It's the tone that counts, the mood one's voice creates, the deception that a disembodied voice can be an intimate companion. Roosevelt was the first national leader to apply this understanding to politics.

He realized that he could use radio to manufacture a sense of intimacy with constituents by relying on the emotional value of carefully chosen and communicated rhetoric.[65] Roosevelt was therefore able to do what Hoover could not: mobilize public opinion behind his political agenda.[66] He did it by creating a mass sense of intimacy with listeners, a paradoxical result only possible with a medium of mass communication.[67]

FDR was aided by the fact that his expansive political agenda was a good match to his engaging radio personality,[68] whereas Hoover's limited government approach was as hard a sell on radio as his voice and presentation. In much the same way, television has been a good match to the Republican strategy of message simplification employed since the 1960s, and the Internet resonates with left-leaning instincts toward decentralization and disagreement. But in each instance, the transformational political value of the new medium was not unlocked until someone recognized what made the new medium different from the old and could apply that quality to practical politics. Roosevelt understood the power of radio to produce fantasy along with the power of fantasy to mold public opinion. And he had the skills to make it happen.

Nixon and Television's Deceptions

The development of television as a political force followed the same trajectory as radio: early skepticism about the viability of the medium and uncertainty about how to use it during a long period before it entered the mainstream eventually gave way to recognition of what made television different and powerful, culminating in another transformation of U.S. politics. The arc of this transformation spanned a generation. Harry Truman was president when television was in its infancy, and he was not very impressed with the flickering box. Like many in his day, he saw television as an extension of radio—essentially radio with pictures—much like early radio had been regarded as a wireless telegraph.[69] Truman saw television as a curiosity but not something of tremendous import, and he doubted that it was good for much of anything. The president was hardly alone in his sentiment toward the embryonic medium. Reviewing a display of television technology at the 1939 New York World's Fair, the *New York Times* remarked, "The problem with television is that people must sit and keep their eyes glued on a screen; the average American family hasn't time for it."[70]

It didn't take long for his successors to see what Truman did not: television offered politicians a new way to shape public impressions. Initial efforts to this effect paralleled the way politicians first used radio, which is to say it took some time for early, halting attempts to mature into sophisticated television strategies.

Largely dormant through the 1940s as investors faced the daunting task of developing a functional nationwide television infrastructure, the new medium finally crossed the threshold of viability by the 1952 election cycle, when 110 stations were broadcasting from sixty-six cities into 62 percent of U.S. homes.[71] With this type of reach, television had become too attractive to be left out of the calculations of ambitious politicians. But that doesn't mean they knew what to do with it. The Democratic presidential nominee that year, Adlai Stevenson, shared Truman's disdain for television and refused to adopt his erudite style to the short, simple statements that communicate best over the air, much to the consternation of advisers who weren't as concerned as the candidate that television promotions would turn politicians into products.[72] But to the extent that Stevenson's advisers were successful in getting the candidate to go in front of the cameras, their efforts were akin to using television as if it were radio, buying half-hour time slots for political speeches in the unfulfilled hope that they would attract an audience the way radio serials kept people coming back every week.[73]

Stevenson's opponent, Dwight Eisenhower, was surrounded by people who were far more savvy about how to use the tube, and although the candidate shared some of the same qualms about promoting himself on the air as his opponent, he eventually submitted to the most ambitious television campaign to date. Throughout his political career, Eisenhower was promoted by advertising people determined to use television to leverage the candidate's popularity and clean image. Even before Eisenhower announced his intention to run for president, the secret TV Plans Board—nine advertising and television men who wanted to get Ike into the race—worked to build a groundswell of support by using television to promote his appeal to ordinary Americans.[74] Early in 1952, when Ohio's Senator Robert Taft was the odds-on frontrunner for the Republican nomination, they arranged a televised rally at New York's Madison Square Garden to display for the cameras a (carefully staged) "spontaneous" show of Eisenhower's grassroots support. At the Republican convention that year, CBS producer Sig Mickelson remarked that Eisenhower's people had a more intuitive sense of how to use television than Taft's people. After the convention, Sigurd Larmon, president of the Young and Rubicam advertising agency, implored the nominee to build his campaign around television by using "the same careful planning and strategy that you and your staff employed in setting up the invasion of Normandy, and the same careful planning that we, in our business, employ in order to ensure the successful introduction of a new product."[75]

Eisenhower protested, but not too much. Unlike Stevenson, he consented to an extensive television campaign centered not on radio-style serial appearances but on the type of spot ads used to sell commercial products. The campaign hired Rosser Reeves, a partner at Ted Bates and Company, to design the first television ad campaign in presidential history. Reeves, known for hard-sell television and radio commercials that repeated simple messages to assure widespread recognition, was the father of a series of ads called Eisenhower Answers America, in which the candidate repeated brief, easily digested sentiments in a format that made it appear he was addressing the concerns of average citizens.[76] The spots all followed the same formula: an ordinary citizen in close-up asked the candidate a question, followed by a close-up of Eisenhower answering, with the exchange sounding like this:

Narrator: Eisenhower Answers America
Citizen: They say we've never had it so good. Yet, I've had to stop buying eggs, they're just too expensive
Eisenhower: No wonder. You actually pay one hundred different taxes on just one egg. We must cut costs, which means we must cut taxes.[77]

It was hokey, but that certainly didn't hurt the Republican nominee, who cruised to victory over Stevenson. And for the first time in political history, the elements of pretend that are so central to the effective use of television came into play in a presidential campaign. Reeves adjusted the lighting to make Eisenhower look dynamic. He instructed the candidate to remove his glasses to appear more approachable, employed professional makeup artists, and coached him on how to read scripts.

In a harbinger of things to come, pollster George Gallup was employed to gather data on the issues that concerned voters so the ads would hit their mark.[78] Even the construction of the spots contained more than a little deception. Eisenhower never actually met the people he appeared to address in the ads. He recorded his answers in a studio; sometime later, tourists at New York's Radio City were selected to film the questions, with the most realistic ones used in the ads.[79]

Television grew up during the Eisenhower era. By the time he left office, 80 percent of U.S. homes had televisions (the figure would reach 90 percent by 1962).[80] Not coincidentally, Eisenhower warmed up to the medium. Whatever initial reluctance he may have had toward doing spot ads melted away in the wake of an elaborate marketing strategy designed by public relations professionals and built around television. Eisenhower was the first president to realize that television gave him the opportunity to circumvent the press and take his message directly to the public, which he did by staging televised press conferences. He built a television studio in the White House, and he was the first president to employ something akin to modern photo opportunities.[81] When jet travel was introduced at the White House in 1959, Eisenhower's media advisers recognized the political value of sending him around the world to feed back television footage of the president in iconic locations meeting with world leaders.[82] John Kennedy would subsequently be given credit for using these techniques, but in fact they originated in the Eisenhower White House.[83]

Nonetheless, despite Ike's experimentation with television and success at cultivating a positive public image, his aides had unleashed only some of television's political potential. For all its efforts at image manipulation, the Eisenhower campaign and presidency projected an image of the general that was at its core more true than not. Although dramatically simplified and stripped of negative characteristics, the televised image of Eisenhower that played on his midwestern small-town roots and his courage and leadership during World War II was a fictionalized version of a real person. His public relations advisers amplified these characteristics for political gain, but they did not fabricate them. So it was with John Kennedy, whose televised image portrayed youthful energy, good looks, and a quick wit that reflected part—although certainly not all—of the president's complex persona. It would not be until Richard Nixon ran for the highest office in 1968 that the power of television to validate an untruth would be revealed. And that line would not be crossed until Nixon had famously taken the medium at face value during his 1960 presidential race and saw how television could destroy a politician who did not know how to control it.

Accounts of the fabled Nixon-Kennedy debates long ago entered American folklore: How Kennedy appeared young, tan, and vigorous, his blue shirt looking vibrant on black-and-white screens in stark contrast to Nixon's pallid appearance. How Nixon, ailing and in need of a shave, looked drawn and shifty as his deep-set eyes darted about the screen. How people who saw the debates were more likely to favor Kennedy while those who heard them on radio favored Nixon. How

Nixon entered into the debates against his better instincts, fearing that he would look weak if he backed away. How Kennedy's people were involved in detailed planning of camera angles, lighting, and set design while Nixon largely ignored the advice of media advisers.[84]

We may never definitively know what, if any, influence the debates had on the outcome of the race, which Kennedy won by the narrowest of margins. But we know what Nixon took from the experience. He learned that live television threatens to reveal too much of a person to the viewing audience and that you must control the beast if you want people to see something other than a candid view of your character.[85] It is not a coincidence that Nixon never debated on television again.

For the time being, Nixon was helpless to undo the damage he had inflicted on his public image and political career. He could only watch as television made Kennedy into more than he was. After the first debate, Kennedy's staffers noticed that an aura now surrounded the candidate that they were certain was not there before. At his public events, people pressed closer to him and tried to touch him. Women and teenage girls jumped in the air to get a look at him. The charm and magnetism he projected on screen followed him in person. He had become a television celebrity.[86]

And he knew how to milk it. Like Roosevelt with radio, Kennedy was a natural, the first bona fide TV president. He knew to look at the red light on the camera and address himself to people at home, not those in the room. He appreciated the telegenic benefits of his glamorous wife and young family and shrewdly allowed cameras to capture personal glimpses of life inside the Kennedy White House. He knew during filmed interviews to give dull answers to questions he wanted to avoid so they would be edited out during production. He moved televised press conferences to prime time to maximize the audience for his message.[87] And like Eisenhower before him, he was happy to let savvy media advisers direct these efforts. As his father, Joseph Kennedy, remarked prior to the 1960 campaign, "We are going to sell Jack like soap flakes."[88] And they did—on television.

Yet for all his celebrity Kennedy was not to television what Roosevelt had been to radio. Both men were gifted practitioners of their respective media, but Roosevelt also recognized the transformational power of radio whereas Kennedy, because of his easy success with television, did not need to do the same. Although Camelot was a show, its young, bright, charismatic star really was young, bright, and charismatic. The true political potential of television—to create a false impression through manipulation and control—would be revealed by the man who was humiliated by the 1960 debates and, once understood, would rarely be lost on his successors. Eisenhower may have been the first president to use television and Kennedy may have been the first president born for television, but dour, staid Richard Nixon was the first person to re-create himself on television and in the process release the medium's transformational potential.

In 1968 Richard Nixon was damaged goods. As political handlers are inclined to say, he had high negatives—people disliked him and didn't trust him. His ambition unabated, if Nixon wanted to stage a political comeback he would have to do so as a different person than the dark, shadowy figure of 1960. Television gave him the vehicle to do exactly that. One year after winning the presidency, Nixon told a meeting of the National Association of Broadcasters, "I am the world's living expert on what television can do for a candidate and what it can do to a candidate."[89] He wasn't exaggerating.

Nixon's strategy centered on convincing enough voters that he had fundamentally changed—that he had become a "new Nixon," a more accessible, agreeable version of his former self—and to do so without actually changing anything save for the way he would be perceived. The strategy was dishonest at its core, because the new Nixon projected on television screens was deeply at odds with the person behind it.

Early in the campaign, Nixon announced to the press that he would not "barricade myself into a television studio and make this an antiseptic campaign."[90] But the dishonesty of this statement masked and mirrored the inherent dishonesty of the Nixon strategy, because that is precisely what he did. The "new Nixon" was a creature of the broadcast studio, where the candidate was sequestered so that every element of his appearance could be customized to conform to the fabrication he was creating for the American voter. This strategy was the product of a group of hardened advisers—advertising men, lawyers, media consultants, and speechwriters—who understood the dynamics of television marketing and weren't afraid to treat the political campaign like the rollout of a repackaged but fundamentally unchanged product.[91] They grasped that the Nixon of 1960 came across, in Marshall McLuhan's terminology, as a hot figure on a cool medium: dark, edgy, sharp, and angular. The real Nixon was a poor fit for television, which rewards open, easygoing personalities. If they were to win a television campaign, Nixon's advisers knew they had to recast the famously aloof candidate as someone welcoming and inviting.[92]

In order to create the relaxed, spontaneous Nixon, they paradoxically had to exercise control over every element of his image, which meant throwing out the book on how to run for president and writing a new one suited to the potentialities of television. Open campaign forums were banned. Rallies and speeches to large crowds were dropped. The press, with its potentially challenging questions, was locked out. Everything was stage-managed. The Republican convention followed a script that was timed to the minute, maximizing the size of the prime-time television audience that would see Nixon accept his nomination and allowing time for a scheduled "spontaneous" outpouring of emotion when the nomination was finalized.[93] That autumn, Nixon held one event per day, scripted and planned by the campaign to ensure coverage on the networks' evening news reports.[94] To compliment this daily messaging, the campaign produced and aired ten regional broadcasts, each showing Nixon interacting with an audience containing seven detractors—all campaign confederates—who over the course of the program are "won over" by Nixon's affability and charm. The purpose was to get the broader audience to identify with

Nixon and complete the metamorphosis themselves.[95] It was not to change anything about the actual candidate. He remained as cranky as ever.

The success of the Nixon campaign shaped the way campaigns and officials would act during the television era, for Nixon and his advisers had demonstrated that television affords skillful politicians the opportunity to turn statecraft into stagecraft and thereby manipulate public opinion. Television is an entertainment medium, an emotional medium, and it is ideal for those who are inclined to sell people things they may otherwise not want or need. During this period, the public would become increasingly likely to make political judgments based on the personal qualities of candidates, believing through the sensory realism of the medium that the image they saw of the candidates projected over the air captured the reality of the person.[96] Elections would more than ever turn on matters of candidate character, but not their real character so much as television's version of their character, which the successful ones knew how to manage. Candidates who could not or would not repackage themselves for television—the Bob Doles and Walter Mondales—would be out of favor. Regardless of their governing philosophies and sometimes in spite of them, candidates who could employ part or all of the Nixon formula would be rewarded.

In reaction to the war- and scandal-producing imperial administrations of the 1960s and early 1970s, Jimmy Carter presented himself on television as the honest, down-to-earth peanut farmer who happened also to be president—an image that resonated with so many celluloid renditions of the office. When Carter lost his hold on the medium and public opinion during a time of economic anxiety and international frustration, Ronald Reagan, who knew a little about show business, cast himself as the rescuing hero. George H. W. Bush shed his preppy New England ways to successfully audition for the part of Reagan's surrogate, the rightful heir to Reagan's third term. His son, George W. Bush, during a time of scandal and aggressive partisan politics, marketed himself as the compassionate everyman—a uniter, not a divider—an ordinary guy not corrupted by Washington who more than his opponent would be fun to sit down with over a beer.

Television did not create this type of posturing, but it did necessitate it. And successful practitioners of television knew how to tell an emotional story and generate the reactions that would best resonate with the moment, even if the candidate's image did not square with his life or his agenda was not in demand. Ronald Reagan, the most natural television practitioner and one of the most carefully scripted presidents in history,[97] was a master at stage-managing television images with the intention of manipulating public perceptions of political reality.[98] When Reagan, for instance, wanted to avoid political fallout for cutting health care funds to the elderly, he appeared at a ribbon-cutting ceremony at a retirement home and basked in the televised imagery that communicated how much he cared for the welfare of seniors. As a result, you couldn't convince people that Reagan had cut the funding, because viewers resolve contradictions between what we see and what we hear in favor of the pictures. As researchers Kurt and Gladys Lang noted from work conducted as early as the Eisenhower administration, "With all its magic, television remains a mass and not a face-to-face medium of communication; yet the belief in the intimacy of television has its own far-reaching consequences.... The viewer cannot comprehend the 'real' personal qualities of the familiar face with which he is confronted, but he may believe he can."[99]

This is why Reagan's handlers, when something happened that was unavoidably bad, made sure he was nowhere to be found to avoid being visually connected to the unfortunate news.[100] And it is why reporters were at a loss to make much of the chasm between the policy substance of his administration and Reagan the public-relations product. With advisers who could expertly craft a made-for-TV message built around compelling, emotional imagery and a president who knew how to read his lines and hit his marks, Reagan withstood the attacks of his critics who saw a dark underbelly to the affable president's administration. As one observer noted, "The messenger became the message."[101] Reagan made personal popularity rather than policy the measure of presidential effectiveness. His was the quintessential television administration.

It is not entirely surprising, then, to find that in the years since Nixon's breakthrough the U.S. public has been, in Seymour Martin Lipset's terminology, programmatically more liberal than most of the people it elected to the presidency.[102] Voters who disagreed with Reagan's policy agenda twice helped vote him into office, the second time in a landslide.[103] So it is that Nixon should be credited as the transformational figure whose mastery of television produced the blueprint for two generations of conservative governance. Ronald Reagan may have had a more natural hand at show business and have been better in front of the camera, but he owes a debt of gratitude to Nixon, who demonstrated how to use television to sell something that wasn't there.

The Internet and Small-D Democracy

As progressive bloggers would be quick to point out, television politics has taken its toll on more than a progressive agenda. The era of television politics has also been characterized by weakened links between candidates and political parties, as television's emphasis on personal characteristics has enabled candidates and officeholders to develop personal followings.[104] It has at times weakened institutional checks and balances by diminishing the political influence of Congress, whose multiple voices cannot rival the president's rhetorical and image-making capability.[105] And although questions of cause and effect remain open, television's fakery has not been kind to the body politic. The era of the TV-centered politics of personality has coincided with greater negativity in our political discourse, increased apathy toward the political process, a rise in cynicism about the motivation of politicians, and a deeper sense of political isolation.[106] These characteristics of political culture have appeared only to intensify with the onset of satellite and cable television, whose decentralized programming environment has shattered the traditional networks' hold on viewers[107] without mitigating the erosion of public trust in politicians and political institutions. Rather than challenging the prevailing culture, these technological innovations have reinforced the centrality of television in American political life.

Progressive bloggers would change this by engaging a new medium that they would like to see challenge television's supremacy over U.S. politics. But that is not all they would change. Consider that from local newspapers to wire services to radio and television networks to international media conglomerates, the effect of technology has been to centralize media and political power, nationalize politics, weaken partisanship (as the party press yielded to the commercial press with its emphasis on objective reporting), homogenize political messages, and reorient the source of political financing from government patronage to the political parties to candidates through big-money political action committees and wealthy contributors.[108] Progressive bloggers would use their medium to reverse these trends. They would empower grassroots political action, strengthen partisanship, and challenge wealthy financial contributors with an overwhelming number of small donations from ordinary citizens.

By virtue of its structure, the Internet is an ideal medium for achieving all these goals, inasmuch as it is the first technological innovation in history with the potential to mitigate, and possibly even reverse, the effects of previous technologies. Although it is a mass medium, the Internet is highly decentralized, an electronic bazaar with immeasurable opportunities for users to find content to match their interests. It is the antitelevision: Even the most avid users will see only a tiny fraction of its content, and everyone's Internet profile is unique—no two users will duplicate the sites they visit, the features they use, and the intensity and duration of their patronage.

Unlike television, all politics on the Internet is local, with a wide range of community, regional, issue-centric, and statewide political blogs and a smaller set of national blogs whose relatively large following is the sum total of many contributors who bring local, grassroots perspectives to their involvement. Unlike mainstream journalism, which still clings to the twentieth-century standard of neutral reporting, political blogs are overtly partisan—some of the strongest partisan voices in national politics since the demise of the party press.[109] Unlike television coverage, with its tendencies toward pack journalism and homogeneous messages, the Internet offers information from every conceivable perspective. And in contrast to the big money that has by necessity gravitated to expensive television-centered campaigns and governance, the Internet has become the bastion of the small-dollar contribution raised from countless numbers of anonymous citizens whose willingness to give is boosted by the sense of common cause with others who would be invisible to them if not for their presence on a website.

The online left understands this. Where Jackson recognized the secret to inexpensive printing was its ability to support a national political organization, where Lincoln understood the secret of the telegraph rested with how it permitted him to dominate national discourse, where Roosevelt appreciated the secret of radio resided in its ability to communicate intimacy and mobilize a nation, and where Nixon comprehended the secret of television lay in its capacity to sell false images, the progressive netroots knows that the secret of the Internet is its ability to decentralize power and build networks.

If history is an apt guide, it is likely that time will pass before this secret is entirely unlocked for political purposes. The 2008 Obama presidential campaign will no doubt be viewed as a major step in that direction, as will the 2003 Dean campaign before it and the work of grassroots progressives during the midterm election in 2006. But the Internet is still in its adolescence by the standards of these other technologies, each of which existed in the mainstream for many years before its full political potential was realized. And history tells us there is no guarantee of how U.S. politics would be affected should the day come when someone unleashes this force on a regular and reliable basis, both to win elections and govern. But if the prerequisite to tapping the transformational power of the Internet rests with embracing the decentralized nature of the medium, then the progressive side of the blogosphere is closer than its conservative counterpart to achieving this goal. Although we are not quite ready to add the Internet to the list of media that transformed politics, by virtue of how it developed and how it operates, the trajectory of the progressive blogosphere, as we will see in Chapter 3, is rapidly taking us in that direction.

3

The Two Blogospheres
How Left and Right Are Structured

The blogosphere is an emergent phenomenon, drawing upon multiple actors with individual motivations whose relationship to each other and the political system is dynamic. The left side developed out of a sense of activist rage at the media, the Democratic Party elites, and the DC "Village."

—Anonymous Blogger

The Dean campaign was not only a watershed moment, it was experienced as a watershed moment while it was happening; the message of transformation was itself part of the transformation.

—Zephyr Teachout, director of online organizing, Dean for America[1]

In the late 1990s, the progressive blogosphere did not exist. After 2000 it existed in what looked like a primitive cousin to today's blogosphere, smaller in size and reach, in competition with its conservative counterpart for numerical supremacy in political cyberspace, limited by the number of people with ready access to high-speed lines. Still, the early contours of what would become a movement and what could be a transformational force were already becoming evident. By 2003 the blogosphere was enough of a curiosity to generate speculation about how anything meaningful could come from the ranting of a bunch of amateurs banging away on laptop computers in their homes. In form and content, blogs had an amateurish look and an uneven, ragtag quality. People would visit to rail about the Bush administration and complain about the Iraq War, both of which were still relatively popular. But it was hard to see how anything of substance could emerge from these sites. The war would go on, the Bush administration would proceed at will—nothing would change.

Then came Howard Dean.

In the Beginning, There Was Dean

If the Internet had a moment analogous to television's arrival as a political factor in the Eisenhower years—the sense that an infant medium was emergent but with uncertainty about the full nature and extent of its effects—that moment occurred during the 2003 presidential campaign of former Vermont governor Howard Dean, and the vehicle was the campaign weblog Blog for America. During that year, a precipitous and entirely unpredictable rise in traffic on Blog for America mirrored and powered the unlikely ascendancy of the obscure New England Democrat in the presidential race. Comment threads—comments posted sequentially by readers in response to a blog topic—bubbled over with the thoughts and suggestions of countless Deaniacs bound in virtual community by the idea that together they could elect a progressive president and, in the process, transform the way politics is conducted.[2]

Their ruminations ranged from the silly to the serious. Every endorsement and positive poll result was cause for celebration. Every mainstream press account that could even remotely be considered negative was met with harsh condemnation. People speculated about the composition of Dean's cabinet. Some expressed concern over the governor's eating habits and worried that he wasn't taking enough care of himself as he traveled around Iowa and New Hampshire. To an outsider, the blog had a motley quality. But this haphazard atmosphere hid a sense of ownership of the campaign and the candidate.

This high level of investment manifested itself in the most precious form of political capital for Dean's campaign, as his adherents did more than vent and hope and daydream. They also organized. They wrote letters to undecided voters, distributed flyers, canvassed, and arranged campaign events. Many of these activities were prompted by the campaign's professional bloggers who maintained Blog for America's front page. But others arose spontaneously through the efforts of ordinary citizens utilizing the series of Get Local web tools that allowed anyone to use the website to plan and advertise a Dean event in their community. People held house parties, hung Dean banners on freeway overpasses, displayed homemade Dean placards at sporting events. Throughout the country during the summer and fall of 2003, Dean activities were imagined, planned, and executed by ordinary citizens in the name of, but without the direct knowledge of, the campaign, vastly multiplying Dean's public presence during a time when most of the country was still unfamiliar with him.

The trade-off for this activity was control, as the campaign could not sign off on the things that were said and done in the name of the candidate. This is a bargain no traditional campaign would make. Presidential campaigns are centralized structures. They are about command and control and discipline, and they live in fear that, in a political world built around television, one slip by or on behalf of the candidate, one unfortunate unscripted moment, could become a media story that would put the campaign on the defensive or, worse yet, on the run. But this was a trade-off that the insurgent campaign willingly accepted. It had little choice. Howard Dean didn't expect to find himself running the first Internet-centered campaign. But once the Internet found him—once the comment threads started filling up with reactions from passionate followers—what choice did he have but to grab hold of this new force and see where it went? In this important respect, the Dean campaign did more than maintain a web presence. It used its web presence to decentralize power to its adherents,[3] permitting a glimpse of what Internet politics could be.

To many outside the campaign, including mainstream journalists, the most remarkable thing about the Dean campaign was how effortlessly it could raise large sums of money from ordinary citizens online. In truth, this was simply another manifestation of how completely Dean's Internet followers bought into the campaign. Anyone who journeyed into the comment threads on a day when the campaign was running a fund-raiser would have found the virtual equivalent of people stepping over each other to give money in order to exceed the campaign's stated fund-raising goals, as doing so was a badge of honor and a mark of legitimacy. Signature features arose spontaneously among cyber-supporters: People started adding one penny to their contributions to signify an online donation; others would send money in response to so-called trolls—political opponents masquerading as supporters posting negative messages to the website in the hope of stirring up controversy. Some people would ask or at times beg the campaign to hold a fund-raiser in honor of a key endorsement, or to counter a run of negative press, or to upstage their rivals. Imagine a place where people plead with a candidate to ask them for money. That was Blog for America.

In the end, the efficacy of the effort remained open to speculation. Dean lost. His campaign imploded spectacularly after a disappointing finish in the Iowa caucuses. This left some observers with reason to doubt the effect of the blogging effort on real-world outcomes and whether the interaction between citizen bloggers and campaign staffers mimicked but did not represent genuine discourse.[4] But the Dean campaign transpired during a time when television remained the dominant political medium, and for all its inventiveness, Dean's Internet army was neither large enough nor strong enough to rewrite the rules of traditional politics, which still demanded a tight organization and an effective television presence. The Dean campaign had neither[5] and could not bridge the differences between two seemingly incompatible styles of campaigning.

Whereas television's rules demanded top-down centralization and a cool media presence, the Internet rewarded decentralization and a hot presence. The candidate's own behavior illuminated the stark contrast between the old and the new medium. To his Internet followers, Dean was passionate, and he motivated them to take action—which they were empowered to do through the campaign's decentralized structure. The Internet is an ideal forum for generating friction. But on television Dean's heat communicated anger, and his staff (and more than a few bloggers) held their breath every time he appeared in a television debate or interview, hoping he did not trip up. On television, the lack of discipline and the candidate's fire were liabilities, and it was on television that the 2004 campaign was ultimately conducted and decided.

Still, it is difficult, several years after the fact, not to look back at the Dean campaign and see shades of what has come to pass, especially in light of how the various online communities of the left have started to mature and how effectively Barack Obama tapped the political potential of the Internet without sacrificing traditional campaign methods. Politics continues to revolve around television and play out according to television's rules. But there is more than a hint of the future in a robust and developing progressive blogosphere anticipated by the decentralized qualities of Blog for America—qualities that leave it better positioned than its conservative counterpart to take advantage of the possibilities of power generated at the grassroots.

From a Distance, Similarities Between Right and Left

Although political websites are only one small solar system in the Internet universe, they come in several forms with different types of content and appeal. Newspapers and television networks are online with interactive versions of their traditional incarnations and typically contain pages dedicated to politics. Likewise, elected officials, parties, interest groups, and nonprofits maintain Internet presences. Ditto political campaigns. These organizations and individuals utilize the Internet to make themselves available to plugged-in audiences and constituencies and tend to be relatively traditional in form and function (to the degree that anything may be considered traditional in an adolescent medium). Although they may offer video links, hyperlinks to sources outside the website, and content not available offline, they are essentially top-down instruments of the sort that were the first to emerge in cyberspace. And although they may well be far more sophisticated than their predecessors several years earlier, they share a DNA imprint with early Internet websites, which aimed to facilitate traditional functions like fundraising and advertising on political campaigns[6] or citizen feedback through email on government websites.[7] Their messages and functions are largely centralized. Like early innovations that sprung from other once-new technologies, they share more with their electronic predecessors (television and telephones) than with subsequent inventions that developed more closely from the novel possibilities of the new medium, like weblogs.

Weblogs, or blogs, capture the decentralized, bottom-up nature of the web. Anybody with an interest in politics, free time, and access to the Internet can start one, making blogs a form of citizen media that contrasts sharply with websites maintained by institutions, organizations, and officials.[8] Although all blogs maintain some type of front page for the blog operator (or blogger) to post material, some permit readers to respond with comments or to post their own diaries (technically making them bloggers, too). And blogs frequently contain links to other blogs favored by the blogger and may freely reference material in other blogs using hyperlinks that enable the reader to jump to the quoted cite. These links form connections on the web, directing traffic in a net pattern among and between blogs. Because blogs are blatantly ideological, and because people tend to link to others who share their views, the clusters of links have taken on a distinctly partisan cast, forming two distinct blogospheres (or, to some, blogtopias)—one on the right and one on the left.

From the outside, the network of conservative weblogs can be difficult to distinguish from the network of progressive weblogs, save for the obvious ideological difference in their conversations. Although the two blogospheres share some common points of reference, for the most part they are two distinct entities that appear to mirror each other. Progressive blogs share a common set of favorite progressive links and conservative blogs share a common set of conservative links. Thus conservative blogs are disproportionately more likely to link to other conservative blogs, or conservative outlets like the *Washington Times* and the *Wall Street Journal* editorial page, whereas progressive blogs are more likely to link to other progressive blogs or progressive outlets like the *Los Angeles Times* editorial page and *The New Republic*.[9] It is common for bloggers on both sides of the spectrum to avoid linking to blogs on the other side so as not to increase their opponents' traffic.

Within each blog constellation rests a hierarchy of websites defined by their traffic and concomitant level of influence over blog discussion. Each includes a network of top-line or what Herring et al. call "A-list" blogs[10] and a larger pool of less salient blogs. A-list blogs are most widely read, routinely cited in mainstream media reports, and heavily linked by a large pool of smaller blogs. Readers and viewers of mainstream political coverage may recognize some of the names, owing to the attention paid to them by political reporters: Daily Kos, MyDD, and FireDogLake on the left; RedState, Powerline, and InstaPundit on the right.

Beyond the A-list entries in both blogospheres rests a seemingly infinite web of less-trafficked blogs, some of which are tightly linked to each other to form topic-based communities. There are state-level blogs, local (or community) blogs, and issue-centric blogs. At any given time, both blogospheres are home to a multitude of loosely interconnected political conversations, in places tightly focused and intense but generally wide-ranging and free-form.[11]

On both sides of the ideological spectrum, blog posts are open and uncensored. The blogosphere is the Wild West of the new medium, an information source largely devoid of editorial sheriffs. In a sharp break with the norms that defined journalism ever since it evolved from a trade to a profession, both the left and right blogospheres are openly partisan, colorful, and often raw in their discussions of politics, with no love lost for the other side. This break with journalistic tradition is reflective of—and facilitated by—the fact that the Internet is the first decentralizing mass technology.[12] Liberated from the necessity of reaching a mass audience, bloggers are free to speak their minds; the motivational value of information is as great as its instructional value. In this regard, both blogospheres are a throwback to an earlier political time when partisanship defined news coverage, as bloggers of the left and right employ twenty-first-century technology in the service of nineteenth-century partisan politics while eschewing the twentieth-century journalistic norms of objectivity and balance.

Up Close:
The Activist Heart of Progressive Blogs

Although these similarities make the two blogospheres appear to be two hemispheres in a symmetrical orb, there are important functional and structural differences between the two sides, differences in purpose and operation that in the long run should better position the progressive blogosphere to capitalize on the political benefits of the medium.

Both sides have bloggers who post on matters of political interest and engage in ideologically tinged discourse. But the progressive blogosphere has also spawned a movement that styles itself after movement conservatives who have made their mark on politics for decades. Indeed, as Jonathan Chait wrote in the *New Republic,* prior to the rise of the blogosphere there were no movement progressives to speak of.[13] That began to change with the emergence of the kind of online activism that surrounded the Dean campaign. Plugged-in progressives connected by the Internet began to engage in political action. This group became the subset of the progressive blogosphere that refers to itself as the netroots—shorthand for Inter*net* grass*roots.*

As the netroots emerged in the two years following the Dean campaign, traffic on progressive blogs began to overtake traffic on conservative counterparts. Although the overall blogosphere expanded enormously between 2003 and 2005, owing in part to the increased availability of high-speed access, the left side grew at an astronomical pace. The conservative blogosphere was estimated at two to three times the size of the progressive blogosphere around the time Blog for America was energizing the Dean campaign. As with radio and television, conservatives were first out of the gate in the race to exploit the new medium for political purposes. But two years later the progressive blogosphere was nearly twice as large as the conservative blogosphere. In July 2005 the ninety-eight busiest progressive blogs logged more than 15 million page views per week, better than 5 million more than the top 150 conservative blogs.[14]

The differences between the two blogospheres intensified as the decade continued. By 2008 the progressive blogosphere had a larger nucleus of A-list blogs averaging more visitors and more page views than the conservative side. The differences are spelled out in Table 3.1, which displays the number of unique visitors and page views for progressive and conservative blogs averaging more than 1 million visitors in January 2008. A unique visit occurs when you connect to a website. Page views measure traffic through a website, such that each time a visitor navigates the site beyond the home page it is counted as an additional page view. The average number of page views per visit indicates how deeply visitors use a site.

On all three measures—visitors, page views, and views per visit—the progressive blogosphere is larger and more intensely utilized than the conservative blogosphere. Seven progressive sites cleared the million-visit threshold, compared to four conservative sites.[15] Together, the progressive blogs experienced more than double the number of visitors and page views and averaged slightly more page views per visit. The bulk of this traffic flowed through Daily Kos, a behemoth that alone averaged close to 23 million unique visitors and 26 million page views. Nothing on the right side of the spectrum can compare in size or activity.

Table 3.1 Traffic on Progressive and Conservative Blogosphere General Interest "A-List" Political Blogs with More Than 1 Million Unique Visitors

January 2008 Monthly Averages

Progressive Blogs

	Unique Visitors	Page Views	Views/Visit	Comments
Daily Kos	22,803,327	25,995,733	1.14	Y
Crooks and Liars	4,642,211	7,891,842	1.70	Y
Eschaton	2,951,500	3,302,430	1.12	Y
FireDogLake	2,055,319	2,935,348	1.43	Y
AMERICAblog	1,735,977	2,129,163	1.23	Y
MyDD	1,409,889	2,350,355	1.67	Y
Political Wire	1,236,540	1,483,849	1.20	Y
TOTALS	36,834,763	46,088,720	1.35	

Conservative Blogs

	Unique Visitors	Page Views	Views/Visit	Comments
InstaPundit	7,135,646	7,545,791	1.06	N
Michelle Malkin	5,165,962	7,152,318	1.38	Y
Power Line	1,990,968	2,092,087	1.05	Y
Redstate	1,573,304	2,654,334	1.69	Y
TOTALS	15,865,880	19,444,530	1.29	

Source: Sitemeter.com

Notes: Progressive blogs selected from rankings of advertising costs on Advertising Liberally, a liberal blog advertising network. Conservative blogs selected from blogroll links on high visibility blogs. Does not include sites that emphasize online journalism, like Talking Points Memo, that are designed to be news portals like Raw Story, the Huffington Post, the Drudge Report, or that are supported by conventional media outlets like washingtonmonthly.com or the National Review Online.

And Daily Kos, even more than other progressive blogs, is teeming with activity. On any given day, the number of comments to front-page diaries is likely to be orders of magnitude higher than the number of comments on any blog of the left or right, a testament to the size of its readership and the involvement of its readers. A constant stream of reader diaries fills the right side of the homepage for anyone to read and recommend to others, and the most frequently recommended diaries receive a premium position at the head of the list, where they remain until being supplanted by others in an endless cycle of user engagement. In the conservative blogosphere, the only blog that comes close to Daily Kos in unique visits is InstaPundit, a top-down website that does not provide for reader diaries or comments, as it is not geared to a netroots audience.

This is a telling distinction. More pronounced than size differential are the structural distinctions that separate right from left. The conservative blogosphere is to a large degree vertically organized, one piece of a well-established conservative media infrastructure. The progressive blogosphere, absent a preexisting movement, is more horizontally organized, depending on links among websites to amplify its messaging and multiply the effect of its activity. The presence of a vital, organized conservatism and the absence of a similar structure on the left explain structural differences between the two blogospheres that dovetail with the activist asymmetry between the two sides.

The progressive blogosphere operates on a bottom-up and decentralized basis, relying heavily on the open source approach to idea formulation and political mobilization we mentioned in Chapter 1 that invites real-time peer review by a large number of bloggers.[16] The term *open source* is borrowed from computer science, where it refers to a software product created by a multitude of designers; anyone can join the community and make additions or modifications. The most widely recognized open source product is probably Wikipedia, the online encyclopedia where anyone can create, alter, refine, and challenge an entry. The theory behind open source is that an unlimited number of minds working in the open will collectively produce a stronger product than a small number of experts working in seclusion (the way software and newspapers are traditionally produced).

The Internet itself has open source origins. Before it was used for chatting and dating, its precursor, ARPAnet, was developed by the Department of Defense to enable researchers to communicate with each other. The source code for its operating system was made available to its users, who were encouraged to work with it and share changes with other users, putting a lot of minds to the task of improving the code.[17] As end users as well as designers, researchers had an interest in contributing to the development of the system, so individual self-interest was served by making an investment in the collective enterprise.

In a similar manner, the netroots are an open source community; countless individual contributions make possible a sturdy and vigorous presence. If the strength of the Internet is the ability to build relationships, the left blogosphere draws on that strength through an interconnecting set of relationships among contributors.[18] Decentralized and permeable, netroots activism depends on a constant flow of information among bloggers within and among websites. Ideas can originate with regular contributors, some of whom are well known to their readers and to journalists, or with relatively anonymous authors of diaries and comments posted to blogs who can participate at little personal cost.[19] This is a characteristic shared with some conservative blogs but is arguably more critical to the development of a political agenda being created outside established institutions.

This is not to say that the conservative blogosphere has not aggressively fought political battles and does not engage in the same type of networked discourse as the left. The right blogosphere can take credit for some high-profile political achievements, not least among them challenging the authenticity of documents used by Dan Rather questioning President Bush's National Guard service, setting into motion a chain of events that culminated in the dismissal of the CBS anchor from his post. But actively pursuing news stories is different from hosting a movement, and it can be done without the open source structure prevalent on the left. The difference rests in the context in which the two blogospheres operate and their overall objectives. With a more centralized structure that is something of a throwback to the electronic media of the twentieth century, the right blogosphere is Microsoft Windows to the progressive blogosphere's open source operating system, Unix.

For instance, the popular conservative blog RedState, whose interactive qualities echo those of Daily Kos, was created by a 527 group (a tax-exempt organization established to engage in political action) and is owned by a conservative publishing conglomerate whose holdings include the Evans-Novak Political Report and the Conservative Book Club.[20] In 2005 several conservative blogs joined forces to create Pajamas Media, a mainstream initiative designed to leverage the reporting power of conservative blogs to cover political news. Michelle Malkin, one of the most popular conservative political bloggers, was a syndicated columnist before she was a blogger and is a regular presence on conservative television and radio programs. The Drudge Report, one of the largest nonblog conservative websites, pipelines information from Republican Party operatives.[21] These are movement conservative figures with access to an existing idea and media infrastructure, including well-funded think tanks, talk radio, news outlets like Fox News, and, until they lost it, control of all three branches of the national government. This infrastructure has permitted the conservative blogosphere to participate in a broader institutional structure already engaged in messaging, public relations, campaigning, and governing. All the things the netroots had to create on the left preexisted on the right.

The centralized characteristics of the conservative blogosphere are not lost on progressive bloggers. A survey of forty-one bloggers whose writing appears in progressive national, state, and local blogs reveals a certain sensitivity to the vertical structure of the online right. One state-level blogger referred to large conservative blogs as "astroturfs"—fake grassroots blogs designed to appear bottom-up when in fact they're supported by monied interests. Allowing for the possibility that perceptions are skewed by distance from and antipathy toward the other side, a number of progressive bloggers shared the sentiment that the telltale characteristics of messaging and money revealed their right counterpart to be a top-down phenomenon.

They perceive uniformity in the messages emanating from conservative blogs, in contrast to what they encountered on the left and in a manner they viewed to be indicative of a coordinated effort to influence mass public opinion. One respondent sensed that conservative blogs had "fallen victim to the top-down talking points and controlled headliners who dominate the approved right-wing spin," while others added:

> The coordination of talking points leads me to believe that even independent actors were willingly co-opted for top-down coordinated messaging.

> My impression is conservative bloggers are a strong echo chamber with messages coming from Drudge and InstaPundit in particular.

> They appear to follow Republican talking points more closely than the progressive blogs [follow Democratic talking points].

Where does this coordination originate? From the institutions that have no parallel on the left: the conservative establishment or conservative hierarchy. One progressive blogger viewed the right's hierarchical structure as a natural extension of "their more authoritarian ideological worldview," but others generally pointed to an abundance of money:

> Conservative organizations are much more generous in funneling money to conservatives while progressive organizations tend to horde their resources.

> The right side came from subsidized think tanks and established companies who hire operatives to blog. This led to the development of blogs like Powerline and RedState, as well as Michelle Malkin's video ecosystem.

> Places like RedState have been bought out by publishing outlets, and "bloggers" like Michelle Malkin are actually paid through the conservative media structure.

> It would seem to me that the rightosphere is extremely top-down, with major sponsorship coming from establishment conservative circles, with establishment conservatives like Hugh Hewitt and the National Review leading the way.

> At some point, Pajamas Media co-opted any bottom-up phenomenon that may have existed, thereby buying off a bunch of people who didn't act all that independently anyway.

The bottom line for these bloggers is a clear organizational distinction between the right and left, where the left is a community and the right is a corporation. As one blogger put it, "Right blogistan is the same message, many voices; left blogistan is many messages, many voices."

The contrast carries through blogger self-perceptions of the online left, which in contrast to the right is perceived as having decentralized roots. Universally, progressive bloggers represented in the sample regard their corner of cyberspace as having originated as a bottom-up phenomenon lacking in centralized control or big-money support. Several trace their blogging roots to the Dean campaign. Virtually every one has an account of freely engaging the progressive blogosphere, from the Washington State blogger who reeled off the names of nine regional blogs, each started by "an independent person with his own funds for his own political reasons," to the Illinois blogger whose goal of creating "a group blog out of the disparate individual bloggers on the Illinois scene" was "very much bottom up and not agenda-driven by existing organizations," to the Texas blogger who called his challenge to the political hierarchy of the Rio Grande valley "the best example of bottom-up grassroots development of a blogosphere in the nation."

> From 2003 to 2006, the number of Rio Grande valley–based blogs went from zero to literally dozens and dozens because grassroots activists who were against the machines [political organizations] or not tied to the machines wanted to have their voice heard. Many of these activists were doing so anonymously out of fear of recrimination from the machines. I was in touch with some of these folks who asked me to help mentor them in early 2006. One blogger, who was blogging under his real name, did some excellent coverage of a school board embezzlement scandal which wasn't even being covered by the media extensively because of fear of the machines.

The same is true of national bloggers. The big names among them, like Markos Moulitsas of Daily Kos, Duncan Black of Eschaton, and Joshua Micah Marshall of Talking Points Memo, were independent actors who began writing online when the medium was in its infancy. They developed a readership that expanded along with the growth of the Internet, but they hardly could be considered stars in a medium that was still largely free-form when they started. With an initial readership that could be measured in thousands rather than tens of millions, online blogging wasn't much different than writing for your own amusement (in July 2002—during the "Jurassic period," as one blogger called it—Daily Kos had 5,150 page views).[22] Consequently, the early blogosphere was something of a meritocracy. The ones that thrived did so through talent, effort, the ability to engage readers, and an excellent sense of timing. The same holds for featured contributors to national sites. As one such contributor succinctly put it, "I started in the diaries and worked my way up."

What the progressive blogosphere lacks in vertical organization it more than makes up for in horizontal relationships with online advocacy organizations that suggest how the blogosphere has emerged as part of a budding movement infra-structure. As Table 3.2 indicates, twenty-nine of thirty bloggers who responded to a question about how frequently they were in touch with advocacy organizations said they had regular (50 percent) or occasional (47 percent) contact.

The list of organizations they engage is far-ranging. It prominently includes Democracy for America (DFA), the political action committee that arose from the ashes of the Dean campaign that focuses on rebuilding the Democratic Party from the bottom up by identifying and supporting progressive candidates for state and local offices. Moveon.org—the widely known progressive advocacy group that boasts more than 3 million online members—is equally prominent. So, too, is Drinking Liberally, a social networking organization that directs progressives from its website to more than 300 locations nationwide where, at a specified time and place, anyone can come to meet over drinks to bond, vent, and talk progressive politics. Most meeting locations are bars and restaurants, a throwback to early-nineteenth-century taverns where Federalists or Republicans would gather to read party newspapers and argue about politics (or, as the Drinking Liberally website puts it, "promoting democracy one pint at a time").

Regional advocacy groups also receive significant attention from state and local bloggers. Like the bloggers themselves, these groups tend to have organized recently and maintain an online presence for the purpose of bringing about political change offline. The True Courage Action Network, for instance, was founded in 2006 for the purpose of advocating for clean elections and campaign reform in Texas. In the San Francisco Bay area, the Wellstone Democratic Renewal

Table 3.2 Extent of Interaction Between Progressive Bloggers and Other Political Actors

	Percent	N
Advocacy Organizations		
Regular Contact	50.0	15
Occasional Contact	46.7	14
No Contact	3.3	1
Party Committees		
Regular Contact	46.7	14
Occasional Contact	33.3	10
No Contact	20.0	6
Elected Officials		
Regular Contact	50.0	15
Occasional Contact	43.3	13
No Contact	6.7	2
Unelected Political Figures		
Regular Contact	50.0	15
Occasional Contact	46.7	14
No Contact	3.3	1

Club, named for the late progressive Senator Paul Wellstone, seeks to generate a grassroots takeover of the Democratic Party around a populist/progressive platform. Washington Public Campaigns was incorporated in 2003 for the purpose of mobilizing the grassroots behind public funding of political campaigns in Washington State. All are linked horizontally to bloggers who broadly seek the same objectives.

In the same manner, Table 3.2 shows how commonplace it is for progressive bloggers to maintain multiple links to Democratic Party officialdom. As with advocacy groups, these are horizontal links. There is no centralized control between party committees, elected officials, and unelected political figures and bloggers, no funding of bloggers by the party, no centralized message coordination. Instead, progressive bloggers engage formal party structures and establishment figures as part of their effort to transform the Democratic Party into a bottom-up, progressive, grassroots organization, and their high level of engagement is a barometer of the seriousness of that purpose. "I saw that there was a need to bring Democratic electeds and activists to the blogging world," said one local blogger, "so we could integrate the various parts of the progressive movement better."

About half the bloggers responding said they had regular contact with party committees including, at the national level, the Democratic National Committee (DNC), the Democratic Congressional Campaign Committee (DCCC), the Democratic Senatorial Campaign Committee (DSCC), and, closer to home, a variety of state party and county committees. A comparable number claim regular contact with elected federal, state, and local Democrats ranging from members of Congress to state legislators and mayors, unelected Democrats like regional superintendents of education and agency commissioners, as well as candidates for office and their campaigns. Collectively, this is a far-flung matrix of connections, a measure of how extensively the progressive blogosphere has enmeshed itself in Democratic Party politics.

No one could have planned a set of decentralized relationships like these. Progressive bloggers did not intend to build a movement from horizontal links spread far and wide through cyberspace, but the lack of organization on the left forced the emerging progressive movement to develop horizontally, which, as it turns out, has positioned the left to take advantage of the full power of the Internet far more thoroughly than the right. For the left, blogs presented the opportunity for an information insurgency—a means to penetrate the national discussion without the benefit of a pulpit. The progressive blogosphere developed from the ground up because progressive bloggers had no other choice.

A "Bourgeois Elite"

Like the citizen activists who rallied to Howard Dean's Blog for America, netroots bloggers do more than write about politics. They write about politics with the intention of facilitating political change, and they engage in political activity with the objective of unifying the left around an activist politics. Their broad goal is to turn the Democratic Party into an openly progressive party. Echoing movement conservatives two generations senior who successfully built a working conservative coalition inside the Republican Party, they are engaged in a power struggle with entrenched Democratic Party interests that, from the netroots perspective, seek to accommodate the right. They object to elected Democrats who triangulate away progressive priorities in what bloggers perceive to be an ill-advised attempt to cobble together winning electoral margins instead of working to build permanent majorities around progressive positions. They oppose with equal vigor mainstream political reporters who are perceived to frame the news in right-wing terms. These are activists who regard the blogs as a forum for planning and generating grassroots political action.

They come to blogging from a variety of backgrounds: from academia and software development, the entertainment field, and traditional media. They defy categorization by age. The blogger survey includes an individual who had been a commentary writer for more than forty years and another who started blogging in college. Some started blogging with the Dean campaign or posted diaries on Daily Kos. Many started casually, then got hooked.

A glance at the biographies of some of the past and present contributing editors to Daily Kos—the individuals responsible for a good share of front-page content—echoes this diversity of background. The group includes a stay-at-home mom, a playwright, a stockbroker, a medical doctor, a sociologist, a classicist—and more than a couple of former Republicans (including the site's founder, Markos Moulitsas). Excerpts from their biographical information, which you can find listed by screen name in Box 3.1, suggest that they are a diverse lot, united primarily by a love for words and a passion for progressive activism.

So it is with respondents to the blogger survey, who, when asked to volunteer why they started to blog and how their reasons for blogging developed over time, consistently spoke about their activist nature and their determination to shape media and political institutions. Progressive bloggers are motivated by personal and social considerations as well as by concerns about the state of political institutions and the media. Personal and social motivations—respectively the most and least frequently mentioned groups in Table 3.3—speak to the individual makeup of progressive bloggers. Desire to change the institutional and information environments addresses what they hope to accomplish by blogging.

More than half the bloggers in the sample expressed a personal reason why they selected to devote their time and energy to blogging about progressive politics. About one-third were lured by the opportunity for self-expression—either to vent or to voice an opinion in a forum where someone may (or may not) be listening. One in five were drawn to blogging because they find it to be fun, to alleviate boredom, or to be a venue for personal learning. Regardless of the nature of the fulfillment they find by posting words online, these individuals receive a sense of

Box 3.1 Select Biographical Information on Daily Kos Contributing Editors

BarbinMD (Barbara Morrill)
As Barbara Morrill entered her forties, she was a stay-at-home mother of two who spent her time helping with school projects and chauffeuring kids to soccer or lacrosse. Soon after the 2000 selection of George W. Bush as POTUS, she got her first computer and discovered the Internet and a shared outrage. Now she's a stay-at-home mother of two who spends her time helping with school projects, chauffeuring kids to soccer or lacrosse, and writing about politics and the media for Daily Kos from her Maryland home.

brownsox (Arjun Jaikumar)
Arjun Jaikumar is an actor and playwright by trade. He grew up in Newton, Massauchetts, the son of two loyal and wonderful Democrats, and his earliest political memory is waking up bright and early in 1988 to see if Governor Dukakis won.

DarkSyde
Stephen DarkSyde is a forty-something former stock and bond trader and one-time moderate conservative. As the scope of incompetence and malfeasance in the Bush administration and the wider neoconservative Republican Party became evident throughout 2003, Stephen began reading and writing on blogs. In short order, he rejected the existing incarnation of the GOP and joined forces with progressive bloggers.

DemFromCT (Greg Dworkin)
Greg Dworkin is chief of pediatric pulmonology and medical director of the Pediatric Inpatient Unit at Danbury Hospital in Danbury, Connecticut, where he has been in clinical practice for eighteen years. He holds academic appointments as clinical assistant professor of pediatrics at New York Medical College and adjunct assistant clinical professor of allied health science at Quinnipiac College. His clinical areas of expertise include respiratory illness in the pediatric population and the implementation of asthma education programs for the public and for health professionals.

Georgia10 (Georgia Logothetis)
Georgia Logothetis is a twenty-four-year-old political junkie living in Chicago. She first became addicted to politics at the tender age of twenty-two, when she stumbled across Daily Kos. An avid writer and poet all her life, she was first published at the age of nine in *An Anthology of Poetry by Young Americans.* She is currently an attorney at a Chicago-based law firm.

Meteor Blades (Timothy Lange)
Meteor Blades is the online moniker of Timothy Lange, born in 1946. He has been politically active since 1964, when he participated in voter registration in Mississippi with the Student Non-Violent Coordinating Committee in Freedom Summer. He was involved as an organizer in Students for a Democratic Society and, for sixteen years, as a member of the American Indian Movement. He was incarcerated at the Industrial School for Boys in Golden, Colorado, for twenty-three months and spent thirteen months at a federal prison camp for refusing the draft.

continues on next page

Box 3.1 continued

MissLaura (Laura Clawson)
Laura Clawson, born at the very end of 1976, is currently the Mellon Fellow in
Sociology at Dartmouth College. Politics were always an important part of Laura's
life: her early memories include a strike picket line, a gay pride march, and untold
Democratic Socialists of America potluck dinners. She participated in the first AFL-
CIO Union Summer and other political activities during college, but was not part of
an active political community in 2003 when, with great relief, she discovered Daily
Kos, which ultimately propelled her back into real-world political action.

Scout Finch (Jennifer Bruenjes)
Jennifer Bruenjes is a native Kansan in her mid-thirties who bleeds Jayhawk
crimson and blue. Frustrated by watching the unquestioned leadup to the Iraq War,
she set out on the information superhighway to find like-minded souls. Once there,
she discovered that she was not alone. In fact, there was a whole underground
movement afoot at Daily Kos that was aimed at restoring our democracy. Soon, she
became entrenched in the movement and began telling her friends that while she
was a mild-mannered sales and marketing executive by day, she was a Democratic
Superhero by night. Some speculate that she may privately wear a cape while she
works.

Smintheus (Michael Clark)
Michael Clark lives with his wife in rural eastern Pennsylvania. As a young boy in
Rhode Island, he witnessed the power of grassroots activism while helping to block
a boondoggle of a highway that would have cut his town in two. He's never figured
out what a "lost cause" is. He is a classicist and ancient historian with degrees
from Brown, UCLA, and Oxford. He tends to be fairly well up on events as of a few
millennia ago, but rarely blogs about them. Instead, he concentrates on the things
that citizens of a democracy ought to care about and that journalists really ought to
write more carefully about.

Trapper John (Jake McIntyre)
Jake McIntyre, thirty-one, was born and raised in Buffalo, NY, "City of No Illusions,"
where he attended the high school that beat Tim Russert's alma mater seventeen
straight times in football. During the course of a generally undistinguished undergrad
career at Cornell, Jake worked a number of dead-end summer jobs, which brought
him to the realization that the labor movement was the only buffer between
contemporary U.S. society and Dickensian England. After Cornell, Jake moved to
Honolulu, where he discovered love and the law. In 2001, he relocated to D.C. (along
with fiancée and law degree), where today he works for a midsized labor union.

---

personal gratification from blogging that dovetails with the social motivations for
blogging expressed by better than three in ten survey respondents: an idealistic
concern for improving society, desire to change the direction of the country, and
the wish to reach out to people who may not be politically involved. In several
instances, bloggers who started out satisfying personal urges discovered a social
purpose in what they did. "At first, it was a way to vent," said one blogger, "then

Table 3.3 Reasons for Blogging

	Percent*	N
Personal	**51.2**	**21**
Self-expression (venting, voicing an opinion)	31.7	13
Fun, boredom, personal learning	19.5	8
Informational	**43.9**	**18**
Providing information unavailable in mainstream media	29.3	12
Raising awareness	14.6	6
Institutional	**41.5**	**17**
Building progressive infrastructure	24.4	10
Influencing the Democratic Party	7.3	3
Promoting progressive candidates	4.9	2
Influencing other bloggers	4.9	2
Social	**31.7**	**13**
Improving society	17.1	7
Distressed with the direction of the country	12.2	5
Reaching people who may not have been involved	2.4	1
N		**41**

*Includes multiple responses

it became a way to effect political change." Said another, "I was terribly distressed with the direction the country was taking, and felt the need to speak out."

A range of agenda-based items aimed at making changes to media and political institutions complements these personal and social motivations for blogging. Better than four in ten bloggers were drawn to the Internet as a medium that could challenge what they regarded as superficial or irresponsible mainstream political coverage that enabled the Bush administration's conservative politics. One blogger expressed the sentiment that at the dawn of the age of blogs "there was literally no representation of the liberal side of political thought in the media," and another set a goal of offering "an alternative progressive message on the news of the day." If, as a third blogger noted, "the press is not covering important issues," blogs could fill the media void with substantive discussion.

Building institutional structures was mentioned almost as frequently as improving media coverage among bloggers inclined to use the Internet to generate social activism. Bloggers aim their institution-building energies in several directions: primarily toward developing a progressive infrastructure, and secondarily toward the companion objectives of rejuvenating the Democratic Party as a progressive institution, promoting progressive candidates, and influencing other bloggers for the purpose of building the blogosphere. One respondent offered this thoughtful and comprehensive account of using a perch in the blogosphere to build a progressive infrastructure:

Leading up to the 2004 elections and in the year or so afterwards, I became interested in "big picture" analysis of the progressive movement, and anything which indicated systemic problems in the machinery of the left, which could be addressed and make the movement more effective. That was around the time I started actively posting material (not just a few comments here and there), and around the time I started a local progressive blog. I thought that I was helping the movement by a) commenting on systemic problems and posing potential solutions, and b) contributing to an infrastructure of local political blogging which could fill the gaps in political coverage abandoned by traditional media. Around a year or so later (late 2005) and leading up to the present, I slowly began developing a theory of problems that face the progressive movement, expressed in terms of political machinery (coordination between organization, campaign effectiveness, etc.) and culturally rooted problems (weakened labor movement, resurgent religious conservatism, etc.). My blogging became more focused on these problems, and on identifying solutions to these problems, which progressive activists could take up in an entrepreneurial fashion.

It takes a unique combination of interests and desires to draw someone to a project like this, where they take it upon themselves to join with others who are similarly motivated to attempt to build a progressive infrastructure. Progressive bloggers are to some degree defined by a combination of the desire for self-expression, the tendency to find pleasure in the public broadcast of the written word, the wish to raise awareness in others, and the desire to improve society, coupled with a progressive bent—the sense that the country was badly off course during the Bush years—and an inclination for movement-building as a corrective.

This makes bloggers unusual. They are a definable subset of the broader population, a self-selected group, whether their words appear prominently on the front pages of major national blogs or outside the spotlight on state, local, campaign, or issue blogs, whether they are diarists on blogs that permit commentary or individuals who take the time to post on comment threads. What ties them together in the netroots is their commitment to taking action and their belief that action can start with the written word.

This differentiation is evident in the backgrounds of the Daily Kos contributing editors detailed in Box 3.1. For all the variety among them, there are demographic characteristics that set them apart from a simple cross-section of Americans. Most are formally educated, many at prestigious universities. A number of them come from homes where activism or political involvement—or both—were commonplace. They include more lawyers and political consultants than you'll find in the general population. Like the bloggers in the survey, they are an elite, the emerging opinion leaders of the twenty-first century.

Among high-profile bloggers on leading national blogs, the markings of that elite are starting to become apparent in conventional ways. Notwithstanding the fact that anyone can post comments and diaries and engage in netroots activism, as the Internet has matured it has become a less permeable institution for those who would turn to the blogosphere to wield a large megaphone. As blogging has inched toward the mainstream, grudging recognition of bloggers by the much-maligned conventional press has conferred legitimacy on their endeavors and has begun to make the highest profile bloggers into quasi-celebrities outside the blogosphere and full-fledged stars within it. The largest blogs are commodities with value, their advertising seen by millions of eyes per month. In this context, established bloggers occupy a valued place in the new media constellation that they did not hold just several years ago, making it all the more difficult for new bloggers to set up shop and compete with them. In 2002 and 2003, bloggers were like the first pioneers of the 1940s to venture into television while the action and glamour was still in radio. By 2007 and 2008, they were more like the early television stars of the 1950s, occupying an enviable place no longer accessible to those who came after.

This shift is apparent to many of the bloggers in the survey, one of whom referred to "the royalty of the blogosphere" as a "firmly entrenched establishment" that serves as a gatekeeper to new voices, at least at the highest levels of recognition. Another reminisced about a time several years ago when there was a "window of opportunity" for would-be bloggers to establish a following, as opposed to today, when the blogosphere is "closing to newcomers unless they are extraordinarily talented." A third blogger summed it up in terms that could apply to any maturing institution: "Right now we have many people becoming active in the process, but we also have a consolidation of power among certain bloggers.... Hopefully, the structure of the new media systems will allow a continual flow of new voices to the process without too many personalities claiming 'territory' and protecting their own power as is so often the case in any power structure."

The cross-pressures created by an emerging pecking order in an otherwise decentralized medium results in an odd mixture of accessibility and rigidity. Always self-selected, bloggers from the start were a different breed from people who partake regularly in traditional media. Now they have the added complication of having matured into leadership positions in a world that only a few years ago did not exist. By dint of their early investment in a new medium, they have become an activist elite, using words to influence and motivate those who, also through self-selection, frequent the communities of the progressive netroots.

Still, if the days when an unknown writer could build a huge community from scratch are in the past, it remains the case that the blogosphere has a lot of access points for people who want to take part in political expression without seeking the benefits accorded to notables. By definition and design it is an accessible medium, even if it has developed its own pecking order. In that regard, only the lack of desire could stop someone from being a part of the progressive netroots, even if there are limits to their participation that were not there when the blogosphere was in its infancy. Having a power structure does not negate having a community. Indeed, what community doesn't have one?

When viewed from the perspective of why people blog, the differences between those who blog and those who do not become more significant than the status differences among bloggers. Ordinary citizens offline, members of the progressive blogosphere are all part of an information elite online by virtue of their writing and their activist bent. Blogger Paul Delehanty, writing under the pseudonym Kid Oakland on Daily Kos, thoughtfully portrayed netroots bloggers as "Mavens"— people in the know positioned to influence others—and concluded:

> We in the blogosphere who are lucky enough to participate in this "community of Mavens" have a vital role to play. We need to understand and enhance that role. Blog posts can take any of a myriad of forms (humorous, wonky, outraged, worried) and still fulfill the core function of effective communication: crossing the chasm. I am convinced that good writing can persuade and connect. And I think that's what everyone who's ever written a diary here or a blog post elsewhere has sought: to communicate effectively. That's our job.[23]

Bloggers trade in words and information, which netroots activists of all stripes use to persuade and engage, powered and empowered by the connections made possible by the Internet. What makes this elite group unusual is that without the Internet they would be ordinary citizens. Their influence doesn't come from having recognizable family names or from having attended journalism school; credentials are not required to blog. The highest-profile among them were in the right place at the right time and persevered in their endeavors when conservatism was still ascendant and the political influence of the Internet was widely dismissed. But otherwise there is nothing extraordinary about them other than their commitment to what they do.

Chris Bowers of the blog Open Left calls them a "bourgeois elite," emerging as it did from people who support themselves with day jobs. This sets the netroots elite apart from (and in opposition to) liberal officialdom such as it is— top Democratic Party officials and leaders and a constellation of their aides and advisers—who are generally viewed within the blogosphere as something akin to the court of Versailles, the out-of-touch aristocracy that has come to characterize an ossified liberalism. In the same way it sets them apart from the mainstream media elite, the star columnists and pundits who inhabit Sunday morning talk shows and weeknight cable gabfests. Bowers explained the distinction in this 2006 post on MyDD:

> Bloggers and blog readers are not "the people." When understood as a group, they are not representative of America either in terms of demography or in terms of political engagement. Political blog readers are the highly engaged avant-garde of U.S. politics. As [the 2005] Blogads survey showed, their level of engagement in politics is incredibly high. Sixty-seven percent said [they] donated to a political campaign in 2004, compared to 15 percent nationwide. Seventy-two percent of blog readers said they signed a petition in 2004, 66 percent said they contacted an elected official, 44

percent said they wrote a letter to the editor, and 43 percent said that they attended a campaign event. Further, among self-identified Democratic blog readers, these percentages were actually much higher. Other studies of netroots activists, such as the study of Dean activists conducted by Pew, have shown similar, or even greater, levels of political engagement among the netroots.... The audience of the blogosphere is full of political activists, and the blogosphere has emerged as the primary means for progressives to communicate with a large segment of their activist class.[24]

Indeed to think of the netroots as a bourgeois elite opposed to an entrenched liberal aristocracy and distinct from the rank-and-file proletariat nicely captures the movement that has grown up around progressive blogs. Class distinctions explain why Democratic Party officials and liberal reporters are so often the recipients of much of the progressive blogosphere's verbal firepower, when the mainstream perspective of those two groups is that there should be a natural affinity with progressive bloggers. And they explain why it is possible to speak of a movement emerging online even though political blogs, to say nothing of widely read political blogs, constitute a fraction of blog traffic overall.[25]

A quick glance at the categories for the 2007 Weblog Awards competition reveals just how vast the larger blogosphere is, with topics as wide-ranging as technology, sports, business, law, science, education, gender issues, medicine, pets, food, music, culture, and, of course, gossip.[26] But political blogs can have an outsized influence on political discourse despite their relatively small overall presence. The Internet is not a mass medium like its predecessors; through decentralization and interconnectivity, the voices of the few can be multiplied and their actions compounded.

* * *

The emergence of a netroots bourgeois elite has no direct parallel on the right despite the presence of bloggers who, like progressive bloggers, trade in the arts of persuasion and political discourse. Of course, the right doesn't need anything like this, because movement conservatism has been around for years. The Internet emerged as a viable mass technology at a time when, with unions in decline and the social movements of the previous generation exhausted, an activist vacuum existed on the left. The netroots filled that vacuum.

Because of its activist orientation and decentralized, open structure, the progressive blogosphere is well positioned to take full advantage of the Internet's ability to decentralize power among a large community of individuals. But potential and results are different, and without the latter the Internet is easily dismissed as so much sound and fury.

There are several ways to measure how well they are doing. As political activists, netroots bloggers seek to shuffle the balance of political power at the national and local levels, within the Democratic Party and without. As media operatives, they seek to alter the narratives that define political debate. As individuals invested in community, they seek to create social capital by empowering a wide range of citizen activists. We will evaluate the effectiveness of the progressive blogosphere on these three broad criteria—political effectiveness, narrative development, and creating social capital—starting with the political record of the netroots circa 2006, the year U.S. politics began to shift to the left.

4

The Progressive Blogosphere and Political Effectiveness

If our goal was to expand the playing field and fly the Democratic banner in places that hadn't seen it in a long time, we have already succeeded. Of course, success raises expectations. It no longer is enough just to be competitive in these tough districts, in these long-shot races. Now, we want to win them. As usual, we're responding to success by moving the goal posts. Whether we reach that new level of success remains to be seen. But I'm damn proud of these [netroots candidates] that are making serious runs at their opponents. There are others, obviously. But man, we have so many good candidates, so little time. I wish there were 10 Daily Kos–style sites to cover the universe of great Democrats. Because we're a movement on the rise, with a deepening bench and an inspiring new wave of leaders. I may not be ready to believe we'll take the House and Senate this year, but I certainly believe that our future looks bright.

—*Markos Moulitsas, Daily Kos, October 17, 2006*

Three weeks later, everyone in the progressive blogosphere would believe. Democrats indeed won majorities in the House and Senate, storming back from the political wilderness to take control of both houses of Congress for the first time since Newt Gingrich's revolutionaries uprooted an entrenched Democratic regime in 1994. How much did the netroots contribute to this outcome? The evidence suggests quite a lot.

This may be a controversial observation. Bloggers, politicians, journalists, and academics have all debated the efficacy of the Internet as a viable political tool, and there are a lot of skeptics. The debate over the ability of the netroots to effect political change is a key part of the larger discussion about the hope and hype of Internet politics, where arguments about the transformative potential of the Internet[1] clash with arguments about its dangers and limitations.[2] This debate has considered a range of potential outcomes linked to Internet communications, including voter learning[3] and political interest,[4] mobilization,[5] message credibility,[6] and, as we will consider in Chapter 6, social isolation[7] and efficacy.[8] To a degree, this debate is fashioned by changes in the technology itself and by research developments that try to keep pace with these changes. As an emerging technology, the Internet has proved thus far to be an amorphous focus of study, with early predictions about its influence stemming from observations of a medium that only faintly resembles the Internet of today.

But if we focus on 2006, the year the netroots came of age, and we assess the political effectiveness of progressive bloggers on their own terms, multiple indicators point to an important set of activities successfully engineered by online activists that made it possible for Democrats to take advantage of a public opinion wave that emerged over the course of the year and to realize a sweeping victory. In House races, the work of netroots activists made Democrats competitive in enough districts to expand the scope of their victory. On the Senate side, a case can be made that netroots candidates were the difference in the Democrats' improbable takeover. These conclusions follow from an evaluation of outcomes that bloggers themselves called for: candidate recruitment in long-shot congressional races; raising small-dollar contributions from multiple sources; infusing traditional campaigns with alternative Internet-based communications; electoral success among a set of netroots candidates fully engaged in online fund-raising and communication; and national electoral success in nonfederal races. When we evaluate the political effectiveness of the progressive blogosphere by its own standards, we find that by 2006 it had become a movement with teeth.

Metrics of Netroots Success

If the Internet is to change the fundamental dynamics of political engagement along the lines discussed in the progressive blogosphere, we would expect to see renewed electoral success on the political left and renewed involvement in politics at the grassroots level. Netroots activists have been engaged in efforts to alter entrenched patterns of elite political activity, including candidate recruitment, fund-raising, campaigning, and ultimately winning elections. These efforts frequently place the netroots bourgeois elite at odds with the Democratic Party aristocracy (with whom they often share ideological affinity but whom they regard as purveyors of a corrupt and broken system sustained through interest group money and rules that dramatically favor incumbents) as well as with the mainstream media aristocracy (despite the critique frequently voiced by the right that media coverage tilts left).

How well they have done can be determined by looking at a set of metrics of political effectiveness as they apply to the 2006 political cycle—the first in which the netroots was large enough to make a difference. These are:

Contested House seats. Netroots activists have sought to expand the political playing field by recruiting congressional candidates in as many districts as possible, even districts where progressive candidates have little chance to win, in order to force the opposition to expend resources defending otherwise uncontested seats and to capitalize on unexpected circumstances that could put unlikely districts in play. Their effectiveness may be measured by determining if there were fewer House seats left uncontested by Democrats in 2006 than in 2004 and other previous years.

Donor base and contribution size. If progressive candidates are to be responsive to grassroots concerns, they need to be supported with small-dollar contributions from multiple contributors. To achieve this outcome, the donor base should be large, and the average contribution made through progressive Internet-based organizations engaged in grassroots fund-raising should be of the small-dollar variety.

Hybrid campaigning. Traditional campaigns are television-centered and rely on top-down campaign approaches, like television advertising, direct mail, robocalls to voters, and campaign messages derived from polling data and focus groups. Nontraditional campaigns attempt to integrate these initiatives with web-friendly activities that require them to experiment with a degree of decentralization, through what may be termed *hybrid campaigning.* Hybrid political campaigns mix traditional approaches with new campaign media (websites with interactive features and weblogs), introducing a decentralized, bottom-up element to campaigning to raise funds online and engage in an ongoing online dialogue with netroots supporters. If the netroots model of decentralized campaigning has merit, then as the new media grow in reach and effectiveness we would expect to see the number of hybrid campaigns increase—and achieve some degree of success. We can assess the prevalence of hybrid campaign methods by counting the number of hybrid campaigns among competitive House and Senate candidates as ranked by national political observers, and an examination of vote margins among candidates employing hybrid campaign techniques can determine the degree of competitiveness and electoral success achieved by Internet-friendly candidates. In particular, the presence and effectiveness of hybrid campaigning will be examined through the use of nontraditional fund-raising efforts (seeking and receiving funds through progressive Internet-based organizations), campaign websites with highly interactive features, and high rates of online discourse about the campaigns in the progressive blogosphere.

Candidate convergence. At the point where aggressive online fund-raising and an active campaign web presence converge with maintaining a high profile on progressive blogs, we can identify a class of netroots candidates who have actively embraced an Internet-centered approach to politics. Their campaigns would be those at the vanguard of the netroots revolution, heavily investing in online political organizing and fund-raising while actively and intentionally engaging the progressive blogosphere. We can determine the number of such campaigns by examining web use and online discourse patterns among 2006 House and Senate candidates singled out by leading national bloggers for netroots funding. Then, we can determine their effectiveness by looking at how their campaigns performed, giving us a sense of the outcomes realized by the most committed web-centric candidates.

Nonfederal candidates. Because progressive Internet-based politics developed in a bottom-up fashion, some of the earliest political results should be at the state and local levels. Democracy for America, the political action committee that emerged as the legacy of the 2004 Howard Dean presidential campaign, endorses and supports progressive nonfederal candidates who would not otherwise receive attention outside their jurisdictions. If their efforts are effective, the electoral success of endorsed nonfederal candidates should increase from year to year. Because they have been operating since 2004, we can compare their rates of success prior to and during the 2006 cycle.

As we will see, when these metrics are examined collectively, it becomes clear that the progressive blogosphere began to have a noticeable effect on the political process and on political outcomes during the 2006 cycle. The netroots succeeded in contesting more House seats in 2006 than 2004, and a group of progressive candidates launched hybrid campaigns during which they engaged in online fundraising and sophisticated bottom-up web activities while generating significant attention from progressive bloggers. Many of these campaigns were competitive, and a number were victorious even though they faced long odds. At the nonfederal level, progressive candidates have been making steady progress since 2004, especially in gubernatorial and state legislative races, thanks in part to netroots efforts.

Contested House Seats

The strategy of running a Democratic candidate in every House district was an online creation that bucked the thinking of established political pros. Because unchallenged districts are invariably the least competitive in terms of their partisan distribution of constituents, conventional thinking suggests that time and money expended in such districts are wasted resources better employed in jurisdictions that offer some promise of victory. Proponents of contesting every House district see the political map differently from many Washington professionals. Their thinking is akin to the logic behind the Fifty State Strategy championed by Howard Dean during his tenure as chair of the Democratic National Committee, which funnels national party resources to even the reddest of states in an effort to build a national party infrastructure at the state and local levels. The debate between concentrating resources in places where Democrats have proven they can win, versus spreading resources to places where Democrats traditionally do not compete, continued through the 2008 election, when Barack Obama at least temporarily silenced critics of a broader approach by contesting and winning Republican states like Virginia, North Carolina, Indiana, Colorado, and Nevada. But this strategy has detractors whose opposition dates back to the netroots initiative of 2006.

Promoted heavily by netroots activist Chris Bowers, the logic behind the House recruitment effort is straightforward: the only way to compete nationally is to engage everywhere. As Bowers explained to his MyDD readers:

Uncontested seats ... hurt Democrats both up-ticket and down-ticket. They thin out our candidate benches, and weaken our activist base. They limit the distribution and dissemination of our message, allowing Republican frames, memes and narratives to thrive unchallenged. Perhaps worst of all, uncontested and lightly contested Republican incumbents in 90 seats across the country has resulted in $63 million being funneled to seriously challenged Republican incumbents in other districts over the past three cycles. In other words, uncontested seats fail to stretch Republican defenses, making it all the easier for them to maintain their majority.[9]

This approach turns conventional thinking on its head by regarding expenditures in hopelessly noncompetitive districts as an element of a broader strategy to elect Democrats nationwide. Disregarding the odds of success in any individual district, it views each contest as part of a network of races that collectively constitute the electoral landscape, assessing the cost of investing in a set of lost causes against the benefits of broadening the national playing field.

In the five election cycles prior to 2006, dating back to the 1994 Republican takeover of Congress, Democrats regularly left at least thirty-three seats uncontested; in 1998 they conceded fifty-five contests by not recruiting candidates. In each cycle, Republicans left fewer seats uncontested. When Bowers put out the call to find a candidate in every district in 2006, his goal was to improve on the high-water mark of 403 Democrats competing for 435 seats in 2000, with the secondary goal of surpassing the Republican high-water mark of 419 contested seats in 1994.[10]

A quick glance at Table 4.1, which lists Republican House seats left uncontested by Democrats in 2004 and 2006, illuminates the long odds any Democrat would face running in these districts. The list includes some of the most entrenched congressional Republicans, running in districts with an overwhelming Republican constituency. For obvious reasons, well-funded national organizations like the Democratic Congressional Campaign Committee (DCCC) would have no interest in recruiting candidates or investing resources in districts such as these. Blogger Jerome Armstrong explains that, when he approached the DCCC in 2005 with the idea of contesting every single congressional seat in 2006,

> I got mostly the same usual standbys for why that wasn't a priority. I'd given [them] a Project 90 document before meeting with them [a reference to ninety uncontested or lightly contested Republican seats in the previous three cycles], which explains in mind-opening detail, what happens when you contest a race that would have been previously uncontested. Simply put, the safe Republican will go and spend their money helping the endangered or challenging Republicans in other districts, but the challenged Republican-held seat will siphon off money from those other Republicans. This document analyzed it in cold numbers over the past three cycles, and the conclusion was blatant—it makes sense to challenge all the seats. Yet, inside DC, that's still a foreign concept. There are 435 federal level seats up next year in

Table 4.1 Uncontested Republican House Seats, 2004 and 2006

Republican Seats Uncontested in 2004 and 2006 (4)

District	2004 Winner	R–D Vote	2006 Winner	R–D Vote
AL-06	Bachus	100–0	Bachus	100–0
MS-03	Pickering	80–20	Pickering	78–22
VA-06	Goodlatte	100–0	Goodlatte	75–25
AZ-06	Flake	79–21	Flake	74–26

Republican Seats Contested in 2004 and Uncontested in 2006 (6)

District	2004 Winner	Party	R–D Vote	2006 Winner	R–D Vote
CA-42	Miller	R	68–32	Miller	100–0
WI-06	Petri	R	67–30	Petri	100–0
TX-11	Conaway	R	77–22	Conaway	100–0
LA-06	Baker	R	72–19	Baker	83–17
VA-04	Forbes	R	65–35	Forbes	76–24
FL-12	Putnam	R	65–35	Putnam	69–31

Republican Seats Uncontested in 2004 and Contested in 2006 (32)

District	2004 Winner	R–D Vote	2006 Winner	Party	Defeated	Party	R–D Vote
KS-01	Moran	91–9	Moran	R	Doll	D	79–20
GA-10	Deal	100–0	Deal	R	Bradbury	D	77–23
TX-13	Thornberry	92–8	Thornberry	R	Waun	D	74–23
KY-05	Rogers	100–0	Rogers	R	Stepp	D	74–26
GA-06	Price	100–0	Price	R	Sinton	D	72–28
GA-07	Linder	100–0	Linder	R	Burns	D	71–29
CA-22	Thomas	100–0	McCarthy	R	Beery	D	71–2

District	Incumbent	2004	Incumbent	Party	Opponent	Party	2006
FL-04	Crenshaw	100–0	Crenshaw	R	Harms	D	70–30
GA-06	Kingston	100–0	Kingston	R	Nelson	D	68–32
CA-41	Lewis	100–0	Lewis	R	Conteras	D	67–33
OK-03	Lucas	82–18	Lucas	R	Barton	D	67–33
TN-07	Blackburn	100–0	Blackburn	R	Morrison	D	66–32
MS-01	Wicker	79–21	Wicker	R	Hurt	D	66–34
OK-04	Cole	78–22	Cole	R	Spake	D	65–35
PA-19	Platts	92–8	Platts	R	Avillo	D	64–33
VA-07	Cantor	76–24	Cantor	R	Nachman	D	64–34
VA-01	Davis	80–20	Davis	R	O'Donnell	D	63–35
FL-07	Mica	100–0	Mica	R	Chagnon	D	63–37
SC-03	Barrett	100–0	Barrett	R	Ballenger	D	63–37
TX-03	Johnson	86–14	Johnson	R	Dodd	D	62–35
SC-01	Brown	88–12	Brown	R	Maatta	D	60–38
PA-05	Peterson	88–12	Peterson	R	Hillard	D	60–40
TX-14	Paul	100–0	Paul	R	Sklar	D	60–40
FL-21	L. Diaz-Balart	73–27	Diaz-Balart	R	Gonzalez	D	59–41
LA-04	McCrery	100–0	McCrery	R	Cash	D	58–17
AZ-03	Shadegg	80–20	Shadegg	R	Paine	D	58–39
FL-24	Feeny	100–0	Feeny	R	Curtis	D	58–42
FL-25	M. Diaz-Balart	100–0	Diaz-Balart	R	Calderin	D	58–42
FL-09	Bilirakis	100–0	Bilirakis	R	Busansky	D	56–44
TX-10	McCaul	84–16	McCaul	R	Ankrum	D	55–41
NY-25	Walsh	90–10	Walsh	R	Maffei	D	51–49
PA-10	Sherwood	93–7	Sherwood	**D**	Carney	**R**	47–53

Note: In VT-AL, Sanders (I) ran uncontested in 2004 because he caucused with Democrats; Democrats challenged and won this seat in 2006.

the House, and contesting them all just doesn't make sense, they say, regardless of the facts. They cannot see the forest for the trees.[11]

Other mainstream figures were equally uncharitable in their evaluation of the plan. Congressional expert Stuart Rothenberg wrote, "Blogger Chris Bowers at MyDD perhaps is the best example of how clueless some bloggers really are about politics."[12] Against this backdrop, Bowers and his fellow netroots activists attempted to prove the experts wrong.

Measured against their stated goals or against previous recruitment figures, their efforts were successful, perhaps remarkably so. In the 2006 cycle, candidates stepped forward to challenge incumbent Republicans in all but four of thirty-six seats left untouched in 2004. An additional six Republicans who faced opposition in 2004 were unopposed in 2006, resulting in a net increase of twenty-six contested districts for a total of 425 races contested by Democrats. This represents the largest number of seats contested by Democratic candidates since Republicans gained control of Congress, surpasses the twelve-year Republican high-water mark for candidate recruitment and falls only ten seats short of Bowers's quixotic objective of running a candidate in every district.

Tactically, then, the effort to recruit candidates to run as what only could be considered sacrificial lambs was a resounding success. Despite resistance from mainstream Democrats, online progressive activists were able to propel more than two dozen individuals to political service of the highest order. At this level, we see evidence of the ability of the progressive blogosphere to organize, persevere, and achieve tangible results through decentralized virtual political activity.

But what of the wisdom of the effort or, put differently, what might we make of the strategic success of recruiting candidates in long-shot districts? Because the stated benefits of expanding the competitive playing field are either abstract or indirect, this is a more difficult question to answer. The data in Table 4.1 do not address whether the enterprise resulted in enhanced progressive activism, strengthening of the Democratic Party's national position, or victory in competitive races because Republicans had to divert resources from tighter contests. And it is perhaps unfair—certainly it is at odds with the professed objectives of the advocates of national recruitment—to evaluate the strategic success of the effort by looking at what happened to those Democrats who ran in previously uncontested districts. Nonetheless, Table 4.1 provides outcome data, and it offers an important glimpse into the possible strategic fruits of the Internet-driven recruitment strategy.

The bottom section of Table 4.1 lists the races contested by Democrats in 2006 in descending order by vote margin, with the most lopsided results listed first. On average, the victory margin in these thirty-two races fell a dramatic twenty-eight points from the previous cycle just by virtue of the presence of a challenger, although the mean margin of victory was a noncompetitive 63.9 percent. However, the distribution of victory margins tells a different story. Using a four-point differential as the benchmark for competitive races, two of the thirty-two contests were competitive: NY-25, where Democrat Dan Maffei came within two points of upsetting nine-term Republican incumbent James T. Walsh, and PA-10, where Chris Carney upset Republican Don Sherwood by six points in a contest that included allegations of personal misconduct by the incumbent.

In the early months of 2006, when candidate recruitment needed to be finalized, national observers did not consider either of these seats to be competitive. Had they remained uncontested as in 2004, Democrats would have lost the opportunity to take advantage of the favorable political dynamics that developed in these districts in 2006. Because Democrats ran credible candidates, the strategy of contesting as many seats as possible directly yielded a net gain of one congressional seat. Although it might be argued that the political climate in 2006 was unusually favorable to Democrats, it is also possible that any cycle can yield unexpected and quirky contests and that parties will capitalize on them only if they are prepared. From this bottom-line perspective, it is possible to make a case for the strategic effectiveness of the recruitment strategy that validates, at least in part, the successful tactical recruitment effort waged on the Internet.

Donor Base and Contribution Size

The potential of the Internet to influence political outcomes caught the attention of mainstream observers in 2003, when Howard Dean demonstrated that a long-shot candidate operating with a solid base of grassroots support could garner enough money through small-dollar contributions to compete with better-known challengers. Perhaps the most pronounced lesson of the Dean campaign for conventional candidates is that the Internet can be a lucrative source of campaign dollars (and, not coincidently, progressive bloggers were not shy about their sensitivity to being treated like a big ATM by mainstream progressive fund-raising organizations). By 2008 the ability of the Internet to bankroll a candidate had crossed into conventional wisdom with the astounding online fund-raising success of the Obama campaign—which in September took in roughly three times the amount raised by the Dean campaign in a year—and Ron Paul's long-shot Republican effort, which raised large amounts of online cash from a relatively small but dedicated base. Still, the experience of these campaigns may not be transferable to candidates without a preexisting online following like Dean, Obama, or Paul or to progressive causes not directly attached to a candidate. A more stringent measure of the effectiveness of the progressive blogosphere is whether money can be raised for progressive causes through affiliated online organizations in a nonpresidential year.

Throughout the 2006 cycle, the progressive blogosphere actively promoted the work of Moveon.org, one of the largest online progressive activist organizations, and Democracy for America (DFA). An examination of their fund-raising figures for the 2006 cycle, displayed in Table 4.2, confirms that both organizations were successful in achieving the goal of raising large numbers of small contributions.

The average contribution for both organizations was much less than the small contribution level of $200 established by the Federal Election Commission. The average contribution size to Moveon.org was dramatically below this mark, at $45 per contribution from more than 600,000 individual contributors, on the strength of a large number of small-dollar contributions to progressive candidates and ad campaigns run on behalf of candidates and progressive causes during the 2006 cycle. Likewise, the average contribution to Democracy for America was slightly more than $90. A smaller operation than Moveon.org, DFA raised more than $1.7 million from slightly less than 19,000 contributors for the purpose of sponsoring progressive candidates at the subnational level.

Hybrid Campaigning

The three components of hybrid campaigning examined here are nontraditional fund-raising efforts, campaign web use, and the amount of attention paid to a campaign in online discourse. Collectively, these activities indicate how deeply congressional campaigns were engaged in Internet activity and the extent of their investment in progressive netroots politics.

Table 4.2 Democracy for America and Moveon.org Donor Base and Contribution Size, 2006

Moveon.org	
Dollars raised	$27,392,712
Individual contributors	608,727
Average contribution	$45
Contributions to Candidates (rounded)	
Dollars	$3,600,000
Contributors	250,000
Average contribution	$14.40
Contributions for TV ads (rounded)	
Dollars	$2,800,000
Contributors	250,000
Average contribution	$11.20
Democracy for America	
Dollars raised	$1,734,551
Individual contributors	18,917
Average contribution	$91.69

Sources: Moveon.org, "Election 2006: People Powered Politics" and Democracy for America.

Netroots campaign involvement ranged from nonexistent to all-consuming depending on the inclination of the candidate, so hybrid campaigns vary in the extent to which they utilized the Internet to organize, fund, and promote themselves. The critical distinction is between campaigns that were Internet-friendly (beyond routine activities like maintaining a website) and campaigns that did not engage in Internet-driven grassroots activities. In this regard, some hybrid campaigns accepted money from Washington-based groups like the DCCC, spent heavily on television advertising and direct mail, and received large-dollar special-interest contributions, whereas others, like the upstart congressional campaign of Carol Shea-Porter in New Hampshire's First Congressional District, could not have been competitive without using the Internet to raise funds, advertise, and build grassroots support.[13] What they hold in common is the willingness to relinquish a degree of control over their communication environment to realize the bottom-up benefits of Internet politics. This sets hybrid campaigns apart from traditional campaigns that are notoriously reluctant to relinquish such control.[14]

In order to relate hybrid campaign activities to political outcomes, 2006 House and Senate seats considered by three leading congressional election experts to be in play were ranked according to their level of competitiveness at two points in the election cycle: spring 2006 and just before Election Day.[15] Each contest was placed into one of five tiers based on the collective wisdom about its level of competitiveness roughly six months before the votes were cast: Democrats Favored (Tier 1); Toss-up (Tier 2); Lean Republican (Tier 3); Likely Republican (Tier 4); and Safe Republican (Tier 5).[16] Typically, contests considered "likely" or "safe" for one party are noncompetitive, but rankings change over the course of a campaign, and in 2006 a number of races that were noncompetitive in the spring were considered to be in play by autumn. These races are included in the rankings employed here.

Spring rankings are significant because they set expectations for autumn, which in turn can influence national campaign committee expenditure decisions, campaign fund-raising ability, and candidate recruitment in seats without challengers. In essence, springtime rankings codify congressional races as either highly competitive contests worthy of a lot of attention or, to varying degrees, contests where a challenge is not likely to materialize. These judgments, of course, change as rankings change, but the early line on competitiveness will structure decisions that can have a meaningful effect on a campaign's trajectory. For this reason, springtime rankings were used in this analysis.

By Election Day, there had been some movement in the rankings to reflect the coming Democratic wave. Of the ninety-one ranked House races listed in Table 4.3, the vast majority initially leaned toward Republicans, making those contests unlikely to attract significant early money or attention from the DCCC. By Election Day the political landscape had shifted dramatically, as thirty-four of fifty-eight Tier 3, Tier 4, and Tier 5 races had become competitive. But when early decisions about candidate recruitment and financial support had to

Table 4.3 House and Senate Campaign Competitiveness Rankings, Spring and Fall 2006

House Races

Spring Rankings	N	Fall Rankings					Democratic	
		Tier 1	Tier 2	Tier 3	Tier 4	Tier 5	Wins	Pct.
Tier 1 - Democrats Favored	19	18	1	0	0	0	19	1.00
Tier 2 - Toss-up	14	8	6	0	0	0	10	0.71
Tier 3 - Lean Republican	18	3	14	1	0	0	11	0.61
Tier 4 - Likely Republican	11	1	6	3	1	0	3	0.27
Tier 5 - Safe Republican	29	1	9	6	12	1	9	0.31
TOTAL	**91**	**31**	**36**	**10**	**13**	**1**	**52**	**0.57**

Senate Races

Spring Rankings	N	Fall Rankings					Democratic	
		Tier 1	Tier 2	Tier 3	Tier 4	Tier 5	Wins	Pct.
Tier 1 - Democrats Favored	3	3	0	0	0	0	3	1.00
Tier 2 - Toss-up	1	1	0	0	0	0	1	1.00
Tier 3 - Lean Republican	3	1	2	0	0	0	3	1.00
Tier 4 - Likely Republican	2	0	0	2	0	0	1	0.50
Tier 5 - Safe Republican	2	0	0	1	0	1	1	0.50
TOTAL	**11**	**5**	**2**	**3**	**0**	**1**	**9**	**0.82**

be made, the conventional wisdom was not yet as favorable to Democrats as it would be later.

Democrats ended up winning a fair share of these contests, along with 71 percent of the races initially considered toss-ups and all of the races where they were favored, most of which never became competitive. They did even better in the Senate, winning nine of eleven competitive seats. The exceptions were an open Republican seat in Tennessee and the unusual saga of Ned Lamont, one of the premier netroots candidates, whose stunning primary defeat of incumbent Connecticut Democrat Joseph Lieberman was followed by a blowout general election loss to Lieberman, who reclaimed his seat by running as an independent candidate.[17]

How many of these less-competitive contests benefited from netroots attention? One may assume that hybrid campaigning would appeal to the candidate who is fighting an uphill battle. Long-shot Democrats would be expected to be more likely to turn to the netroots and employ hybrid campaign methods out of the necessity created by having less chance of attracting significant resources through conventional means, in much the way the netroots itself developed from the lack of a progressive infrastructure. Likewise, individuals engaged in Internet-based political activity might be more drawn to candidates who demonstrate a propensity to listen to them. The logic of enlarging the congressional playing field that leads to successful Internet-based efforts to recruit a record number of Democratic congressional candidates suggests a strategic netroots affinity for long shots. And as early as 2004, Markos Moulitsas of Daily Kos wrote of the benefits of his efforts to focus netroots attention on the races official Washington ignores:

> One of the problems with organizations like EMILY's List is that they focus too much on the won/loss equation. Their funders expect a winning record, so they have abandoned their "early money is like yeast" model to fund only the safest of bets. I swore early on that my model would be different, and made that clear from the beginning. I had three criteria, which I made crystal clear. Candidates would be chosen if they met two out of the three: 1) They could tie up an incumbent and keep that incumbent from campaigning and fundraising for other candidates, 2) were from a swing state, and 3) had a chance of winning.[18]

The data indicate that this philosophy applied to the 2006 cycle. Table 4.4 compares the rankings of online-funded House and Senate races with all targeted races. Candidates were deemed to have engaged in active online funding activity if they were endorsed by Moveon.org or Democracy for America, maintained a link from their website to the progressive fund-raising organization ActBlue, or were targeted by progressive weblogs as netroots candidates worthy of funding.[19] Twenty-five of ninety-one targeted House races and all eleven targeted Senate races fell into this category. For both sets of contests, involvement in online fund-raising

Table 4.4 Online Fund-Raising and Electoral Success

House Races

Ranking Tier	Online Funded					Within 4 Points		All Targeted Races				
	N	Average Margin (D)	Won	Lost	Pct.	N	Pct.	N	Average Margin (D)	Won	Lost	Pct.
1 Democrats Favored	2	11.0	2	0	1.00	2	1.00	19	19.1	19	0	1.00
2 Toss-up	2	-2.5	0	2	.00	2	1.00	14	8.1	10	4	.71
3 Lean Republican	8	2.6	5	3	.63	7	.88	18	2.3	11	7	.61
4 Likely Republican	3	1.0	1	2	.33	3	1.00	11	-0.9	3	8	.27
5 Safe Republican	10	-5.7	3	7	.30	5	.50	29	-5.2	9	20	.31
TOTAL	**25**		**11**	**15**	**.42**	**19**	**.76**	**91**		**52**	**39**	**.57**

Senate Races

Ranking Tier	Online Funded*				
	N	Average Margin (D)	Won	Lost	Pct.
1 Democrats Favored	3	28.3	3	0	1.00
2 Toss-up	1	18.0	1	0	1.00
3 Lean Republican	3	7.0	3	0	1.00
4 Likely Republican	2	-1.0	1	1	.50
5 Safe Republican	2	-4.5	1	1	.50
TOTAL	**11**		**9**	**2**	**.82**

*All targeted Senate races were online funded.

Candidates were deemed to have engaged in active online funding activity if they were endorsed by Moveon.org or Democracy for America, maintained a link from their website to ActBlue, or were targeted by progressive weblogs as Netroots candidates.

skews toward the less-competitive races. This dynamic is most apparent among House races because of the contrast between online funded races and all targeted races. Twenty-one of twenty-five online-funded contests (84 percent) were in the three least competitive tiers of House races, with the least competitive Tier 5 races constituting the modal group. This compares with 64 percent of targeted House contests overall.

Within each tier save for two online-funded toss-up races, recipients of online funding performed as well as comparably ranked candidates in terms of won-loss records and appreciably better in terms of victory margins. The strongest effect in these races appears to be the ability of online funding to make races competitive, an important political objective that complements the strategy of contesting every open House seat in that it increases the costs of competition, forcing opponents to expend resources to contest seats that otherwise would not be endangered. Most long-shot candidates receiving online money were able to finish within four points of their opponents. Seven of eight Democrats in "Lean Republican" districts ran competitive races, and all three "Likely Republican" districts and five of ten "Safe Republican" districts were competitive.[20]

These figures attest to the prevalence and effectiveness of online funding methods, particularly as they apply to underdog campaigns. But fund-raising is only one portion of hybrid campaigning, which includes message dissemination and grassroots mobilization. Hybrid campaigns exploit the two-way communication potential of the Internet by attracting supporters with interactive features and hyperlinks from their campaign site to other Internet websites that engage readers in political action and discourse using links to progressive blogs. Such hyperlinks, which in general are more commonplace on campaign websites today than several years ago,[21] represent a more advanced and open use of Internet technology than the conventional top-down and controlled characteristics of candidate websites (candidate messages to voters, photos, fund-raising links) prevalent since candidates first developed a web presence in the late 1990s.[22] Table 4.5 illustrates the extent to which campaigns in each tier engaged in these activities.

A web score was calculated based on a weighted count of Internet features supported by each campaign, in an attempt to capture how fully these campaigns embraced the more empowering, bottom-up aspects of Internet politics. One point was assigned for the presence of traditional campaign website interactive features (such as clickable links for making campaign contributions and registering to vote), one point for website daily news updates, two points for maintaining a campaign weblog, and three points for maintaining hyperlinks to other websites.[23] Higher weights reflect characteristics that emphasize two-way interactivity, with blogging and linking to other sites suggesting a high degree of involvement in netroots politics.

As with Internet fund-raising, long-shot Democrats were more thoroughly web-oriented than Democrats running in favorable districts. Democratic House and Senate candidates running in Tier 1 races utilized the Internet less than

Table 4.5 Campaign Web Use

House: All Races

Ranking Tier	N	High	Mean
1 Democrats Favored	16	3	1.8
2 Toss-up	11	6	2.5
3 Lean Republican	16	7	4.1
4 Likely Republican	11	5	2.9
5 Safe Republican	23	7	3.2
TOTAL	**77**		

House: Races Within Four Points

Ranking Tier	N	High	Mean
1 Democrats Favored	16	3	1.8
2 Toss-up	10	6	2.7
3 Lean Republican	14	7	4.2
4 Likely Republican	9	5	2.9
5 Safe Republican	13	5	2.9
TOTAL	**62**		

House: Winning Races

Ranking Tier	N	High	Mean
1 Democrats Favored	16	3	1.8
2 Toss-up	9	6	2.6
3 Lean Republican	11	7	4.0
4 Likely Republican	3	5	3.3
5 Safe Republican	8	5	2.3
TOTAL	**47**		

House: All Races

Ranking Tier	N	High	Mean
1 Democrats Favored	3	4	2.7
2 Toss-up	1	4	4.0
3 Lean Republican	3	7	6.0
4 Likely Republican	2	7	4.5
5 Safe Republican	2	7	5.5
TOTAL	**11**		

Web scores were calculated on a seven-point scale where one point was assigned for the presence of campaign website intereactive features, one point for website daily news updates, two points for a campaign blog, and three points for links to other websites. Campaigns for which web data were incomplete or unavailable are omitted.

Democrats in any other tier. By contrast, the most engaged Democrats were in Tier 3 ("Lean Republican") contests. Long-shot candidates running in "Likely Republican" and "Safe Republican" House and Senate races averaged higher web scores than candidates in toss-up contests. However, unlike Internet fund-raising, there is little difference in web use between victorious and unsuccessful Democratic campaigns, or between competitive House races (with margins of four points or less) and House campaigns overall.

A similar pattern of outreach from the netroots to the campaigns is evident in the amount of online discussion that campaigns in the five tiers merited from bloggers on Daily Kos. Whereas the campaigns' web-use measures capture top-down interest in participating in netroots politics, candidate mentions on the Daily Kos front page and in diaries posted by readers are a bottom-up metric of grassroots interest in a campaign.

Table 4.6 displays the average number of Daily Kos front-page and diary mentions of the targeted races between March 15, 2006, and Election Day. Once again, campaigns where Democrats were favored attracted the least discussion, complementing the top-down dynamic of their campaign web use, and the more interactive Tier 3 ("Lean Republican") House campaigns drew the most netroots discussion. Senate races, no doubt by virtue of their greater prominence, were more thoroughly discussed than House races in comparable tiers and, apart from Tier 1 races, were among the most-discussed contests overall. But the greater variation among tiers of House races suggests a match between campaigns that reached out through the Internet and netroots interest in House campaigns, with Daily Kos bloggers and diarists focused especially on Tier 3 races where victory was too unlikely to merit tremendous mainstream support but where the odds of success were better than the even more problematic Tier 4 and Tier 5 contests. Netroots attention thrived in this region.

And few details were omitted from discussion once bloggers took to a campaign; it was as if the blogosphere was running an adopt-a-campaign program. Front-page and dairy posts covered a range of campaign discourse including fund-raising updates, analyses of debate performances, discussion of the candidate's statements on the Iraq War and other issues, firsthand accounts of appearances by the candidate, analyses of the state of the horserace, announcements of upcoming events, commentary on the effectiveness of the candidate's advertising, criticism of (or, in some instances, praise for) media coverage of the campaign, and criticism of the candidate's opponent, all delivered in frank, partisan language designed to energize and motivate like-minded readers. Savvy campaigns would post diaries as part of their netroots outreach strategy, fueling the conversation and signaling to readers that they understood the importance of and were part of the progressive blog community.

For instance, consider the contents of the 290 postings about Tier 3 challenger Joe Sestak, running in Pennsylvania's Seventh Congressional District against long-time Republican incumbent Curt Weldon. A favorite of Daily Kos diarists, Sestak

Table 4.6 Daily Kos Front-Page and Diary Mentions, March 15–November 6, 2006

House: All Races

Ranking Tier	N	High	Low	Mean	Std. Dev.	Quartile
1 Democrats Favored	18	105	8	57.9	23.4	1
2 Toss-up	14	196	51	121.0	39.1	2
3 Lean Republican	18	388	1	172.6	107.8	3
4 Likely Republican	11	411	87	157.7	93.5	3
5 Safe Republican	29	343	6	123.6	75.9	2
TOTAL	**90**					

House: Races Within Four Points

Ranking Tier	N	High	Low	Mean	Std. Dev.	Quartile
1 Democrats Favored	18	105	8	57.9	23.4	1
2 Toss-up	13	196	51	123.8	39.3	2
3 Lean Republican	15	388	1	170.1	108.5	3
4 Likely Republican	9	411	90	170.4	98.8	3
5 Safe Republican	14	343	6	136.2	91.9	2
TOTAL	**69**					

House: Winning Races

Ranking Tier	N	High	Low	Mean	Std. Dev.	Quartile
1 Democrats Favored	18	105	8	57.9	23.4	1
2 Toss-up	10	133	51	106.8	26.3	2
3 Lean Republican	11	388	66	177.6	91.2	3
4 Likely Republican	3	256	90	147.7	76.7	3
5 Safe Republican	9	225	52	104.4	49.0	2
TOTAL	**51**					

Senate: All Races

Ranking Tier	N	High	Low	Mean	Std. Dev.	Quartile
1 Democrats Favored	3	215	114	167.7	41.5	3
2 Toss-up	1	386	386	386.0	—	4
3 Lean Republican	3	441	375	329.7	114.0	4
4 Likely Republican	2	681	566	623.5	57.5	4
5 Safe Republican	2	1139	2196	1687.5	528.5	4
TOTAL	**11**					

Quartiles for Daily Kos mentions are: 1 (1–89); 2 (90–114); 3 (115–79); 4 (180–2196).

began as a heavy underdog and surged to become a serious challenger to Weldon, ultimately winning the suburban Philadelphia seat by twelve points. Kos readers took to Sestak early, before political insiders gave him a credible chance of winning, and they were not subtle about their support. Their discussion is notable for how it references and advances the candidate's online campaign through comments such as these:

It's ground war time! The battles are going well, but the war is far from over. We face a very determined enemy who will do anything to hold onto power. Now is not the time to let up. We need EVERY. SINGLE. VOTE. Below the fold you will find the BIG LIST OF CANDIDATES for House, Senate, and Governor races [including Sestak], with links to volunteer and/or donate.[24]

On Saturday afternoon, Joe Sestak held court and did a bit of live blogging over at Firedoglake. The entire engagement is very much worth a read.[25]

[Sestak has] a pretty simply layed out webpage. The banner isn't the prettiest thing I've seen, but it does have the candidate's name, the office he is running for, and there isn't anything on it that looks bad. The navigation has links to about, issues, take action, and contribute (which is made red to stand out).... The general idea of the design is good I think. It would be made a little bit better if it was a little flashier I think, though.[26]

By discussing such things as the candidate's blog posts, analysis of his website, and online action items like links to volunteering and fund-raising opportunities, online discourse defined and facilitated Sestak's netroots campaign by creating a web presence that operated organically with the campaign's Internet efforts. The campaign was both beneficiary and promoter of this approach, posting online to engage supporters. For instance, note how the campaign posts this fund-raising update as a Daily Kos diary, employing the same language used by other diarists:

Netroots-endorsed Fightin' Dem Joe Sestak recently announced that he has raised $700,000 in the 2nd Quarter—beating his opponent, career politician Curt Weldon by almost $300,000! ... Joe is showing what Democratic candidates can do when they stand up for their principles and fight for what they believe in. We are proud to say that Joe's message of real security—based on health, education, economic and defense security—is resonating among thousands of Democrats yearning for change. Thank you again![27]

Centralized campaign efforts to reach out to supporters through the web dovetailed with the natural inclination of supporters to analyze, discuss, dissect, and promote their favorite candidates in blog posts, creating a system that was simultaneously spontaneous yet manufactured, the marriage of a natural outpouring of blogger sentiment and the strategic calculation of some campaigns to embrace netroots partisans.

Candidate Convergence

This convergence of top-down planning and bottom-up sentiment is evident in the overlap found in the fund-raising efforts, web activity, and blogger engagement of hybrid campaigns. Essentially, campaigns that engaged the netroots were likely to do so all-out, investing in online fund-raising techniques aimed at bringing in many small-dollar contributions, maintaining an active web presence, and receiving a lot of blogger attention.

Table 4.7 displays the extent of this convergence among sixteen House and three Senate candidates who were deemed netroots candidates for fund-raising purposes. These campaigns—all long shots or severe long shots—were endorsed by the blogs Daily Kos, MyDD, and Swing State Project and raised funds online through the progressive political action committee ActBlue. Table 4.7 displays their fund-raising record in terms of the number of people who contributed to their campaigns and the number of dollars they raised online, their web score, and the number of times their campaigns were referenced in Daily Kos front-page entries and diaries.

All of the campaigns raised $50,000 or more though online contributions; thirteen raised more than $100,000, and nine raised more than $200,000. Most of these were from small contributions, with thirteen campaigns averaging less than $100 per contribution and six averaging less than $50. Thirteen of the campaigns had web scores of four or higher. Thirteen were in the highest quartile of Daily Kos mentions. The average campaign raised $277,942 from 3,044 contributors, or $99 per person, had a web score of five, and was in the highest quartile of Daily Kos mentions. It is possible, therefore, to speak of netroots candidates where fund-raising and Internet strategies converged with visibility on progressive weblogs—where a campaign's investment in netroots politics intersected with the netroots' interest in the campaign. For a subset of targeted races, netroots campaigning was a comprehensive strategy.

Tellingly, half of these campaigns were successful, and the average vote margin of −5 is just slightly outside the range of competitiveness, despite the fact that ten of these netroots candidates began their campaigns as Tier 5 challengers. Even in a Democratic year, this is a remarkable record. It is not possible, of course, to know how many would have been victorious without small-dollar fund-raising and online support, but at the very least an already difficult task would have been far more problematic for all of these candidates without the progressive blogosphere. On the Senate side, it is difficult to see how Ned Lamont would have won the Connecticut Democratic primary without netroots support, and the data support the claim that a hybrid campaign approach made the difference for Democrats Jon Tester (Montana) and Jim Webb (Virginia) in their razor-thin victories. Democrats would not have reclaimed a majority in the Senate if not for these hybrid campaigns.

By the 2008 cycle, support for netroots-friendly candidates had grown more strategic. With their successful 2006 campaign behind them, Democratic congressional majorities firmly in place, and a second consecutive Democratic wave forming, online activists shifted their attention from supporting long-shot Democrats to supporting Democrats who were invested in progressive causes.

Table 4.7 Netroots Candidate Funding, Web Use, and Daily Kos Mentions

House Races

Ranking Tier	Candidate	Outcome (W/L)	Margin	Number of Contributors	Funds Raised Online	Average Contribution	Web Score	Daily Kos Mentions	Daily Kos Quartile
3 Lean Republican	Joe Sestak	W	+12	3,617	$867,072	$240	4	290	4
3 Lean Republican	Jerry McNerney	W	+6	3,456	$206,581	$60	7	388	4
3 Lean Republican	Patrick Murphy	W	0	3,063	$165,882	$54	7	247	4
3 Lean Republican	Darcy Burner	L	–2	3,414	$223,529	$65	7	295	4
3 Lean Republican	Francine Busby	L	–11	1,409	$124,407	$88	2	320	4
4 Likely Republican	Paul Hodes	W	+8	2,562	$87,260	$34	4	256	4
4 Likely Republican	Eric Massa	L	–4	2,878	$415,487	$144	5	411	4
4 Likely Republican	Linda Stender	L	–1	2,549	$64,629	$25	4	187	4
5 Safe Republican	Timothy Walz	W	+6	2,164	$53,307	$25	N/A	131	3
5 Safe Republican	Ciro Rodriguez	W	+8	508	$185,739	$366	1	52	1
5 Safe Republican	Larry Kissell	L	0	2,868	$174,507	$61	5	300	4
5 Safe Republican	Jay Fawcett	L	–18	2,644	$63,714	$24	3	222	4
5 Safe Republican	Larry Grant	L	–5	2,625	$72,103	$27	N/A	179	3
5 Safe Republican	Gary Trauner	L	0	2,568	$275,781	$107	4	151	3
5 Safe Republican	John Courage	L	–36	2,377	$72,202	$30	6	113	2
5 Safe Republican	Daniel Seals	L	–6	2,341	$538,660	$230	2	166	3

Senate Races

Ranking Tier	Candidate	Outcome (W/L)	Margin	Number of Contributors	Funds Raised Online	Average Contribution	Web Score	Daily Kos Mentions	Daily Kos Quartile
4 Likely Republican	Jon Tester	W	+1	5,472	$343,235	$63	7	566	4
5 Safe Republican	James Webb	W	+1	5,557	$893,817	$161	4	1139	4
5 Safe Republican	Ned Lamont	L	–10	5,770	$452,988	$79	7	2196	4
AVERAGES			**–5**	**3,044**	**$277,942**	**$99**	**5**	**400.5**	**4**

Daily Kos mentions in front-page stories and diaries, March 15, 2006, through November 6, 2006.
Quartiles for Daily Kos mentions are: 1 (1–89); 2 (90–114); 3 (115–179); 4 (180–2196).

In early June, Markos Moulitsas introduced the Orange to Blue list, hosted online by ActBlue, which would replace the joint online fund-raising collaboration of Daily Kos, Swing State Project, and MyDD. In a front-page Daily Kos post, Moulitsas explained the reasoning behind dividing the efforts of these progressive blogs. Pointing to the smaller size of the blogs in 2006, Moulitsas acknowledged that it made sense to pool resources in order to raise whatever was possible, but in 2008:

> We suddenly came to a new realization—now that Democrats look to expand their majorities, we can afford to be more picky about who we support. If our unofficial motto is "More Democrats, Better Democrats," we have graduated from the "more Democrats" part to "better Democrats." And on that front, in a target rich environment, we realized that our various communities had different criteria for who we wanted to support. While we all share concerns over the war in Iraq and civil liberties, Open Left focuses a great deal on Net Neutrality and gravitates toward hitting "Bush Dogs" [conservative Democrats] and Republicans representing Kerry/Blue districts. Daily Kos is concerned about immigration issues and is more drawn toward Western candidates, Swing State Project loves to sniff out winnable races ignored by establishment forces.[28]

This strategic shift provided a growing blogosphere with more flexibility to identify netroots candidates based on a wider assortment of criteria and, in Moulitsas's words, "be more nimble and responsive to the issues and concerns of our communities."[29] It permitted them to take another step forward, identifying and contributing to candidates who shared a progressive agenda rather than just the Democratic Party label.

Nonfederal Candidates

Nonfederal races offer additional evidence of the political effect of Internet politics. As a grassroots phenomenon, the blogosphere would be expected to influence state and local contests as a precursor to making a mark on the national scene. Evidence of this may be found in the track record of state and local candidates endorsed by Democracy for America, which recruits, endorses, and raises money for progressive candidates for offices as small as school board in an effort to—in the organization's words—"rebuild the Democratic Party from the bottom up."[30]

Their electoral track record from the 2004, 2005, and 2006 election cycles may be found in Table 4.8. The table presents a combined won-loss record and winning percentage for these three cycles in statewide races (governor, lieutenant governor, secretary of state, treasurer, secretary of agriculture, and state supreme court), state legislative races, and local races (mayor, city council, school board, city and county commissioners, county and district court judges, district attorneys, public advocates, sheriffs, township clerks, and supervisors of elections). In keeping with their philosophy of spreading resources widely, DFA contested races in thirty-eight states during the three cycles, including red states like Georgia, Kentucky, South Carolina, Kansas, Texas, and Utah.

If DFA's grassroots efforts were effective, its success rate should have improved with each election cycle as the organization became increasingly savvy and as its donor base grew. In the aggregate, the data confirm that this has happened. After winning slightly less than half the races where DFA endorsed a candidate in 2004 (48 percent), its record improved to 53 percent in 2005 and 63 percent in 2006. Although statewide contests could have been influenced by national political dynamics (certainly the 75 percent success rate in 2006 statewide races could reflect the Democratic tide that swept the country in that cycle), most down-ballot races would be expected to respond more to local currents than to national trends. Among these contests, DFA state legislature candidates won at

Table 4.8 Electoral Success of Democracy for America (DFA)–Endorsed Nonfederal Candidates, 2004–2006

2006	*W*	*L*	*Pct.*
Statewide Races	6	2	.75
State Legislative Races	14	8	.64
Local Races	4	4	.50
TOTAL	**24**	**14**	**.63**
Number of States Contested: 25			
2005	*W*	*L*	*Pct.*
Statewide Races	1	1	.50
State Legislative Races	4	4	.50
Local Races	14	12	.54
TOTAL	**19**	**17**	**.53**
Number of States Contested: 18			
2004	*W*	*L*	*Pct.*
Statewide Races	2	4	.33
State Legislative Races	19	22	.46
Local Races	10	8	.56
TOTAL	**31**	**34**	**.48**
Number of States Contested: 31			
Number of States Contested, 2004–2006: 38			

Statewide races: Governor, lieutenant governor, secretary of state, state treasurer, secretary of agriculture, state supreme court

State legislative races: State Senate and House or Assembly

Local Races: Mayor, city council, school board, city and county commissioners, county and district court judges, district attorneys, public advocates, sheriffs, township clerks, supervisors of elections

a markedly improved rate in 2006 (64 percent) over 2005 (50 percent) and 2004 (46 percent), whereas the DFA record for local races declined marginally from 56 percent in 2004 to 50 percent in 2006. Collectively, these results suggest a strong return over three election cycles in DFA's investment in individuals running for nonfederal offices, often in jurisdictions that would not be expected to support progressive candidates.

Conclusion

The combined picture presented by these metrics is of an emergent progressive blogosphere that has demonstrated proficiency in political organizing and campaigning. It was a force in the 2006 elections, which served as a turning point in netroots political effectiveness and a harbinger of the successful 2008 cycle. In 2006 the netroots came of age, recruiting and supporting long-shot candidates who were able to take advantage of a favorable political climate and contribute to the size of the Democratic wave in House, Senate, and nonfederal contests. To the extent that hybrid campaigning made the difference in narrow Democratic victories in Montana and Virginia, a case can be made that Internet-based campaign practices delivered the Senate for Democrats. Small-dollar contributions supplemented traditional big-dollar fund-raising avenues and distributed campaign cash to long-shot candidates, some of whom competed effectively. Internet-driven support at the nonfederal level helped progressives win in traditionally non-Democratic states, in the process building a farm team of progressive candidates who will utilize Internet-based campaign methods to run for national office in future years.

Progressive bloggers certainly view things this way. Opinions expressed by participants in the blogger survey were generally consistent with empirical measures of their effectiveness, with large majorities of those surveyed saying positive things about their political effectiveness in the 2006 cycle. On three key measures—recruiting candidates, making elections competitive, and winning elections—a majority of bloggers felt the progressive blogosphere had been either effective or very effective in 2006. As Table 4.9 indicates, they felt they had their greatest success in making elections competitive (84 percent said the progressive blogosphere was effective or very effective), followed by winning elections (68 percent) and recruiting candidates (52 percent). These figures reflect a sharp improvement from where bloggers felt their medium was in 2004, when only 16 percent felt they had achieved any notable recruiting successes and just 4 percent felt their efforts contributed to electoral victory.

That being said, progressive bloggers as a group are circumspect about their accomplishments, and some remain skeptical about the extent of the blogosphere's political influence. On making campaigns competitive, they point to a few salient races where netroots candidates overcame distant odds to win elections, like the Webb, Tester, and Lamont races in the U.S. Senate. One Texas blogger listed five

Table 4.9 Progressive Blogger Perceptions of the Political Effectiveness of the Progressive Blogosphere, 2004–2008

Recruiting Candidates

	2004	2006	Estimated 2008
Very Effective	0%	12%	16%
Effective	16	40	60
Ineffective	40	36	24
Very Ineffective	44	12	0

Making Elections Competitive

	2004	2006	Estimated 2008
Very Effective	0%	24%	32%
Effective	40	60	60
Ineffective	36	16	8
Very Ineffective	24	0	0

Winning Elections

	2004	2006	Estimated 2008
Very Effective	0%	8%	12%
Effective	4	60	72
Ineffective	56	32	16
Very Ineffective	40	0	0

N = 25

state legislative races made competitive by the work of progressive bloggers. But they were careful to acknowledge the limitations of their efforts, noting that even in the case of Lamont's Internet-powered challenge to Lieberman, the netroots could help to make some elections competitive, but they couldn't do it by themselves (as evidenced by Lamont's loss to Lieberman in the general election). One blogger noted that "the larger the race, the less substantial the effect." Others added that bloggers can create early buzz, help raise money, quickly disseminate ideas, and efficiently and effectively connect candidates and voters, but they "cannot by themselves close the deal."

They sound similar precautions about their ability to win elections. "I don't think the blogosphere is big enough to win elections yet," one blogger suggested, "but it's big enough—and important enough people read it—that it has an impact." Said another: "Winning elections is due to multiple elements coming together. While online organizing (which was phenomenally successful in 2006 and continues to build) became an important element, it was still only one aspect [of winning campaigns]."

And there were dissenting voices, like the blogger who said "handpicked progressive candidates are usually disasters and they have won few elections"—although this blogger did acknowledge that "they did a little better in the [2006] election." And another blogger, looking ahead to governing decisions that follow political victory, asked, "How has the success of the blogosphere electorally translated into success in policy? I think that certain candidates, who the blogosphere tout as electoral successes, have ridden the blogosphere into DC where they ineffectually or actively fail to represent those blogospheres." In this voice we hear the frustration with the Democratic Party establishment in Washington, which to this blogger is a bigger issue than whether or not progressive candidates win elections, and which inspired the shift in 2008 to supporting other (read: better) Democrats. Winning in this sense is a means to a larger objective that can only be accomplished if successful candidates remain true to a netroots agenda by not giving in to what was widely viewed in the blogosphere, circa 2007, as capitulation by Democratic congressional leadership to the Bush White House on the Iraq War, domestic surveillance, and other defining issues.

On recruitment efforts, bloggers tended to single out their favorite examples of candidacies that were launched with netroots backing, like Rick Noriega (recruited to run in an ultimately unsuccessful bid for a U.S. Senate seat in Texas in 2008), Brian Keeler (who ran unsuccessfully for the New York State Senate in 2006), and, of course, Tester and Webb. But they held different perspectives on what these recruitment efforts meant. Whereas one blogger pointed to Webb's election as tipping the balance of power to the Democrats in the Senate and said that alone "single-handedly qualifies the blogosphere as very effective" in its recruiting, others drew different conclusions from the same election: "I don't think 2006 was a big recruitment year for the blogosphere. We played the hand we were dealt in terms of candidates, with a couple of notable exceptions. Even in Tester and Webb, however, I think the success there was less in recruiting as in making it possible to compete even with limited traditional resources."

Nonetheless, even if the influence of the blogosphere were limited to providing resources to underdog candidates, this would stand as an important contribution. And there is a widespread sense among bloggers that, as with winning and making elections competitive, the future holds a great deal of promise. "I think the blogs have the potential to be better at recruiting candidates and at contributing to winning elections," one blogger wrote, "but they aren't there yet." This was a typical sentiment. On recruitment, 76 percent of the bloggers surveyed believed the 2008 cycle would be a fruitful one for the progressive blogosphere, up twenty-four points from 2006. Eighty-four percent felt the netroots would make a positive contribution to winning elections in the 2008 cycle, an increase of sixteen points from 2006. And almost all the bloggers expressed the belief that the efforts of the blogosphere would help make elections competitive in 2008.

The political achievements of 2006 constitute an admirable record for a political community only several years old utilizing a medium that is still coming into its own. It is, of course, impossible to know how Internet-based campaigning will fare in future years—whether the future will be as bright as many bloggers think it will be, or whether the 2006 and 2008 cycles were anomalies caused by intense hostility to the Bush administration. What can be said at this point is that it is possible for the Internet model to compete effectively with traditional campaigning, at least under the favorable circumstances in place in 2006 and 2008. Hybrid campaigns demonstrated the power of modifying traditional campaign techniques with Internet-based fund-raising, communications, and mobilization efforts, pointing the way to what may be emerging as the campaign model for the post-television era.

5

The Progressive Blogosphere and Media Narratives

Virginia Sen. George Allen (R) apologized Monday for what his opponent's campaign said were demeaning and insensitive comments the senator made to a twenty-year-old volunteer of Indian descent. At a campaign rally in southwest Virginia on Friday, Allen repeatedly called a volunteer for Democrat James Webb "macaca." During the speech in Breaks, near the Kentucky border, Allen began by saying that he was "going to run this campaign on positive, constructive ideas" and then pointed at S.R. Sidarth in the crowd.

"This fellow here, over here with the yellow shirt, macaca, or whatever his name is. He's with my opponent. He's following us around everywhere. And it's just great," Allen said, as his supporters began to laugh. After saying that Webb was raising money in California with a "bunch of Hollywood movie moguls," Allen said, "Let's give a welcome to macaca, here. Welcome to America and the real world of Virginia." Allen then began talking about the "war on terror." Depending on how it is spelled, the word macaca could mean either a monkey that inhabits the Eastern Hemisphere or a town in South Africa. In some European cultures, macaca is also considered a racial slur against African immigrants, according to several Web sites that track ethnic slurs.

—*Tim Craig and Michael D. Shear,*
"Allen Quip Provokes Outrage, Apology,"
Washington Post, *August 15, 2006, A1*

On progressive blogs, it's known simply as the "macaca incident." When Republican George Allen, the junior senator from Virginia, was caught on videotape using a slur toward a young volunteer staffer from his opponent's campaign, netroots bloggers saw an opportunity to change the course of the media narrative surrounding a heavily favored incumbent from a conservative state.

The incident occurred on a Friday. Progressive blogs flew into a frenzy almost immediately. By Monday, video of the exchange was posted on leading progressive websites; one blogger posted it on Daily Kos with a simple headline: "Just Watch the Video." Their efforts were reinforced by the presence of the video on

89

YouTube, permitting anyone with Internet access to see it. By Tuesday, the macaca story had penetrated the mainstream press. Allen apologized, but the story never entirely disappeared. He remained on the defensive about his remarks through the election, battling charges that he held racist views, and lost to Webb by a slim margin less than three months later.

As far as setting the campaign narrative goes, this may have been the progressive blogosphere's most effective moment in 2006, as representatives of the new media were able to work the macaca story into the campaign narrative of the old media and keep it there through the election. First came the stories about the incident. Then the apology. Then a story line developed about the emerging technology that permitted this event to become a story in the first place, captured nicely by this piece that ran in the *San Francisco Chronicle* nine days after the initial burst of mainstream coverage:

> What are the three scariest words in U.S. politics? Caught on tape. It's a video epidemic, coming directly to your computer on YouTube. Virginia Sen. George Allen was looking right at a hand-held video camera last week when he called a staffer of Indian descent from his opponent's campaign "Macaca," a term considered derogatory.... Someone like Allen has spent millions of dollars to hone his message, shoot his TV ads and craft his sound bites. And then, because he came up with a remark about a member of his opponent's staff that appeared to be racist, all that is out the window. While Allen has been staging a series of public apologies—"I just say from the deepest part of my heart that I am sorry and I will do better"—the clip has been playing on the video downloading site YouTube and subsequently on national television.[1]

This piece, and the lesson it taught, was in turn trumpeted in the blogosphere. "YouTube is the greatest netroots tool since blogs," wrote Markos Moulitsas in a post that linked to the *Chronicle* article, "and potentially even more transformational for American politics."[2]

In the months following, progressive bloggers used the macaca exchange the way mainstream journalists use news pegs—as a hook for exploring other seemingly racist comments and behaviors by the senator, helping to build a story line that would provide context for other incidents, like a subsequent statement by Allen that appeared to renounce the Jewish ancestry of his maternal grandfather. Within a week, Moulitsas was blogging about Allen's association with a group called the Council of Conservative Citizens, an alleged segregationist and white supremacist group, amplifying the publication of a report about Allen and the group that appeared in *The Nation*.[3]

The effort to build a narrative around the macaca incident was explicit and was itself a theme that Moulitsas blogged about. One occasion for blogging about the larger narrative was an Allen campaign event with former New York mayor Rudy Giuliani, during which Allen said, "You can tell a lot about people by the folks they stand with."[4] Juxtaposing those words with a picture of Allen posing with members of the Council of Conservative Citizens, Moulitsas wrote,

> Sen. Felix Macaca Allen has a history of racism, and much of it has come out. The images and words showing that pattern are far more powerful than a long list of Senate votes, and hits voters viscerally, effectively. And once you have well-defined narrative, you can slot anything into it to further reinforce that narrative.... By feeding into the narrative, we could take what was probably a political plus for Allen—a campaign stop with Rudy Giuliani—and use it as a hook to reinforce the anti-Allen negative narrative.[5]

Moulitsas continued this post with a discourse on narrative-building that reads like a tutorial on what the progressive blogosphere needs to do to get the media to frame political issues its way. Expressing a complaint often heard on progressive blogs, he admonishes Democratic strategists for not understanding how to frame events for reporters and voters:

> Now, this [narrative building] is something Republicans have mastered, and have used for over a decade. Their favorite narrative is the "too liberal" canard, but the one they'll use the most this year is "Democrats won't protect you" line, slotting issues like the NSA spying scandal and the Patriot Act to support that narrative. They don't focus on boring roll call votes but on the story, and it's brutally effective. So we must build our own narratives against their guys. For that gubernatorial candidate who opposes abortion in all instances, even when the mother's life is at risk, he's so ideologically rigid that it trumps a woman's life. Frame it however you want (it's not my forte), but rigidity and ideological blinders are not positive values. Then we must puncture their own positive narratives. Bush won 2004 on the "protect America" line. We'd say, "he's screwed up in Iraq," and people would respond, "Yeah, but he wanted to keep America safe. His heart is in the right place." We'd bring up the NSA spying on Americans, and they'd respond with the same, "but he wants to keep America safe." Go down the list of Bush's failures on Iraq and the war against terrorists, and you'd get the same line. People were willing to forget his policy and issue failures because they believed that narrative.
> That is, until the Dubai Port deal. At that moment, it was clear he no longer placed preeminent priority on "keeping America safe," and would trump that desire in favor of corporate interests. His positive narrative was punctured, and suddenly one of the ages-old negative Republican narratives—that they're for corporations above people—was reinforced. Bush's [job approval] numbers haven't recovered since. So to Democratic consultants—learn from your opponents. Get away from [talking about] those silly roll call votes and random issues, expecting people to process their voting decisions intellectually, and start building narratives about both your candidate and his or her opponent. Tell us what they are all about, and use the issues to support that narrative. Don't give us spreadsheets and pie charts. Give us a story.

News Narratives, Framing, and Power

As an emerging medium, the Internet presents a challenge to the political narratives heard in the mainstream media (or, as progressive bloggers call it, the MSM).[6] But the traditional media presents an even bigger challenge to progressive bloggers, who work tirelessly to reframe story lines that they feel undercut progressive objectives, reinforce conservative perspectives, or are factually incorrect.

Netroots bloggers can influence media narratives in at least two ways. As with the George Allen story line, they can highlight material that changes the thematic thread of a story sufficiently to alter the coverage of reporters and the words of pundits who produce mainstream narratives. Or, as Moulitsas contends, they can implore party elites to use clear, simple, thematic language when talking about people and issues. Neither approach is easy to implement because of the strong inertia produced by journalistic routines and a class of Democratic officials not accustomed to thinking or speaking in readily accessible language. Sometimes bloggers find themselves screaming (which, on blogs, involves the use of uppercase letters) at high-profile Democrats when they fail to talk about politics from the gut.

For their part, bloggers represented in the blogger survey expressed the opinion that on balance the progressive blogosphere is doing a good job influencing political narratives and that their efforts improved between 2004, when 32 percent considered them effective, and 2006, when that figure shot up to 72 percent (see Table 5.1). As with political outcomes, bloggers saw an even brighter future in 2008, with 76 percent predicting they would effectively influence how politics is discussed in the presidential cycle.

Their comments reflected this generally positive assessment. "I thought the way the local blogs pushed stories into the media about their own congressional candidates was wonderful," one blogger wrote. Another drew connections between media narratives and political outcomes, observing that the ability of bloggers to make elections competitive "has been to a considerable extent through influencing the media narrative, both pro some candidates and anti others." A Texas state blogger took note of how professional journalists have started turning to blogs as a source of information and free research.

Table 5.1 Progressive Blogger Perceptions of the Ability of the Progressive Blogosphere to Influence Mainstream Media Narratives, 2004–2008

	2004	*2006*	*Estimated 2008*
Very Effective	0%	20%	28%
Effective	32	52	48
Ineffective	44	28	16
Very Ineffective	24	0	8

N = 25

In 2006 in Texas I was part of a group of bloggers who hounded the fact that many state legislators were illegally paying for second homes in Austin with campaign funds by leasing them from their spouses. [One legislator] in particular was also doing a tax dodge. We hounded this and the media picked it up. John Coby at Bay Area Houston blog spent MONTHS exposing Texas legislators' ethics violations and after he hounded this topic for months, the *Houston Chronicle* and *Dallas Morning News* picked it up as their own, essentially using his research without credit. I have, especially with regard to the Texas Legislature, followed a number of stories that the media picks up after I've explored them fully.

But on the big-ticket items involving major national policies and the way progressives are portrayed in the mainstream, netroots bloggers fight a constant battle for control of the message. Indeed, if the macaca incident is an example of a successful attempt to influence mainstream discourse, there were many others that bloggers found more frustrating. Diaries and comment threads on top progressive blogs are filled with rants about how the media talk about the Iraq War, electronic surveillance, Social Security, and even such deeply entrenched frames as the War on Terror (contending that one cannot fight a war against a tactic) and the 2007 surge of troops in Iraq (they strongly preferred a Vietnam-era term: "escalation").

What's at stake in this effort is how the broader public thinks about the problems of our day, their causes, appropriate solutions, and the relative appeal of liberal and conservative ideas. This makes the battle over news narratives a struggle for power with mainstream opinion leaders over how the electorate will assess political problems and solutions. Although netroots bloggers clearly seek to promote a progressive perspective, the ideological benefits that accrue to them through framing the news can be realized only by first succeeding in a tug-of-war with reluctant journalists and politicians.

Bloggers are aware of the forces arrayed against them. If you take as a point of departure the widely expressed netroots claim that power in contemporary Washington is built on a corrupt alliance of politicians, journalists, and corporate money, then efforts to frame the media narrative in a way that points this out require participants in this system to put their interests at risk or at least to question them openly. A Daily Kos diarist who uses the screen name TocqueDeville pointed this out in the context of how the mainstream media covered the presidential campaign of former North Carolina senator John Edwards:

> Am I the only one who noticed that, during the debates, almost every time John Edwards began to speak about one of his central campaign themes, corporate power and corruption in Washington, Wolf Blitzer would begin to interrupt him? Brian Williams at NBC did it too. Edwards could ramble on all day long, but as soon as he mentioned corruption, he was suddenly out of time. Then, after Edwards dropped out, the eulogies for his campaign, at least in the corporate media, reduced his message to fighting poverty. How quaint. No message of corporate power or corruption

in Washington. Suddenly Edwards's whole campaign was about poverty. You would think he had been running for president of the Salvation Army.[7]

The diarist continued by applying these observations about press coverage of Edwards to the initial press reaction to Barack Obama's widely discussed March 2008 speech on race relations, contending that the central message of the speech—that people of all races share a common economic plight—was scrubbed from mainstream media discussion:

> A freshman writing student could identify the dramatic climax of Obama's speech. "Not this time." [As in, this time we're not going to ignore the economic hardships that cut across racial boundaries.] In fact, if you had to title the speech, that would be it. But in the corporate media, that part of the speech doesn't even exist. Because if they acknowledged that part of the speech, then that would mean the candidate was getting to set the terms of the debate.... This [part of the speech] was nothing less than Obama reasserting what this election is about. Issues that affect all races, all Americans. I'm sure Obama understands that hardship breeds contempt. And that one of the best ways to heal class and racial divisions is for everyone to get a piece of the pie. But the corporate media doesn't want an election about crumbling schools, jobs, or special interests.[8]

The challenge for bloggers, then, is to persuade journalists and politicians who are invested in the mainstream to discuss ideas in language that questions the status quo. Perhaps this is why there is so much online fascination with the process of framing, whereby changing the context used to portray facts can dramatically alter how those facts are absorbed and understood by the audience for conventional news. In theory, if Democratic leaders en masse were to speak about the corrupt or bankrupt characteristics of the political system using everyday language like Edwards and Obama, then reporters would have no choice but to begin to repeat it. This, of course, presupposes that Democratic leaders would find it in their interest to frame political discourse in such a way, that they would be disciplined enough to do it consistently, and that they would know what to say and how to say it. It's a tall order. But to attempt to make it happen, high-profile bloggers will jump at every available opportunity to show them how it could be done.

Their efforts follow closely from the prescriptions of framing guru George Lakoff, a netroots hero (Moulitsas called Lakoff's 2004 book *Don't Think of an Elephant* "the best book this cycle"[9]) who provides a theoretical blueprint for something bloggers try to put into practice. Lakoff filled a void on the left by writing about message framing and was warmly embraced by progressive bloggers as something of a left-wing Frank Luntz, someone who could help package liberal ideas for public consumption. Their objective is to get Democrats to implement Lakoff's theories about how to use language to structure political discourse.

Lakoff contends that political arguments are won or lost by how effectively the different sides communicate their values and principles, and he argues that conservatives have been so effective at consistently telling the public what they stand for that you can actually boil it down to a ten-word philosophy that most people (at least prior to the second Bush term) would accept at face value: strong defense, free markets, lower taxes, smaller government, and family values. Progressives, by contrast, like to talk about programs and policies, leaving people unclear about core values. Thus Lakoff suggests mining fundamental progressive principles, which he says are rooted in a vision of America as a caring community, to develop an equally terse philosophy that could be presented to Americans as an alternate to the right-wing vision.[10] Progressives could then weave this philosophy into mainstream political narratives by working to shape news stories around progressive frames. Progressive bloggers have taken this advice and run with it, imploring progressive elites not to reinforce conservative frames and to advance progressive frames of their own making. Blogger Jeffrey Feldman operates a blog called Frameshop (frameshopisopen.com) that regularly deals with detailed examples of how progressives can shape political narratives. Cross-posting his work at Daily Kos led to the emergence of Frameshop diaries where Feldman and other bloggers post their messaging ideas. Feldman consciously attempts to put Lakoff's theories to work for netroots progressives, stating in a 2004 Daily Kos diary that "we want to put the idea of 'framing' to good use, on the ground, right now. We want to use Lakoff's ideas to make things better, to take back control of the political debate, and to repair the system."[11] In this regard, he viewed his frameshop idea as something akin to an auto body shop for broken discourse, not an academic exercise but a practical experience in getting ordinary people to help repair political language:

> I begin with the idea that political debate in this country is like a highway filled with cars, where much of the highway and most of the cars are broken. Fixing the highway is a big project. It takes time, it takes connections, and it takes money. Lots of money. It's not a short term project. Rearticulating the core principles of the Democratic Party is too big for me right now. It's important work, and I hope to be involved. But we have real problems to fix that can't wait for broad repairs to our party infrastructure. In the short run, we need to fix as many cars as possible— we need to make repairs to the language we are using. If we repair enough cars, driving will become safer.[12]

So, for instance, during the 2007 battle between Congress and the White House over the State Children's Health Insurance Program (SCHIP), Feldman suggested a narrative equating the cost of a day fighting in Iraq with providing health care for children, linking readers to the American Friends Service Committee website, where they could download website banners that read, "One Day of the Iraq War Equals $720 million: How Would You Spend It?" "Good framing," Feldman concluded, "ready made banners, and it's all free."[13]

Following Hurricane Katrina, a diarist named Doolittle posted a Frameshop diary about why Republican government doesn't work that linked—in typical horizontal fashion—to another diary by the blogger Sterling Newberry that said, "Republicans say government doesn't work, the evidence is that Republicans in government don't work." Then, the diarist urged readers to think about how to get Democratic candidates to "'frame' this for the electorate."[14] Other Frameshop diaries wrestled with how to address the charge that antiwar progressives hate America,[15] how to keep conservatives from brushing off deficit spending,[16] and how to address matters like immigration,[17] criticism of the Iraq War,[18] and literally every major issue in the news. Some suggestions were more sophisticated and detailed than others, but between the 2004 election and March 2008 more than 450 Frameshop diaries appeared on Daily Kos, with the overwhelming share written by Feldman.

Several themes emerge when looking broadly at the narrative elements that progressive bloggers seek to change in mainstream political coverage. Clearly, they want to change the way major policy initiatives are discussed. They want to redirect political narratives away from inside-baseball horse-race coverage toward a more substantive understanding of the costs resulting from political choices. They hope to reframe the discussion of public opinion to position progressives in the mainstream. They object to stories that balance progressive positions with conservative positions when they feel that such equal balance does injury to progressive ideas. And they really object to lazy journalism.

Framing Policy

If there is a single, overarching policy issue that netroots bloggers feel passionately about, it is the Iraq War. For years they have struggled against a mainstream news narrative that they feel misrepresented the risks posed by invading Iraq, overplayed the dangers of Saddam Hussein's regime, supported an inventory of ever-changing Bush administration justifications for the war, provided misleading accounts of how the war was progressing, ignored official mistreatment of the troops by the administration and the Republican Congress, downplayed combat deaths and injuries, and falsely asserted that to oppose the war is to oppose America. Theirs is a lengthy and detailed litany of complaints against the traditional press, which they hold accountable for selling an unnecessary war to a susceptible public, then propping up the administration to cover for its own complicity. In challenging conventional coverage, netroots bloggers strive to replace mainstream narratives about the war with the narrative heard frequently on progressive blogs—that the war is a failed policy. To this end, one of the story lines they attacked mercilessly was the give-it-time-to-work frame, which suggested it was premature to assert that the situation in Iraq would not or could not improve. What made this frame particularly frustrating to netroots bloggers was how amorphous measures of success made it virtually impossible to challenge calls for patience.

New York Times columnist Tom Friedman became a favorite blogger target, and his repeated calls for patience made his name synonymous with goalpost-moving. In May 2006, the website Fairness and Accuracy in Reporting (fair.org) posted a list of fourteen of Friedman's public predictions about the future course of the war dating back to 2003. Read together, they become a comical loop of pleas for patience, reiterating for almost three years that Iraq policy would sort itself out in six months:

> "The next six months in Iraq—which will determine the prospects for democracy-building there—are the most important six months in U.S. foreign policy in a long, long time." (*New York Times*, 11/30/03)

> "What we're gonna find out, Bob, in the next six to nine months is whether we have liberated a country or uncorked a civil war." (CBS's *Face the Nation*, 10/3/04)

> "I think we're in the end game now.... I think we're in a six-month window here where it's going to become very clear and this is all going to pre-empt I think the next congressional election—that's my own feeling—let alone the presidential one." (NBC's *Meet the Press*, 9/25/05)

> "The only thing I am certain of is that in the wake of this election, Iraq will be what Iraqis make of it—and the next six months will tell us a lot. I remain guardedly hopeful." (*New York Times*, 12/21/05)

> "I think we are in the end game. The next six to nine months are going to tell whether we can produce a decent outcome in Iraq." (NBC's *Today*, 3/2/06)

> "Well, I think that we're going to find out, Chris, in the next year to six months— probably sooner—whether a decent outcome is possible there, and I think we're going to have to just let this play out." (MSNBC's *Hardball*, 5/11/06)[19]

Progressive bloggers, who chafe at the ability of mainstream pundits to shape conventional wisdom without accountability, jumped on this inventory of shifting expectations. Duncan Black, blogging under the screen name Atrios at his blog Eschaton, coined the term "Friedman Unit" to mean an interval of six months in the future. Bloggers picked this up and ran with it, submitting tongue-in-cheek posts to mock elite opinion leaders who ask the public to withhold judgment about the future course of events until that critical six-month window has passed. "If we were to award an anti-Pulitzer to the pundit who has been the most predictable purveyor, in the last three years, of numbingly constant and aggressively unfounded 'progress is just around the corner' talking points," mused the blogger Hunter in September 2007, "who would it be? I'm talking about the king of the Freidman Units, that pundit that has the most colorful history of predicting progress around every corner, of using absolutely every new tidbit of good news, bad news and no news as proof positive that success will be evident in a mere few more months, if only we keep doing what we're doing, because this-time-by-gum-it's-going-to-work."[20]

In similar fashion the traditional press, during the months following the 2007 Iraq troop surge, began reporting official claims that the United States was making progress in Iraq. As public opinion polls began to mirror this claim, the notion that the surge had worked passed into conventional wisdom. Believing otherwise, bloggers pushed back against the mainstream narrative. "Will the media finally report that the surge has failed?" implored Daily Kos contributor Georgia10 in March 2008:

> The centerpiece of John McCain's campaign is that "the surge is working" in Iraq. He has repeated this lie hundreds of times on the trail, and in doing so, he has rarely been challenged. The press has largely reported his contention as fact, despite overwhelming evidence to the contrary. The surge, the president's "New Way Forward," was supposed to provide stability, promote political progress, and otherwise assist the Iraqi government in meeting certain benchmarks. As to those expressed goals, the surge has, by any measure, failed. Yet John McCain, this administration, and members of the press who dutifully repeated their spin as fact maintain that the surge "worked" because there has been, in the last several months, a sharp decline in violence. The reality presents a much more complex situation.... If what we wish never happens occurs—that is, if the violence in Iraq continues to rise after such a positive downtrend—will the media finally report that the surge has failed? Regardless of the level of violence, will the press admit that the escalation has failed to bring about the promised political progress? Or will they, in typical, stenographic fashion, allow John McCain to repeat the lie that has become the cornerstone of his candidacy?[21]

But the appearance of posts like these are testimony to the inability of the progressive blogosphere to move the narrative on the Iraq War in the direction of its position. Indeed, to the dismay of progressive bloggers, the surge-has-worked frame persisted as an established fact through the last days of the 2008 campaign. Despite witnessing a wholesale shift in public opinion against the Iraq invasion over a period of years, progressive bloggers contend that changes in attitudes occurred more in spite of media coverage than because of it—a point they make when they claim, repeatedly, that the public is ahead of the press and political class in its attitudes toward the war.

In December 2007, blogger DemFromCT posted a piece on Daily Kos arguing that the surge narrative was not working for the administration because attitudes toward the war in general had not changed. In one sense, the post is a plea for a different narrative about the surge, something that had not materialized by late 2007 (or ever). At the same time, DemFromCT presents data showing no change in support for a troop pullout since the start of the surge to argue that the public, despite the narrative about the surge's effectiveness, had not warmed up to the Iraq War:

> One thing about the American public: after considering all the alternatives, they eventually get it right. Sometimes it's too late to prevent tragedy, but once aware, it's tough to go back to an innocent "how things were." And so it is with Iraq. For all the bloviating about the surge by DC types (with the requisite understanding that violence is also down for nonsurge reasons because of nearly completed ethnic cleansing and an announced stand-down by Al Sadr's Mahdi army prior to the surge), the American public is unmoved.... In the end, don't believe everything you hear from Washington, DC talking heads. Crowing about surge success is not what the public wants from Washington. That's confined to war supporters, who are fighting for their own credibility, and for the GOP nomination. You can argue about what that means, but you can't argue about what the public wants. That's crystal clear from the polls. What the public wants is "withdrawal as soon as possible," except if they're Republicans. And—message to the media—Republicans are not the majority of the public.[22]

But is the traditional media listening to the framing messages emanating from progressive blogs? Certainly blogs are an idea factory. Bloggers are diligent in suggesting to each other new ways to frame policy and in complaining to the mainstream media about frames they dislike. This no doubt is a gratifying exercise, but not because it translates into bringing about changes in media policy frames.

Framing Politics

The same may be said about how traditional reporters frame politics, another source of ongoing frustration to progressive bloggers who consider mainstream political narratives to be largely content-free. The critique that political news in the television age overwhelmingly focuses on horse-race competition and personalities at the expense of issues and substance is not new and is certainly not limited to the blogosphere. Scholars who studied political news content in the late twentieth century have drawn many of the same conclusions.[23] But bloggers are much noisier in their complaints, criticizing traditional journalists for dumbing down political discourse by trivializing elections. They believe the messages in mainstream political coverage do a disservice to democracy—and they are on a mission to change that.

Netroots bloggers regard too many mainstream journalists as lazy and in love with superficial, gossipy story lines that would make great cocktail party chatter but not, in their view, serious news content. "Gore's 2000 campaign was hounded by pundits far more interested in fake propaganda claims that he said he 'invented the Internet,' and in the political meanings of 'earth tones,' and in fretting over his 'wooden' demeanor," blogged Hunter on Daily Kos, "than they were in any more substantive comparisons of the two candidates."[24] This line of reasoning is prevalent on progressive blogs as netroots activists call out for a more substantive approach to political reporting, directly blaming what they regard as the devastation of the Bush administration on an established press corps that did not do its job. "There is a special place in hell," the post continues, "for anyone who, at any point, figured that America should elect their president according to who they'd like to 'have a beer' with, or opined in the national media that such reasoning was anything but a godforsaken sophistry."[25]

But using blogs to change the way reporters cover politics is a Herculean task, given the entrenched nature of how mainstream reporters regard political news. Hunter presented a wish list in 2006 for how he wanted to see the 2008 presidential election covered:

> In my fantasy, when it's twenty-three entire months before the next election, there's no such thing as "frontrunners." It doesn't matter if their press offices call them frontrunners. It doesn't matter if bored media figures figure that adding the word "frontrunner" will spice up an otherwise transparently same-old-story. It doesn't matter if the cable networks want to spend hours talking about the presidential election prospects twenty-three months from now because panel-riddled horserace divination with little to no actual significance is pretty much the only thing they're good at.
>
> In my fantasy, we're not pondering who has the most "presence," or the strongest "narrative," twenty-three entire months before the next election. We're not looking to decide who should be supported based on breathless rumors of support that so-and-so lined up from so-and-so, or whether or not the fundraising numbers twenty-three months in advance indicate that so-and-so has the support of the monied classes that really ought to be listened to first, in these things....
>
> In my fantasy, we start looking at presidential candidates now—sure. We take a look, for the next year, at what each potential "contender" actually does. What do they get done? What issues do they solve that nobody else could? What did they spend that year doing, aside from shoring up support for getting out of their current job and landing another? Did they spend all their time preparing to be president, or did they spend all their time serving their country?[26]

But Hunter was realistic enough to recognize that this is a fantasy (he titled the post "And the Sky Will Be Made of Candy"), as much as netroots activists would like to see it come to pass. There is simply too much resistance from reporters. The blogger DemFromCT elaborates on the problem:

> The media really doesn't care for policy (especially complex policy that has to be explained), but they love a good fight. They will report on one even when there isn't much of a fight anymore (and don't ever ask them to referee, because they'll not call one until it's way too late to matter).... As for analysis, well, forget broadcast media for that. Takes too much time (and spoils the narrative). Print media is much better at it, but there's way too much horse race these days and not enough coverage of fundamentals (like how bad the economy really is).[27]

As frustrated as progressive bloggers may be with journalism that they feel reduces politics to trivial, partisan mud-wrestling, they can be downright hostile to traditional journalists who encourage bipartisan compromise to resolve the political dilemmas suggested by their own coverage. Perhaps no journalist promotes bipartisanship more prominently or proudly than David Broder of the *Washington Post*, one of the most senior political reporters in Washington. And perhaps no journalist takes more heat from the progressive blogosphere for doing so.

Broder would like nothing more than to see civility return to national political discourse, which he feels is dominated to the detriment of the vast political center by extremists on both sides of the aisle. During a web chat on Washingtonpost.com in 2007, he rejected the premise of a questioner who pointed to polls showing widespread support for progressive issue positions and asserted that "mainstream America's views" are being "subverted by the Republican agenda": "I have to disagree. I think the country is closely balanced, with a controlling group in the center that rejects extreme positions and seeks practical solutions drawn from the agendas of both liberals and conservatives. Most Americans I meet are not ideologues of any sort; they are practical people seeking practical solutions to real challenges."[28]

But to bloggers like Atrios, whom Broder no doubt would perceive as being one of the extremists responsible for political incivility, the idea that our political problems derive from an overriding ugliness in political discourse produced equally by Democrats and Republicans is an artifact of how reporters like Broder cover politics, leaving Broder with solutions to problems that exist on television but not in the real world. Atrios, who is quick to fault Democrats when he believes they do not act aggressively to defend their principles, believes Republicans are the source of the bitterness in Washington, a result of a deliberate strategy to bully their way to power. This critique—expressing a widely held tenet of netroots philosophy—views bipartisanship as a laughable antidote to the problem, as it would simply reward Republicans for their bullying by forcing Democrats to meet them halfway on a playing field of GOP design. A simpler and more effective solution would be for reporters to recognize the imbalance and permit it to inform their coverage, which would emphasize real problems and their remedies rather than horse-race politics, personality pageants, and political death matches.

Atrios terms the quest for centrist politics "High Broderism," which he views as a political frame employed by aristocratic Washington journalists to maintain their privileged position in the political status quo:

> We normally think of "High Broderism" as the worship of bipartisanship for its own sake, combined with a fake "pox on both their houses" attitude. But in reality this is just the cover Broder uses for his real agenda, the defense of what he perceives to be "the establishment" at all costs. The establishment is the permanent ruling class of Washington, our betters who know better. It is their rough agenda which is sold as "centrism" even when it has no actual relationship with the political center in a meaningful way. Democracy's messy, in Broder's world, and passionate voters

are problematic. It is up to the Wise Old Men of Washington to implement the agenda, and the job of the voters to bless them for it. When the establishment fails, the most important issue is not their failure, but that the voters might begin to lose faith in and deference for their betters. Thus, people must always be allowed to save face, no matter what their transgressions, as long as they're a part of his permanent floating tea party.

While this basic attitude isn't unique to Broder, his apparent lack of interest in the actual details of policy makes him a more absurd figure than some. For him it's not about results, but about the right people being in the right places. It is terribly elitist in all the wrong ways. Arguments can be made for certain types of elitism—you do want a brain surgeon conducting brain surgery—but Broder's elites are simply aristocrats. It's their town.[29]

A Daily Kos diarist, commenting on Broder's web-chat reference to the "controlling group in the center," elaborates:

> How does Broder reconcile his conception of where the political center is with the questioner's reference to polling that suggests America swinging more towards the liberal end of the spectrum? He does it by giving added weight to "a controlling group in the center." If that group happens to be more to the right of the ideological center of America, but also happens to weigh a lot more in importance (at least in the mind of David Broder), then that weight shifts the "center" away from the majority of Americans.
>
> How did that "controlling group in the center" come to have such control in the first place? Part of the reason is because the members of that group are a self-selected elite who then nominate into the group those they find of acceptable political quality. Membership in the "controlling group in the center" won't be offered to just anyone who demonstrates an above average level of influence on American public opinion. Members must also play nicely with those in the "controlling group in the center." No one is allowed in who would suggest that the "controlling group in the center" maybe shouldn't have so much influence. And it goes without saying that Broder is a member of that "controlling group in the center."[30]

Political frames, then, become a vehicle for the struggle between two elites over how the rest of the country will be encouraged to think about politics and the political system, with ramifications for which elite will hold sway. The netroots' indictment of Broder's aristocracy as a "self-selected elite" could apply with equal measure to the bourgeois writers of the online left, who would, if successful, replace what they regard as a false centrist solution to false horse-race politics with center-left solutions (what they regard as *true centrism*) to an issue-based politics (what they regard as *true politics*). A collateral ramification of this initiative would be to make netroots elites the new dominant voice of politics, to depose Broder along with Broderism.

For this reason, bloggers face tremendous pushback from Washington journalists, who would feel compelled to defend their coverage under any circumstances. The battle over political frames is ultimately about power—especially which group has the power to set the national agenda—because the winner of the battle over political frames will determine the viability of policy outcomes by controlling the narrative about the nature and cause of our political problems, thereby legitimizing or delegitimizing possible solutions. If the online left is to realize its goal of establishing a lasting progressive regime, then this is ultimately a battle that they will have to win. Considering the powerful individuals who they seek to topple in the process, any victory, if it comes at all, will have to be built on a string of other, more readily achieved successes in the relatively more accessible political arena. There they can engage the advantages of a decentralized medium to recruit candidates, raise money, and contest elections that give them a more direct way to displace an entrenched elite.

Opposing False Balance

Bloggers are a throwback to the partisan press of the early nineteenth century, when political news was loud and opinionated (see Chapter 2). As commercialism eroded partisan reporting and printers became professional journalists, reporters came to regard themselves as independent actors, and objectivity became the Rosetta Stone for viewing and deciphering political events. In the twenty-first century, however, these two reportorial hallmarks—independence and objectivity—are clashing. Bloggers contend that objective reporting, far from presenting the world accurately, masks what they perceive to be the damage left by years of a runaway Republican president and Congress. Indeed, this attitude is implied in their critique of Broderian centrism.

It isn't difficult to find examples of this perspective expressed on progressive blogs, but none states the case as clearly as a review, by Daily Kos executive editor Susan Gardiner, of former *Los Angeles Times* political reporter Ronald Brownstein's 2007 book, *The Second Civil War: How Extreme Partisanship Has Paralyzed Washington and Polarized America*. Brownstein, in what could be regarded as an exercise in High Broderism, equates the partisan exploits of Tom DeLay and Karl Rove with what he calls the "hyperpartisanship" found on Daily Kos. Gardiner is none too pleased: "Nearly everything is wrong with this book," she writes, "and every one of us should read it."[31] She continues:

> *The Second Civil War* is probably the best example to date of the thinking that we're up against as we try and change the way politics is practiced in this country. The mindset of Ronald Brownstein is Exhibit A for every entrenched establishment prejudice held against the more inclusive participatory movement that we're building as revitalized progressives.... From the first few pages in the introduction, in which the counterweight to an indicted Tom DeLay's arm-twisting thuggish leadership style as one of the most powerful House Majority Leaders in American history is balanced against ... wait for it ... Daily Kos users attending the first Yearly Kos

convention, the moral bankruptcy of searching for an equivalency is on constant display.... A professional journalist who either honestly sees the two examples as appropriate weights, or feels the need to provide egregiously unbalanced "balance" and obliges, should be considered irrelevant to the continuing national conversation. This tired, endless quest to create false equivalencies—by a press the Constitution gives special mention because of its sacred duty to inform—is far more damaging to our national discourse than what ordinary citizens are saying on a blog.

What Gardiner speculates to be the result of moral bankruptcy would probably be understood by journalism students as simply attempting to achieve objectivity by pitting two sides of an argument against one another. This technique has long served political reporters well, because it relieves them of the burden of having to tell a story from no one's perspective, which in an absolute sense is what objectivity requires. The alternative is to risk appearing to take sides, because, as Edward Jay Epstein long ago noted, despite the appearance that television-era reporting does not have a point of view, there is no such thing as "news from nowhere."[32] Substituting balance for objectivity solves this problem, especially in a political system where the presence of two parties makes the he-said, she-said narrative form easy to write.

Often lost in this simple formulation, however, are the assumptions journalists make when they equate balance with objectivity. They have to assume that there are two sides to an issue—no more, no less. And they further have to assume those two sides are of rough equivalence, equally plausible and equally valid. The easiest way for a reporter to satisfy these assumptions is to cover the statements made by partisans about an issue, because then the equivalence matter can be reduced to whether the parties in question actually made the statements attributed to them—an easy thing for a journalist to document. At that point, the plausibility of what was said is no longer at issue, and the reporter can claim to be presenting both sides in an objective manner. And if both sides dislike the story, the reporter can lean on that as a point of professional pride, because he or she must be doing the job well.

What also gets lost in this formulation is that objectivity is a value. And with the emergence of the blogosphere it is no longer a value that is universally shared among those who write about politics, just as it was not valued prior to the rise of the commercial press. To the contrary, just as today's traditional reporters associate objectivity with principled coverage, editors during Andrew Jackson's time felt the same way about partisanship. In a mirror image of today's mainstream values, party newspaper editors felt objectivity was inappropriate, given the purpose of newspapers to mobilize partisans. This is why a Washington, D.C., newspaper during the Jackson era derided a nonaligned Baltimore paper by asserting that neutrality in political affairs was opportunistic and demonstrated a "complete lack of principle." Similarly, a Kentucky paper chastised a neutral Indiana paper: "'We do not know [how] it is in Indiana, but in this State, people have more respect for an open, independent adversary than for dumb partisans or shuttlecock politicians, who are considered too imbecile to form an opinion, or too servile to express an opinion when formed."[33]

On Daily Kos we can imagine reading a statement like that about the traditional press. In fact, we just did—in Gardiner's assertion that equating the writings of the progressive blogosphere with the tactics of the House Republican majority is morally bankrupt. Ron Brownstein, trained as a traditional journalist, would be no more willing to accept this assault on one of the pillars of conventional political reporting than the editor of the *Louisville Public Advertiser* would have entertained a challenge to his partisanship from an early-day penny paper. Yet because objectivity and partisanship are values, it is fruitless to regard the battle between them as a contest that can be won. They are, at core, different choices, neither right nor wrong. And as with any value choice, each has consequences.

This is where progressive bloggers make their stand, arguing that objective coverage does damage to the polity by promoting false equivalencies and ignoring important political stories that cannot be told in balanced fashion. In Gardiner's critique of Brownstein, this includes demonizing progressive tactics in order to balance them against conservative tactics in an attempt to impose balance between right and left in defense of a sensible center. She calls Brownstein's formulation an "argument sandwich" whose logic works to minimize what she regards as the cardinal sins of the right by balancing them against the venial sins of the left:

> About now, if I were in the rolodex of the chattering classes, I suspect I would be getting a phone call from Brownstein saying, Hey, I said the Republicans started it. I said their tactics were more drastic. And you know what? He'd be right. He said exactly that. But the charge has been diluted with so many qualifications, and so many "balanced" examples from Democrats in order to not offend The Hammer [Tom Delay] and his hangers-on, that this layered effect cancels out any reasonable way to evaluate the stark undemocratic (with a small "d") tactics the modern GOP has foisted on America.
>
> The right-wing movement has brutalized democracy and its institutions, turned them inside-out, spat upon them, and then ground the rest of us under its boot heel with a savage glee. To disguise this fact like one limp piece of lettuce in a triple-decker sandwich is shameful and not worthy of passing as "journalism."
>
> Usually, this sandwiching is accomplished with the following formula:
>
> - Both political parties are nasty and brutish.
> - The Republicans? Slightly more so (examples).
> - But Democrats do it too! (Often lame and reaching examples provided).
> - Both political parties are nasty and brutish.

In one case, he refers to the infamous night of the Republicans holding the vote open on the Medicare bill for nearly three hours in order to arm-twist votes (earlier in the book, he'd dug up an instance a decade and a half earlier when Democrats had held a vote open for 15 minutes. You know, it's just the same! Even though … um … it's not). He follows his reference to the GOP episode with the sentence,

"Though these tactics recalled the Democratic maneuvers against Republicans after the mid-1980s, they often exceeded them." There you have it: a sandwich stacked in one sentence. And no mention at any point in the book that the Medicare legislation in question turned out to be based on outright falsified numbers provided knowingly by the White House.[34]

The netroots are noisy, Gardiner acknowledges, and they can write unpleasant things, but they engage the system—petitioning, canvassing, talking politics, registering voters—while in her estimation the DeLay-Rove conservative axis has worked to undermine it through antidemocratic politics that do not find a counterpart on the Internet.

Just as gradually staking out territory to the right gave conservatives the political advantage of moving the region of political compromise to the right, the rise of the netroots to counteract this trend has, for established journalists, resulted in a rough equivalency between the two sides. Nothing in the traditional journalistic model would permit Ron Brownstein to see it any other way, to write that the responsibility for contemporary hyperpartisanship falls largely or exclusively on the right. It's unlikely that he would even have a frame of reference for thinking it. In contrast, progressive bloggers cannot see anything but an obvious false equivalency because their method of reporting about politics isn't affected by the need to remain detached and balanced. To the bloggers, reporting the story otherwise merely serves to delegitimize their actions.

What, then, of these two perspectives, infused as they are with different values? In nineteenth-century America, partisan editors did not easily give way to the emerging values of professional reporting until they found themselves outgunned by a converging set of forces: industrialization, commercialization, urbanization, and the loss of patronage. In the early years of the twenty-first century, we are witnessing declining audiences for network news programs, the spread of high-speed Internet access, and increased reliance on computers to deliver newspaper and television content. By one count, roughly half the population relied on the Internet as its primary source of news in 2008, compared to one in three who relied on television and one in ten who relied on newspapers; nearly 70 percent of Americans felt that traditional journalism was out of touch with their everyday concerns.[35] At this stage, these changes have been enough to boost the importance of blogs but not enough to revolutionize journalism, which in the nineteenth century required wholesale changes in the economy.

But consider that since the late 1990s we have also witnessed the ascendance of Fox News Channel, catering to conservative tastes in a manner that Neil Hickey, writing in the *Columbia Journalism Review,* called "a bully pulpit for conservative sentiment in America."[36] And we have seen the emergence of open source investigative reporting, where readers can offer tips to bloggers on Talking Points Memo, the heavily trafficked news-oriented site that models itself after early-twentieth-century muckrakers. In 2007, Josh Marshall, the site's founder, received the George Polk Award for Legal Reporting for his work in uncovering political connections in the Bush administration's firing of U.S. attorneys in states across the country.[37] For a progressive website to win a prestigious mainstream award for investigative journalism despite its outward partisanship signals a degree of acceptance of non-neutral reporting models. Perhaps at some point Fox News will be able to stop claiming to be "fair and balanced" without risking its status as a major cable news outlet. Against this backdrop, the challenge posed by bloggers to the traditional journalistic model bears watching, especially as the two media contest each other in a battle over news values.

Opposing Lazy Journalists

As much as netroots bloggers erupt when they perceive misplaced balance in traditional media reports, they hold a special place for reporters who, they feel, simply do not do their jobs. Considering the conventional arguments against the reliability of information on blogs—that blogs lack strict editorial controls, are irreverent and partisan, and permit people to publish without formal journalistic training—bloggers can be highly dismissive of professional journalists when they fail to live up to their own ethical standards for careful reporting. When the journalist is a notable opinion leader, blogger venom can be particularly potent.

Just ask Joe Klein. The veteran *Time* magazine reporter who is venerated by peers in the media aristocracy has been the subject of numerous assaults by Arianna Huffington at Huffingtonpost.com, Glenn Greenwald at Salon, Markos Moulitsas, and assorted Daily Kos diarists for what they consider to be lazy reporting on a range of subjects. They're not subtle about it. "Joe Klein Hates Black Members of Congress," one blog post screams.[38] "Joe Klein, Idiot Tool of the GOP," announces another.[39] The blogger BooMan at BoomanTribune.com calls him "Joke Line."[40] It has to sting to be called out as a joke by someone whose professional identity is BooMan.

But the bloggers are deadly serious, and they document their claims, sometimes extracting apologies (of sorts) from Klein. Some disagreements are over relatively small matters. In March 2008, for instance, Klein wrote about a backlash by women voters in the Ohio and Texas Democratic primaries ("a feminine fury was abroad in the land"), documented by women representing, respectively, a "staggering" 59 percent and 57 percent of the two electorates. A quick check of composite exit polls, supplied on Daily Kos, showed that women had represented 58 percent of the electorate in all Democratic primaries and caucuses to that point.[41] Countered Moulitsas: "It was a slow boil of epic remarkableness!"[42]

Other disagreements involved less trivial errors. In November 2007, with the Foreign Intelligence Surveillance Act (FISA) amendment before Congress, Klein published a column claiming the House version of the bill would require court approval of individual surveillance requests involving communications outside the United States. He accused Democrats who backed it as "mealymouthed on issues of national security," claiming the bill would give terrorists "the same legal protections as Americans," which Klein said was "well beyond stupid."[43] The problem with this conclusion is that his premise was based on a misreading of the bill, which did not require a court order for individual intercepts of conversations involving individuals outside the United States.

Initially, Klein stood by his reporting. But as bloggers started turning up the heat about the basis of his criticism of Democrats, Klein pulled back, admitting that he may have made a mistake but that it's "difficult to tell for sure given the technical nature of the bill's language and fierce disagreements between even moderate Republicans and Democrats on the Committee about what the bill actually does contain."[44] Glenn Greenwald, in a post at Salon, clarified matters for Klein—and his readers—by posting the relevant section of the bill:

> *CLARIFICATION OF ELECTRONIC SURVEILLANCE OF NON-UNITED STATES PERSONS OUTSIDE THE UNITED STATES*
> *Sec. 105A. (a) Foreign to Foreign Communications—*
> *(1) IN GENERAL—Notwithstanding any other provision of this Act, a court order is not required for electronic surveillance directed at the acquisition of the contents of any communication between persons that are not known to be United States persons and are reasonably believed to be located outside the United States for the purpose of collecting foreign intelligence information, without respect to whether the communication passes through the United States or the surveillance device is located within the United States.*

Nobody who can read basic English can fail to understand what this says. As clearly as it can, the bill says that no warrant is required for communications involving non-U.S. persons outside of the U.S. In fact, individual warrants are not even required when a foreign target communicates with someone inside the U.S.; only general approval by the FISA court of the procedures used to eavesdrop is required (see Sec. 105). Thus, Klein's statements about the bill were indisputably, unquestionably false, and all one had to do is read the painfully clear language of the bill to know that.[45]

Greenwald went on to accuse Klein of never bothering to read the legislation, getting his information on what the bill did from Republican sources, and accepting it as fact:

> Klein's GOP source(s) blatantly lied to him about what the bill does and doesn't do in order to manipulate him into uncritically feeding *Time*'s readers the Rush Limbaugh Line—namely, that Democrats are giving equal rights to Terrorists and preventing the Leader from eavesdropping on foreign Terrorists. And Klein dutifully wrote down what he was told in *Time* without bothering to find out if it was true and without ever bothering to talk to any of the bill's Democratic proponents. And no *Time* editor knew enough or cared enough to bother correcting any of it. And thus, the unfortunate four million Americans who read

and trust *Time* now think that the Democrats' FISA bill does the exact opposite of what it actually does.[46]

Challenged to explain how a simple reading of the relevant language in the bill wouldn't have pointed out his error, Klein backpedaled farther. *Time* appended his column with a correction explaining that the bill doesn't exactly say what Klein originally claimed it said, then blamed the error on the need to balance the story: "Republicans believe it can be interpreted that way, but Democrats don't."[47] Greenwald's sarcastic conclusion:

> Klein's so-called reporting error wasn't that he falsely described the bill. No; describing the bill accurately isn't the role of a journalist. Klein's only "reporting error" was that he only wrote down what one side said (the Republicans). He "forgot" to write down what the Democrats said. Now that the Editors noted in passing that the Democrats disagree, everything is fixed. Their job is done. That's what they just said about explicitly as it can be said. And they don't even realize that saying this is a profound indictment on what they do. They think that's what they're supposed to do.[48]

If the public back-and-forth with Klein is about bloggers proving their mettle versus journalists who purport to live up to higher ethical standards, then the subtext is about power. Klein is perceived in the mainstream as a liberal. He was often critical in print of the Bush administration and its allies, and toward the end of the 2008 election he was highly critical of what he perceived to be divisive tactics used by John McCain's campaign. When bloggers accuse Klein of regurgitating right-wing talking points, their purpose is to undermine him, to keep him from doing damage to the progressive cause by lending liberal legitimacy to conservative frames—in much the way that bloggers go after Democratic officials who do the same. On another level, some of the animosity stems from how Klein is perceived in the blogosphere as one of the cool kids—an opinion leader whose position of privilege comes from being one of the charter members of the punditocracy (he was, after all, the anonymous author of the novel *Primary Colors*). This, in the eyes of netroots bloggers, makes Klein part of the problem, the poster boy for that aristocratic group of journalists they regard as lazy, counterproductive, and out of touch.

Conclusion

Progressive bloggers demonstrate savvy and sophistication when they recognize they must influence the traditional media agenda if they are ever going to successfully move the public behind a progressive platform. It is perhaps their most daunting task, because complete victory requires displacing an entrenched elite and upending a mode of political reporting more than a century in the making.

The undertaking parallels their struggles with Democratic Party elites over how to contest and win elections—but without the opportunity to vote their opponents out of office. And there is always a chance that netroots elites can win the attention, if not grudging respect, of at least some in the party aristocracy by using the new media and employing alternative strategies to win elections, because both groups—despite being engaged in a struggle for control of the direction of the party—benefit from victory. Not so with journalists. Bloggers seek nothing less than a complete takedown of pundits like David Broder, Ron Brownstein, and Joe Klein.

So they struggle, and they gain mixed results. On balance they have been more successful in challenging than changing media narratives. And where they have been effective at changing them, they have often been assisted by events they did not generate. Progressive bloggers were able to make the macaca story stick to Senator Allen because his critical error was captured on video and circulated virally on YouTube. Markos Moulitsas acknowledges that none other than George Bush helped puncture the narrative that his foreign policy was steeped in compassion for ordinary people through his involvement in the Dubai port deal. Each of these hinged on events happening beyond the netroots.

It's hard to see how they could have successfully pushed a narrative about Allen's alleged racism without the video footage, or about Bush's self-interested national security objectives without the Dubai deal. Like other political and policy frames they find noxious, the netroots' objections would have been duly noted in cyberspace but not on the evening news or in the daily papers. Bloggers can make the most of what they're given, but that's different from *initiating* the story line. As media scholar Joseph Capella notes, mainstream media are in the "replication business," effectively inserting the media's framework for understanding events into general conversation, where a talking point is mimicked and reinforced to the point where it establishes itself in the popular culture.[49] Bloggers aggressively offer counternarratives, but in television they are up against a powerful force.

These were also episodic events, important, no doubt, in putting a senator on the defensive and eroding the president's approval ratings, but far from the paradigm-changing narratives that netroots bloggers promote. To initiate such frames in traditional coverage—to turn everyday political news into a contest of ideas in which most Americans side with center-left solutions—would require influence over the thematic elements of the media narrative, which in turn would require mainstream reporting to acquire the news values espoused on the blogs, rejecting objectivity manifested in balance. It is hard to see at this juncture how such a revolutionary change would come to pass. In the days immediately following Barack Obama's victory, traditional columnists and pundits, following the lead of conservative opinion leaders, speculated on how America remained a center-right nation despite an electoral earthquake that had sent an African American Democrat to the White House with oversized congressional majorities.[50] The discussion served to maintain continuity in political discourse, and even though progressive voices pushed back they could at best influence the discussion, not change its terms. It is possible to imagine a shift in the center-right frame if journalists perceive Barack Obama to govern effectively from the center-left, especially if the president himself pushes center-left framing, but this is a different thing than expecting a collapse in the prevailing hierarchy of conventional wisdom production.

A more modest outcome would be for bloggers to claim a greater portion of the stage from journalists, something they are already doing. It is worth noting that traditional reporters who several years ago simply ignored bloggers now take them seriously. Some of them, in their own way and on corporate outlets, attempt to blog themselves (including, ironically, Joe Klein). This shift is captured in the optimism of bloggers who perceive their influence over mainstream journalism to have been far greater in 2006 than it was in 2004, and who perceive an even brighter future ahead. Thus journalists no longer dismiss without comment the ranting of the Internet left, and on occasion progressive bloggers will score victories over the forces of objectivity and balance. They may complain more about traditional political frames than change them, but as the netroots face a deeply entrenched media elite they exhibit little fear and show no desire to stop pushing back.

6

The Progressive Blogosphere and the Creation of Community

We are a community. We celebrate our successes. Like the two marriages that have emerged from the Daily Kos community.... And you've shared your happy moments as well with your pictures. Of your babies. And your cats. We also grieve together.... Without my planning or prodding, you started organizing. You started talking to each other and deciding, on your own, to take charge of your politics.... But it wasn't just talking.... You realized that our nation wasn't going to fix itself. We couldn't depend on our Democratic Party to save us. The media was AWOL. We shared a common disgust at the irrelevance of our once proud party and its allied organizations. But what could we do? We were nobodies.... Then technology changed everything. Whether it was blogs, or podcasting, or social networking sites like MySpace and Facebook, or MoveOn, or YouTube, people quickly adopted myriad communication technologies emerging from the web and turned them to political purposes. Millions did so. And while individually we were still nobodies, together, we became ... somebody.

—Markos Moulitsas, August 4, 2007[1]

Pictures of cats? Two marriages? Celebrating success and mourning death? Let's recall that this is a website we're talking about—and a political one at that. But Markos Moulitsas does not exaggerate when he recounts the way the rhythm of ordinary life is acknowledged and shared by those who regularly exchange ideas on Daily Kos.

In September 2007, for instance, Moulitsas blogged about the death of a diarist who posted using the screen name New Direction, saying "we mourn as a community" and honoring his 138 diaries by linking to one that "seems to capture who he was quite nicely."[2] The remarkable thing about this sad but otherwise routine announcement was the outpouring of grief and sympathy that followed in 106 comments by people who almost certainly never met New Direction in real life. "My condolences to his family and friends," they wrote. "Peace be unto New Direction." "Many candles burn for him." "God bless." "He will be missed and remembered by many." A number of bloggers knew that New Direction had just had a child several months earlier and mentioned this in their remembrances. "That loss is especially painful," said one, "with a new baby at home." Added another, "He had a child—could you find out if donations are needed?"[3] It was as if they were talking about a neighbor, relative, or friend.

A similar phenomenon emerged during Howard Dean's presidential campaign on Blog for America, Dean's official campaign weblog (see Chapter 3). Ordinary people who had never met became involved in the everyday events of each other's lives.[4] They blogged back and forth about their aspirations and accomplishments, exchanged favorite recipes, and encouraged one another when things got tough. They developed a kind of proprietary ownership of the candidate, worrying that he wasn't getting enough sleep and that his diet was poor, as if they were responsible for his health and well-being. And always, they believed—in Dean, in their cause, in what was possible for each other and their families and their country. To outsiders, their discourse might have appeared a bit odd, even cultlike, but the most striking thing was how ordinary it seemed. It is easy to believe that politics is a cynical endeavor meant for the thick of skin and cold of heart, yet here were average people daring to engage one another in a most human way. Back at Dean headquarters in Burlington, Vermont, paid professionals were making hard calculations to position their candidate to win the Democratic nomination. But that wasn't happening at Blog for America—it seemed like a Frank Capra movie.

The Dean bloggers called themselves a community, the same phrase Moulitsas uses to describe Daily Kos. If they are a community, it is a virtual one, in the same way that eBay is a virtual store, lacking physical bricks and mortar. But just as people can effectively buy and sell real products on eBay, they can bond with one another online and derive the same emotional benefits they might get from associating in the physical world. This effect is provocative—and telling, because it sets the Internet as a medium apart from television and suggests that a political environment built around Internet communications would be an entirely different entity than the one to which we have become accustomed. The Internet, at its core, is about relationships, be they political, commercial, or interpersonal.[5] Television may have the capacity to unite the world around a single image in real time, but no one ever accused it of building social ties. Quite the opposite.

Cynicism Versus Social Capital

As watching the tube gives way to browsing through YouTube, television's hold on cultural attitudes is being challenged. To those who value social engagement and political participation, this is a positive development, for although the evidence linking television viewing with cynicism and apathy is inconclusive, a strong circumstantial case can be made that they are interrelated because of the way each has increased since the 1960s. During the television era, hours spent watching television rose while interpersonal and institutional trust diminished. In 1960, as television was becoming an indispensable appliance in most American homes, close to six in ten Americans felt they could trust most of their fellow citizens. By 1998 only one-third felt that way. In the years immediately preceding the introduction of color television, three in four Americans felt they could trust elected officials to do the right thing most or all of the time. By 1995, with around-the-clock cable television chattering in the background, three in four Americans felt mistrustful of Washington.[6]

The correlation between America's dependence on television and the decline in interpersonal and institutional trust spawned a wealth of literature from researchers interested in understanding television's role in shaping attitudinal changes. Because attitudes are complex and influenced by a host of stimuli, drawing causal connections between television and cynicism is not an easy task. Political scientist Michael Robinson pegged television's cynical coverage of politics as the cause of an American social malaise that he sensed during the mid-1970s, manifested in lower rates of efficacy, higher rates of cynicism, and a greater sense of powerlessness on the part of ordinary individuals.[7] Other researchers produced complementary findings with claims that network television is among the most cynicism-inducing medium, with its emphasis on the negative voice of reporters,[8] and evidence suggesting negative television ads can generate cynical reactions in people who view them.[9]

More recently, researchers Kathleen Hall Jamieson and Joseph N. Cappella made the case that television's strategic, conflict-ridden framing of politics activates cynical reactions about politicians and the political process. They claim that news coverage, by emphasizing the strategic component of politics, cues people to see politicians and officials as self-interested, a rational precursor to feelings of mistrust.[10] The scholar Roderick Hart makes the complementary claim that television distances us from others even as it seductively makes us feel as though we're connected to a nonexistent electronic community. Hart claims that cynicism is television's natural language, its insidious messages detaching us from our leaders and each other, leaving us longing for genuine human connections.[11]

But there are detractors from the hypothesis that television is a root cause of cynicism and social malaise. Contrary findings offer only qualified support for the argument that television leaves viewers feeling cynical,[12] or support the case that television viewing is related to feelings of powerlessness but not cynicism,[13] or uncover no evidence of a relationship between television viewing and cynicism when the question is examined at the statewide level.[14] Other studies find television viewing generates no negative attitudinal effects at all.[15]

Nonetheless, the malaise hypothesis lingers, most likely because the overpowering presence of television in American life since the 1950s makes it such an obvious target for blame. Perhaps the most celebrated allegation of the negative influence of television in recent years comes from political scientist Robert Putnam in his influential book *Bowling Alone.*[16] Putnam contends that television is in large part to blame for a loss of social capital, or the value derived when people form connections with one another. Putnam calls these connections the "glue of society" because people build trust by making connections, which in turn provides crucial individual benefits (companionship, emotional support, networking) and collective benefits (neighborhood watches that lower crime, Rotary Clubs that raise scholarship money), thereby making social capital simultaneously a private and a public good. As a public matter, social capital enhances cooperation for mutual benefit that facilitates civic engagement, such that stronger relationships with one another fosters political participation, which builds stronger relationships with our political institutions.[17]

Putnam documents the decline in interpersonal and institutional trust that occurred during the second half of the twentieth century in tandem with diminished voting rates and other measures of political and civic engagement. His case against television as the chief culprit in these antisystemic developments is partly circumstantial, partly direct. Noting that the last generation to exhibit high levels of civic engagement was the cohort that came of age prior to television's rapid emergence in the 1950s, Putnam distinguishes between the behavior of people who consume large quantities of television and those who are avid newspaper readers. Heavy viewers tend to be isolated, whereas heavy readers are joiners—and over the years we have become a society of viewers. The more we watch television, the more we stay at home, the less we trust, and the less we engage others.[18]

But the emergence of the Internet has begun to erode long-entrenched patterns of leisure activity, especially among younger people and those with the means to afford high-speed Internet access—those on the privileged side of the so-called digital divide. Could this translate into a reversal of the decades-long decline in social capital that Putnam documents? Possibly. On one hand, sitting in front of a computer screen can limit human interaction, causing social isolation[19] and leading to a condition one participant in the blogger survey referred to as "pretty much talking to ourselves." Alternately, working toward a common goal can be empowering and can build political efficacy,[20] and the Internet can make this possible by facilitating virtual connections that build real social capital.

Some recent evidence supports the latter, more system-affirming possibility. The Internet sharply cuts the cost of gathering information, making it much easier for those predisposed to engage in political activity to take steps toward learning about politics and politicians—steps associated with greater political knowledge, interest, and involvement.[21] It also makes it simple to find others with similar political concerns and beliefs and, once discovered, to engage them in political discussion in a manner associated with increased efficacy and political participation.[22]

However, the self-selection inherent in Internet use makes it difficult to apply these effects broadly. As a decentralizing medium, the Internet would not likely generate the mass audience effects of television and radio. Consequently, any social benefits derived from Internet use should be expected to originate from select groups like the netroots bourgeois elite rather than from a broad swath of the population. This suggests the Internet—or at least the blogosphere—would be a more natural source of bonding social capital than bridging social capital. *Bonding* occurs when like-minded individuals come together for a shared purpose, whereas *bridging* unites people more broadly across social divisions, such as when people from all walks of life turn out to support the hometown baseball team. Bonding is a tighter, more exclusive experience—like banding together to promote a progressive political agenda.

Certainly, bloggers tend to see it this way. For the most part, survey respondents embrace the notion that the blogosphere is a virtual community and has been so at least since 2004, long before bloggers felt they were achieving political results. As evidenced in Table 6.1, 60 percent reported that a virtual community of online bloggers existed in 2004; 88 percent felt this way by 2006. If, as it appears, the community-building element of blogging is not dependent on getting results, then we can surmise that bloggers bond with each other online through the shared experience of fighting for a common objective. The promise of success and the process of trying to achieve it appear sufficient to create the sense of shared purpose that defines what most bloggers describe as a communal endeavor.

But this does not blind them to the limitations of how the blogosphere is structured or whom they reach. Referencing the bourgeois elite, one blogger who is not an upper-echelon member noted that "virtual community is pretty good among the top bloggers, but less so for those further down the pecking order." Another confirmed that bloggers "are good at 'bonding social capital'—that is, reinforcing each others' views—but they are not effective at reaching people who don't already have progressive beliefs and even less effective at reaching people who are not substantially online."

Table 6.1 Progressive Blogger Perceptions of the Effectiveness of the Progressive Blogosphere at Community Building, 2004–2008

Virtual Community Building

	2004	*2006*	*Estimated 2008*
Very Effective	8%	40%	36%
Effective	52	48	48
Ineffective	28	12	16
Very Ineffective	12	0	0

Real-World Community Building

	2004	*2006*	*Estimated 2008*
Very Effective	4%	4%	16%
Effective	28	56	48
Ineffective	48	32	24
Very Ineffective	20	8	12

N = 25

The degree of bridging on progressive weblogs depends on the ease with which individuals with diverse demographic characteristics participate as full community members. Given the virtual nature of the blogosphere and the tendency for people to bond over common interests rather than invisible social characteristics such as gender, race, and age,[23] it is possible that bridging can occur through self-selection—that is, if individuals from diverse backgrounds self-select as members of the community. Interestingly, bloggers on Daily Kos maintain a certain fascination with these statistics—itself an indication of community bonding. Periodically, Daily Kos bloggers post community polls to try to get a sense of who else is out there. These polls are not scientific, although they are prominently displayed and receive a large number of responses and thus can provide a rough glimpse into the demographic breakdown of those bloggers motivated enough to respond.

The results of a series of demographic polls posted in February through April 2008 suggest there is some limited and uneven bridging in the flagship community of the progressive blogosphere. Daily Kos bloggers range in age from adolescent to senior citizen, come from all parts of the country (and beyond), and represent all income brackets. But the central tendencies in the demographic figures suggest that even though everyone is welcome to participate there is such a thing as a typical blogger: middle-aged, male, financially comfortable. The modal age group is forty-five to forty-nine years, with 57 percent of 9,710 respondents to a survey about age reporting to be between thirty-five and fifty-nine years.[24] Sixty percent of 5,602 respondents to a separate poll are male.[25] Half live in homes where income is in the top 20 percent of all households (N=3,631).[26] Participation in this community is open to anyone, but through self-selection Daily Kos does not look like America. And, of course, Daily Kos does not bridge ideological lines. There may not be an ideological litmus required for blogging, and the comment threads can be filled with honest disagreements over policies and candidate preferences (for a good example, look at the comment threads in just about any candidate diary during the long 2008 Democratic primary campaign), but Daily Kos is not about reaching out to conservatives.

Blogs as Communities

Because of its size and reach in the blogosphere, Daily Kos makes a particularly apt case study for examining the ways participants experience themselves as a community. Several characteristics of Daily Kos mirror those one might expect to find in real-world communities. Daily Kos has a history that's told as a narrative about an insignificant website that grew up to become highly influential. It has community standards and norms that members are expected to follow. It has its own set of resources available to anyone who frequents the site, along with activities for members to pursue. Significantly, there is a prevailing awareness of the website as a community, manifested in self-referential meta-discussions about what it means to be a community (not unlike the discussion in this book).

A key element of that self-awareness rests with what Jerome Armstrong, founder of the blog MyDD, calls the "power of many." He explained his understanding of the link between technology and community—in language reminiscent of Putnam's social capital argument—in this 2004 post on Daily Kos:

> We use technology to enhance the things we care about. What's happened online didn't really invent something new, it's merely revitalized the local community that's dissipated in this nation over the past century. That's really a concise explanation of why Dean for America's netroots during 2002–2003 happened, and why we continue here today beyond that moment.... The political blogs reside within a greater sphere, if you will, and what we experience through political participation on Daily Kos, MyDD, and others, is happening with all sorts of issues and life topics on different parts of the Internet.... For us, blogging is the epicenter of all this that's happening toward a renewed democratic expression. It is community, it is about action, it is about transforming the political system. It's through the real work of many that this will happen.[27]

Implicit in Armstrong's understanding of online community is the essential role of the bottom-up, decentralized structure of the Internet that represents the greatest strength of the new medium. Technology makes possible the association of individuals with a common passion for progressive politics (or playing sports or cooking Italian food or making widgets) who otherwise would never be able to locate each other, and individuals take it from there. He suggests that the social capital lost to television masks an enduring desire to engage in collective action that was unleashed when the Internet provided a convenient and inexpensive way to express it.

Those who experience Daily Kos as a community would likely have an instinctive feel for what Armstrong is saying. They would side with those who find meaning and purpose in the blogged words of thousands of writers against those who regard blogs as a self-serving waste of time. Indeed, to appreciate the power of many is almost a prerequisite to deriving satisfaction from participating because it means finding value in the collective body of work that is the blog. It means appreciating the most fundamental element of open source politics.

Consider this instructive exchange between Zach Exley, the online communications chief for the 2004 Kerry-Edwards presidential campaign, and Markos Moulitsas over the value of bottom-up organizing. Exley dismisses the left's "goatee-chinned web designers" who were just "interested in putting cool software up" to "let people use" while they got "trounced by the Republicans' superior top-down organization" in 2004.[28] In turn, Moulitsas dismisses Exley:

> People like Zach, who was unfortunately the "director of online communications" for the Kerry campaign ... never truly understood the power of many. Zach was

responsible for those obnoxious emails that asked for money, more money, and yet more money. He was behind the god-awful Kerry blog. He was behind the campaign's obvious decision to abandon MeetUp as an organizing tool. I sat on a panel discussion with him in 2003 where he sat opposite me, with a Republican, arguing that people couldn't be trusted in the political space and had to be controlled top-bottom.[29]

In short: Exley doesn't get it. Without appreciating the fundamental value of the Internet's decentralized structure, there is no way to understand how so many blog participants experience the website as a community.

Conversely, once you appreciate the degree to which participants buy into the idea of the blog as an extended community, you can begin to identify formal characteristics of community that define participation, starting with the ritual myth of the blog's history and development. On the "About Daily Kos" page of the website, Moulitsas says with some flair that he created Daily Kos on May 26, 2002, "in those dark days when an oppressive and war-crazed administration suppressed all dissent as unpatriotic and treasonous."[30] From humble roots it grew into "the premier political community in the United States."[31] In an August 2004 post, Moulitsas elaborated on the story for those who, in his words, "always ask me how I built this site." His story is one of "opportunism, mixed in with blind luck and a dose of branding" built around the notion of community-building that has itself become part of the lore that infuses the Daily Kos community:

There was once a group of political aficionados who hung out at various political forums—starting with Delphi Forums, then moving on to ones run by a guy named Orvetti. When Orvetti closed shop, they all moved over en masse to [Taegan Goddard's] Political Wire, which at the time had comments. But in the runup to the 2002 midterms, Taegan got sick of the constant flame wars [arguments] in his comment threads and he shut them down. So everyone headed on over to Jerome Armstrong's MyDD, which is where I entered the picture. Digging the site, I decided to start up my own election-themed site, Daily Kos. The site actually lived on fishyshark.com for a month as I tried to come up with a "serious" name for my new endeavor. Even though I eventually settled on "Daily Kos," I considered it a failure at the time—I thought I should've come up with a more creative name. I selected orange as the site color so that it would stand out from the bloggy masses (branding 101).

In short time I caught Jerome's attention, and we made a habit of linking back to each other on a constant basis. A few months later, Jerome (who invented the "open thread") got sick of the flame wars on his message boards and followed Taegan's lead by shutting his comments down. So everyone headed on over to Daily Kos. And I was ready. I had learned my lessons from Political Wire and MyDD's community failures, and immediately shut the door on the Republican commentators who had destroyed the previous sites' communities. I zealously worked to create a "safe zone" for liberal political junkies, despite howls of "censorship" from both liberals and conservatives, and the community grew.... But even back then, the site was no longer about me, it was about the community, discussion, and debate.[32]

Written in the once-upon-a-time voice of oft-told stories about a well-established past, Moulitsas's account is built around the idea that tangible and virtual communities are indistinguishable. He writes of people moving from website to website as if they were frequenting local taverns, of how "everyone headed on over to Daily Kos" as if physical movement were involved. And he writes of the bonding he intentionally encouraged among progressives by making his site a "safe zone"—a virtual haven where progressives could feel safe congregating, indistinguishable from a physical haven save for the fact that it lacks a physical space. In this creation tale, physical community is indistinguishable from virtual community.

It should therefore be unsurprising that there are norms of behavior on Daily Kos much as there would be in any community. The blogger DarkSyde spelled out the basics in a 2006 welcome to new members, at a time when Daily Kos was experiencing dramatic growth. Saying "you're among friends here and your participation is *valued*,"[33] he warns new members that they may be assaulted by trolls looking to disrupt the site by picking on vulnerable, inexperienced contributors who may be more likely than veteran bloggers to engage them. He says bluntly, "If you're new and someone tells you or implies—for no obvious reason—you're not wanted or that no one cares you're here, they're absolutely full of crap.... Like any pathetic coward they zone in on new members whom they perceive as 'weak.' Don't waste time on them."[34]

At the same time, it's vital to treat other legitimate members with respect and to abide by established blog practices, like creating a free member account "to be part of the community."[35] It's also important to make diaries substantive and to document all claims, never to copy and paste articles from somewhere else, to avoid duplicating the work of other contributors, and to put time and effort into writing diaries. Then, try to keep your ego in check as other members of the community determine whether your writing merits greater exposure:

> Once you post a new diary it will appear on the recent diary list and scroll down as other members post theirs. It may scroll away quickly. Members can vote to recommend your diary though, and if enough votes are garnered it will appear on the recommended diary list giving it a much longer life. Understand this: Getting on the reco list involves a great deal of chance. Even if you have name recognition here there's a ton of luck involved. Every one of us who writes articles has watched our cherished work scroll down that list into the abyss and watched as second rate snark we or someone else wrote in less than half an hour pop to the top. What will or will not be reco'd by other members at a specific time is unpredictable. But the best way to get a diary on that list, that you have control over, is to follow the rules and post well written, original work, that you've put some time into. Also I personally like to use Carl Sagan's Rule: Extraordinary claims require extraordinary evidence.[36]

Extraordinary arguments can be helpful, too, because once a diary gets attention it is subject to the comments of other readers who can be quick to express their disagreements. This is politics, after all, and people don't always feel the need to be gentle with their feedback. You can feel the heat rising from comment threads where two or more people are arguing over a position or an idea, as when Obama supporters who contended their candidate had the Democratic presidential nomination locked up prior to the end of the primaries met with Clinton supporters who vehemently expressed a different perspective. But this is the sort of exchange that blogs encourage, and the rules of engagement provide latitude for testiness that would feel familiar to anyone who ever argued with relatives about politics over a holiday meal. "If you come here and trash a Democratic candidate," blogged Moulitsas, "expect to be trashed back (just like I get trashed when I criticize the [Democratic] Party). If you can't take the heat, then don't write that post or diary."[37] As long as you avoid starting a flame war and you're not a shill for a candidate pretending to be an ordinary blogger,[38] it's acceptable to engage other bloggers with gusto. It's what gives blogs like Daily Kos a personality.

The site's host, like the proprietor of a tavern, is responsible for maintaining some semblance of order and making sure guests know and follow the rules. Also like a tavern, blogs get a lot of traffic. Some regulars stay around while others move on as new people come on board, making protocol violations inevitable. For the most part, the community is left to police itself, but warnings are posted when problems flare. To Moulitsas, there is a pattern to the flow of blog participation that resembles the cycle of life:

> I've seen it three times already, and now I'm seeing it happen again. We have an established community. The influx of traffic means lots of new faces who don't know the established etiquette start posting on the message boards. There is tension as the established guard clashes with the old guard. Eventually, the old guard is outnumbered, and seeing fewer and fewer of their old online friends, kind of fade away. It's like seeing your favorite pub taken over by a new scene. As the old guard fades away, the hangers-on complain how the old-timers are being "chased off." But there's nothing I can do. Online communities are not static. People come and go. And those "old-timers" once upon a time chased off the established community that preceded them. And those guys chased off the original community. Like I said, four waves.[39]

An element of this cyclical quality can be found in the changing voices featured on the blog's front page. It is an annual tradition at Daily Kos to rotate the guest bloggers who, by virtue of their featured position as contributing editors to the site, get to post material directly on the front page. Because these bloggers are assured an enormous platform for their ideas, there is tremendous competition for these spots among active blog participants when new bloggers are rotated in (and the existing contributors become an alumni class, free to post whenever they please).

Because Daily Kos is fashioned as a self-described community, the decision is a democratic one, at least to a point. Moulitsas makes the final decision but only selects from among contributors "recommended by the community."[40] They must exhibit, in addition to a thick skin and the ability to match nouns with verbs, an awareness of the communal nature of the blog. "They have to appreciate that they are part of a people-powered, not person-powered movement," he writes. "This is not a good gig for people with big egos."[41]

Like any competition for something with value to group members, the losers can leave feeling bruised, potentially creating rifts with fellow bloggers. In his 2007 call for applicants, Moulitsas attempted to assume this burden while reassuring those who are to be passed over of their value to the community:

> I know some people will be hurt when they are passed over, and will look for excuses or people to blame. The blame will rest on my shoulders. I will make the decisions myself. The final decisions will not be a value judgment over any individuals. It doesn't mean that someone sucks, or that I hate them, or that they're bad for the site, or any such thing. It'll just mean that the number of slots is small, and that I'll be looking for a very specific set of traits that I think will set the right tone for the nation's largest political community site. Remember that ultimately, this is a site about the Democratic Party and elections. I'll be looking for people who get that we're building a movement and can help further that goal.[42]

Consistent with that objective, and with the sense of the blog as a community engaged in collective action, Daily Kos bloggers have created or discovered political tools and resources that they share with others in order to ensure that anyone so inclined can use the Internet for maximum political leverage. One such tool, dKosopedia, is a community-specific "progressive-political version of the Wikipedia."[43] (To understand the inner workings of Democratic Party superdelegates, for example, look here.) The brainchild of community members Centerfielder, wegerje, Pyrrho, Tunesmith, and Waltisfrozen, but open to anyone to edit and build, its purpose is to serve as a political resource "for community members and the general public at large"—although Moulitsas also saw the potential for it one day to grow into a kind of "virtual, open-source, community-driven think tank."[44] And he was quick to point out that he "didn't lift a finger to make this happen"—that the credit for dKosopedia belongs to the "community members" who "did all the work."[45]

Similarly, bloggers will link to external political tools in order to bring them to the attention of other community members and expand their potential for real-world political action In a post about cool tools that will "have great promise for helping us get our collective acts together," SusanG links to websites offering Internet tools useful for online political organizing, including a site that simplifies the process of creating multimedia projects, another that facilitates communal action by permitting people to pledge to do something if others will join them, and a directory of "self-organizing tools for activists" (including "everything from software designed to create a petition drive, to 'constituent management' databases, to collaborative writing programs").[46] "Go forth, organize and create!" she exclaims, "and discuss in comments any helpful websites or tools you've run across that may be of benefit to the community as we prepare to take our country back."[47]

And they do. "DNC has also [*sic*] an organizing tool," responds one reader. "CitizenSpeak is a free email advocacy service for grassroots organizations," adds another. "In Texas," another reader replies, "we had (have?) True Blue Action, which let you log in & pull up a phone list & make calls from home. I really liked it."[48] With links posted alongside contributed comments, the discussion of three tools shared by one blogger blossoms into a community thread that taps into the combined experiences of a range of like-minded activists. Individual knowledge becomes communal knowledge.

Consistent with this emphasis on political action, on rare occasions someone who affiliates with Daily Kos will step into the political arena as a candidate. When this happens, it becomes a point of collective pride and responsibility among other Kossacks (the perhaps unfortunate self-selected term widely used to describe community members). SusanG heralded one of the first such occasions in a May 2006 post that reads like it was written by a proud relative:

> For me, and for the rest of the Daily Kos community, politics doesn't get much more personal than with Brian Keeler's announcement yesterday of his candidacy for the 41st State Senate seat in New York. Brian—or NYBri as he's known around these orange parts—is one of the first examples of a candidate homegrown and nurtured by this very community.... Like many of us, he cut his teeth here during Bush's first term, participating in comments, learning, writing diaries, howling at the direction in which our country's been taken ... and now he's taking OUR agenda out into [the] hard, cruel political world.
>
> For people who claim blogs do nothing but yak yak yak, and navel-gaze, consider this: Brian wouldn't be the candidate he is without the nearly encyclopedic knowledge and the passion this community offers its members. There isn't a talking point his opponent can throw at him today that he won't be able to shoot down instinctively because we've all discussed typical Republican spin, there isn't an issue he won't know how to frame. His candidacy is our candidacy, and we should be ecstatic.[49]

They were. Among the eighty-six comments posted in the ensuing thread were expressions of appreciation ("Outstanding! I hope more Kossacks follow in Brian's footsteps. We are behind you 110%!"), enthusiasm ("I'm so excited by this campaign. It's got my blood pumping!"), and community pride ("'One of our own' has a nice ring to it.")—all reflecting the shared nature of the endeavor. "The netroots sprouts a stalk," said one commenter. "Water it, and let's make it grow." Someone posted a link to NYBri's first Daily Kos diary. Others did more than simply talk. Several donated money to the campaign. And one person posted that she's running for public office, too, describing herself as "another Kossack running to clean up the dysfunctional mess that is Albany."[50] It was a group celebration extending beyond shared attitudes to a collective commitment to take political action.

A strong sense of communal self-definition runs through the telling of the blog's narrative history, its community practices, and its accounts of virtual and real-world collective action. The feeling of collective self-awareness is palpable. Consider how frequently and casually the term *community* is tossed around by bloggers. As a coarse measure of how bloggers regard one another, a quick search of Daily Kos for "community" reveals 2,248 stories and 60,683 diaries containing the term between May 2003 and May 2008.

Another indicator is the telling number of posts and diaries about the blog itself.[51] Bloggers are perpetually fascinated with the process of blogging and, by posting about it, try to get their arms around this phenomenon they've created. In a post appropriately titled "Meta Kos," the blogger Hunter describes the website as "a cross between a newspaper, a blog, a political movement, and a corner bar. And, perhaps, a bit more."[52] He poses the self-referential question "What *is* Daily Kos?" and answers with a list that describes the website as the sum of its parts but, by his own admission, doesn't quite explain to the outsider the intangibles that somehow are greater than the particulars. So he touches the obvious bases—an open source news source, an editorial page, a tool for grassroots political action, a sounding board for new ideas—but concludes by talking about the blog as a self-selected community where "on any given night you may find diaries discussing 80's rock bands, the perils of parenthood, or vacation destinations in Europe."[53] These topics are off the point for a political site but precisely on point as well, for it is *community* that makes the other facets of the blog possible and from which they spring.

If there is a single feature that bloggers attribute to the creation of community, it is the opportunity for anyone to speak on blogs without metaphorically having to raise their hands. In other words, without diaries and comment threads there could be no community. When Talking Points Memo, the highly trafficked site primarily for open source journalism, added diaries and comments in 2005, Moulitsas marked the occasion by noting that "all the top progressive bloggers now run community sites."[54] The contrast with conservative blogs—which mostly do not encourage interaction—is a point of distinction raised by Moulitsas and others. In their view, it is the reason the right blogosphere is not and cannot be a community. "Quite a difference from the other side of the ideological divide," says Kos. "All the Rush Limbaugh wannabccs [there] hate community interaction."[55] He adds, "If conservative bloggers were smart, they would use their medium to engage new voters for their causes and candidates … they would strive to empower their ideological brethren to shape the political landscape."[56]

In concurring with this assessment, Chris Bowers offered observations about the structural differences between right and left circa 2005, a time when the progressive blogosphere had surpassed the conservative blogosphere in traffic by upward of 65 percent despite having a smaller number of high-profile sites. His conclusion: Comments create communities; without them, the right has suffered.

Of the twenty-four liberal blogs in the top quintile, Daily Kos, TPM Café, Smirking Chimp, Metafilter, Booman Tribune, MyDD, and Dembloggers are full-fledged community sites where members cannot only comment, but they can also post diaries/articles/polls. By comparison, there are no community sites among the top twenty-four conservative blogs. None, zip, zero, nada. This is particularly stunning when one considers the importance of the Free Republic community to the conservative netroots.... In fact, of the five most trafficked conservative blogs (over 200,000 page views per week), only one, Little Green Footballs, even allows comments, much less the ability to actually write a diary or a new article.

Anyone who spends a significant amount of time on Scoop blogs [blogs using software that enables user contributions] should not have any difficulty figuring out why this is the case. Because of Scoop's diary feature, it is possible to become at least a semifamous blogger without having a blog of your own. An entire generation of popular liberal bloggers grew out of the Daily Kos diaries and comments....

There are swarms of new conservative voices looking to breakout in the right-wing blogosphere, but they are not even allowed to comment, much less post a diary and gain a following, on the high traffic conservative blogs. Instead, without any fanfare, they are forced to start their own blogs. However, because of the top-down nature of right-wing blogs, new conservative blogs remain almost entirely dependent upon the untouchable high traffic blogs for visitors. In short, the anticommunity nature of right-wing blogs has resulted in a stagnant aristocracy within the conservative blogosphere that prevents the emergence of new voices and, as a result, new reasons for people to visit conservative blogs.

Progressives, then, join together in a manner befitting the decentralized bottom-up structure of the net, something they don't see happening on the other side of the ideological fence. To those engaged in Daily Kos and elsewhere in the progressive blogosphere, participation comes with an element of shared identity. It is—by any conventional definition—a *community.*

Real-World Communities

Online political action, or virtual community building, can lead to forays into the physical world. Evidence from the blogger study suggests this is happening among netroots activists, although real-world community building lags behind virtual community building as a by-product of associating in cyberspace. Only 32 percent felt the blogosphere effectively built real-world ties in 2004, roughly half the number reporting virtual relationships that same year. Two years later, both figures were twenty-eight points higher, showing parallel growth in both realms with real communities continuing to lag behind. Online communities can stand alone, and not everyone who associates online feels the need or has the opportunity to associate offline.

Still, bloggers mentioned few limitations to offline community building. They cite the natural progression to the real world of friendships built online as well as organized opportunities for bloggers to meet. To this end, they talk about their involvement with online sites that initiate offline activity: horizontal links to organizations that bridge the virtual and real worlds, such as gathering through MeetUps—the in-person meetings arranged through the website MeetUp.com—or participating in Drinking Liberally. In some cases, bloggers experienced an almost total shift to the physical world. As one blogger put it, "In terms of community building, my networking circle and political-based friendships have moved from online interaction to regular in person interaction and meetings such as New York City Kossacks having in-person MeetUps and happy hours that allows relationships and trust to be built. That in turn has made recruiting campaign volunteers easier and expanded volunteer efforts to races individually we would have no connection to or awareness of."

On a larger scale, the establishment of Yearly Kos was a conscious effort to do what some had done spontaneously (i.e., move the Daily Kos community offline for a few days each year), permitting people to put faces to screen names. Conceived as a national convention of progressive bloggers, candidates, organizations, and officials, Yearly Kos was started in 2006 for the express purpose of real-world community building. In recognition of this effort, and in an attempt to broaden the identity of the gathering beyond the website that birthed it, Yearly Kos changed its name to Netroots Nation in 2008.

Its purpose is simple. As one blogger put it, "Real-world community building generally requires some in-person experience. That's what Yearly Kos has offered to allow bloggers who otherwise would be geographically remote from each other the chance to meet in person." The Netroots Nation website underscores this need for periodic face-to-face interaction to complement online community building, to "strengthen community, inspire action, and serve as an incubator for progressive ideas that challenge the status quo."[57]

The conference is not planned from above. Appropriately, it is designed in open source fashion, drawing on the volunteer work of Kossacks operating online and in the real world, making event planning itself a bridge between the two spheres. This also makes event planning a communal effort. Recognizing the role of virtual community in the planning and execution of a nonvirtual event, Moulitsas acknowledges "the power of open source convention planning, the way technology allows passionate people to pool their skills, time and resources in pursuit of a grand vision."[58] In turn, as the model that facilitated the creation of the Internet community was employed to bring about the conference, the act of creating a real world presence became the source of new social capital.

Thus the Kossack Pastordan could provide online updates on the activities of the first Yearly Kos Steering Committee and solicit ideas, volunteers, and money from the virtual community. "Need a volunteer with previous experience as a finance director/financial guru/moneygrubber," he wrote, as if chairing a meeting of a social club, "to give us some tips on how to set up our financial system and/or budget. Anyone? Also need a rough estimate of how many folks would be willing to pungle up $50 or so for seed money. We'll apply it to your registration on the back end."[59]

The responses come back in the comment thread. "I have run a lot of conferences and have a lot of ideas," read one response that included an email address for off-blog contact. "Me two," added another. "Me three," was the predictable next response, "altho all of the conferences I have been involved with planning were specific to my industry. But I did leave some text on the dkosopedia re: this and can volunteer a spread sheet and some ideas to help start."[60]

Others, responding from Chicago, volunteered to take advantage of their proximity to the conference site, saying, "I'm in Chicago and would love to help with planning, logistics, etc. on the ground," and, "Hell yeah. I'm another Chi peep, and very excited to have this in the windy city. Mark me down for $50, and if you need volunteers on the ground, let me know."[61] As the thread continued, dozens of self-selected organizers planned, pledged their support, advised one another on how to coordinate their efforts, considered logistical issues large and small ("are you going to have vendors or booth space?"; "how about inviting some of the Air America folks?"; "Cubs in town?"[62]), and offered reassurance to each other as they undertook a massive organizational job together.

Without the sense of already being part of a community, it is doubtful that strangers or even acquaintances would have come forward to volunteer time and money, much less react with such exuberance to the opportunity to participate in a time-intensive event where it would be easier to coast while letting others do the dirty work and bear the cost. Their words reveal a sense of ownership of the Daily Kos community, evidence that if people are empowered to take action on their own behalf they will respond in kind.

It is understandable that they would want to extend this sentiment to the physical world, and it is easy to imagine how the eagerness communicated in Pastordan's response thread would culminate in these far-flung, self-selected event organizers meeting each other for the first time in Chicago as the real faces behind anonymous screen names. Tellingly, it is interesting how many people in this thread posted email addresses and actual names, a sign of trust foreshadowing the transition to gathering in the everyday world, an indication of how real-world communities can flow naturally from online engagement. And it is compelling to see how important it is for people connected online to see each other and develop friendships grounded in person-to-person contact.

Conclusion

It is this phenomenon—the existence of other like-minded individuals and the ability to seek them out and interact—that permits us to view the progressive blogosphere in communal terms. From Howard Dean's Blog for America in 2003 through today's Daily Kos and other progressive blogs, the experience of netroots involvement brings to some participants a sense of gratification normally reserved for everyday real-world affiliations with family, friends, and social organizations. This gratification has to be viewed as a desirable and important outcome in its own right, separate and apart from whatever impacts the netroots have on the political world.

The existence of others—more to the point, the knowledge that others exist—generates the incentive to participate, just as the feelings of goodwill that derive from virtual human contact nurture and perpetuate these interactions. The result is something larger than its individual contributors, something impossible to imagine without the unleashing of Internet technology. Daily Kos and other interactive progressive weblogs may be the product of countless thousands of people typing in front of countless glowing screens. But they are not blogging alone.

Following the 2006 Yearly Kos convention, the blogger Gina commented on the fruits of the combined labors of untold Kossacks whose contributions made the event possible. Tellingly, the thing that made her weak-kneed is remarkable for being so ordinary:

> Probably the most amazing moment was Wednesday afternoon, before the conference. I was in my room wrangling with a gazillion loose ends when Nolan called and said, "Gina, you have to come down here right now." "Great," I thought. "Another problem to deal with." But no, no problem. There were dozens and dozens of people, from all over the country, who just showed up and started working. They were stuffing bags, organizing name tags, arranging registration materials.... I literally got weak in the knees when I saw everyone. I was overwhelmed and humbled. All these people generously and cheerfully doing what needed to be done. How could I ever thank them? Right then I knew that what we had all built together was a success and something more powerful than we had imagined in the first place.[63]

What Gina experienced was the power of many, translated from virtual community to physical community by permitting the Internet to do what it does best: provide the means for a large, decentralized group of people to interact—and then get out of the way. If it was more powerful than what she had imagined, it was because of the way the interactions among people added value to what they did individually. It was because of community.

Remember, Putnam contends that the great virtue of social capital is that it builds trust among people. Consider, then, this observation that Gina relates about how a thousand-plus strangers behaved at Yearly Kos:

> I said in my closing remarks Saturday evening that this convention was built on a foundation of trust. Markos set it out when he first created the structure of our community where we riff raff are trusted to create our own content and manage our own community. In return, the community trusted us by investing and showing up. And speaking of trust ... now that Hyperbolic Pants Explosion's camera has been returned, nothing at this convention was stolen. I mean, of course, we're not

like that. But can you imagine any other event with over a thousand random people from anywhere and everywhere coming together and nothing being stolen? I mean, yes, that's how it should be, but we all know that how things "should" be and how they "are" are two totally different things. So a minor detail, yes. But once again an example of who we are and what we can expect even on the smallest of levels.[64]

We act trustworthy when we are invested in others, and the investment made by those at Yearly Kos came packed in their luggage, developed previously through virtual association. It came from feeling a sense of familiarity and shared purpose, from believing they were at home with others with whom they shared the bond of common goals and perspectives. It came from having a sense of respect for those around them—even when their screen name is Hyperbolic Pants Explosion.

From this perspective, progressive blogs are a retreat from political apathy, and writing a diary or comment is an act of civic engagement that rewards the author for being part of an ongoing organic dialogue. Television offers no parallel.

It is, as well, a reflection of what the netroots hope to bring to the broader political and civic arena. For their actions mirror their words when they write about the new political community they hope to establish in this country—one built around shared purpose and responsibility that extends beyond the narrowly partisan bounds of left and right. From this perspective, the progressive politics they espouse would promise to do what the blog cannot: bridge the gaping social and economic divisions that they feel have served conservative interests during the television age. Using the new medium, they would spearhead a return to a communal politics of the distant past, where people invested in each other and debate was not stunted by sound bites and by the blathering of cable news. We will consider their prospects in Chapter 7.

7

Open Source Politics
in the Obama Era

Back in 2004, Dean webmaster Nico Mele talked to me about feeling a new kind of
progressive muscle flex in support of that campaign. Now we're seeing that muscle
on steroids.

—Micah Sifry, Talking Points Memo, February 6, 2008

I think we're learning what's effective and what's not, and unlike traditional
Democratic political operatives we're actually changing our tactics to fit what's
most effective.

—David Dayen, D-Day Blog

I believe that the next president will stand at the end of the Television Presidency
and at the beginning of the Networked Presidency in which the President and the
people will connect and work to pass their agenda together, where they can and
do agree.

—Joe Trippi, BuzzMachine Blog, June 30, 2008

It's natural to wonder, when reflecting on the trajectory of past political transformations, how difficult it was to recognize in real time those moments that
would come to define a new era. In one respect, it's easy to get an impressionistic sense that something significant is changing, especially when a new
technology works its way into mainstream political discourse. So it was in 1952,
when Eisenhower's television ads marked a clear and jarring departure from
the whistle-stop campaign just four years earlier. But it would be four more
presidential cycles before the transformative power of television would make
itself known, and by that point television was such an established institution
that Nixon's ingenious use of the medium to weave fictional political narratives could easily have gone unnoticed by a public already jaded by decades
of prime-time programming.

The Internet may well follow the path blazed by television broadcasting. By the early twenty-first century, the World Wide Web had already gone from being dismissed as a curiosity to being embraced as a political necessity. By 2000 every serious candidate had a website. By 2003 the Dean campaign had demonstrated that under certain conditions it was possible to engage in large-scale online fundraising. By 2004 a few candidates and journalists tried their hand at blogging. By 2006 bloggers were engaged rather than dismissed by mainstream journalists. Then, in 2008, Barack Obama ran a watershed campaign, the first successful hybrid presidential initiative. Whether or not this represents the turning point in the emergence of the Internet era will depend on how Obama uses the Internet to govern and whether subsequent campaigns echo his methods and success.

Prior to Obama's victory, this sequence felt more like the progression from stump speeches to television spots rather than Nixon's great revelation about selling fiction as truth under the guise of message control. Yes, there were candidate websites, but most of them treated the Internet like it was "TV with keys."[1] Most never invited Internet patrons to act on behalf of the campaign (other than asking for money). Yes, mainstream elites had engaged the netroots—but on their own terms. The Internet had garnered general recognition and has become part of American political and social discourse. But following the political earthquake of 2008, has it revolutionized the form and function of that discourse?

From a netroots perspective, the answer would have to be "not yet." Netroots activists have not succeeded in upending the Democratic Party power structure. They have not succeeded in replacing Beltway punditry and the values of objective journalism with blogger commentary and values. They were not fully integrated into the Obama campaign, for all its organizational brilliance and understanding of how to maximize the Internet's political power.

But the signs of change are there. The netroots have achieved some level of political success up and down ballots despite the opposition and scorn of entrenched political elites. They have succeeded in irritating a media elite that once dismissed them. The outpouring of volunteer energy from millions of ordinary people who powered the Obama campaign is something quite different from the hallmark cynicism of the television age, and it is difficult to watch these events without believing that the progressive blogosphere is at the forefront of a wave of engagement in the political process. By their own standards, they have achieved a level of recognition and success, in the process demonstrating that those who denigrated them as ineffectual and ignorant were wrong.

Something significant is happening. But for efforts to meet expectations, for netroots activists to realize their agenda, they need to achieve much more than they have thus far: they need to redefine the mainstream in their image. Their effectiveness in doing this will determine the form and content of politics in the next generation.

There is certainly a sense among bloggers that they are poised to make this happen, even that they are making it happen, and that they were better positioned than their conservative counterparts to capitalize on Internet technology even before Obama's breakthrough. Across all measures of political significance to the netroots, bloggers represented in the survey feel they are ahead of conservatives—sometimes far ahead—in the race to achieve their goals.

On bringing about the three large political outcomes we discussed in Chapter 4—recruiting candidates, making elections competitive, and winning elections—large majorities of bloggers believe the progressive blogosphere is more effective than the conservative blogosphere. As Table 7.1 indicates, six in ten progressive bloggers rate their record in candidate recruitment ahead of the recruitment efforts of Internet conservatives. Nearly seven in ten draw the same conclusion about efforts to make elections competitive, and better than seven in ten feel that way about winning elections. Just as notably, only 16 percent rate the conservative blogosphere ahead of the progressive blogosphere in each case.

There is a comparable sense of optimism about the netroots' ability to build virtual and actual communities. Almost all the survey respondents felt the left was about the same or more effective at building online communities; virtually no one felt the right had the edge on this score. A slightly smaller majority evaluated real-world community-building the same way.

The only exception to this optimistic portrayal rests with the left's ability to influence media narratives, something progressive bloggers believe the right does as or more effectively than the left. Only 32 percent give the edge on this function to progressives, consistent with the difficulties posed by an entrenched media establishment and the institutional advantages enjoyed by the right that we discussed in Chapter 5.

There are data to support the bloggers on each count. These attitudes capture a movement on the brink. But to succeed, this bourgeois Internet elite must redefine its relationship to power. It must use the transformative potential of the Internet to take power from the old guard and establish a new politics built on the values of the progressive movement it represents, in the manner of other elites in previous times who combined political ingenuity and technological insight to take advantage of a moment when the public was ready for a new direction and institute their version of change. In order to succeed, the netroots elite must do more than threaten, as they now do, the political and media aristocracy. They must eclipse that elite in power and influence and establish their principles, their approach to politics, and their agenda as dominant and mainstream. Should they succeed, we would see dramatic changes in how politics is conducted, how information is disseminated, and how the larger public relates to the political system.

Transforming Process: Hybrid Campaigning

An era of netroots politics would be defined by hybrid campaigning and by governance that reunites voters and officials in a manner not seen since the rise of

Table 7.1 Progressive Blogger Comparisons of the Progressive Blogosphere
to the Conservative Blogosphere, 2006

Recruiting Candidates
The progressive blogosphere is ...

Much More Effective	44%
More Effective	16
About the Same	24
Less Effective	12
Much Less Effective	4

Making Elections Competitive
The progressive blogosphere is ...

Much More Effective	40%
More Effective	28
About the Same	16
Less Effective	12
Much Less Effective	4

Winning Elections
The progressive blogosphere is ...

Much More Effective	36%
More Effective	36
About the Same	12
Less Effective	12
Much Less Effective	4

Influencing the Media Narrative
The progressive blogosphere is ...

Much More Effective	20%
More Effective	12
About the Same	40
Less Effective	24
Much Less Effective	4

Virtual Community Building
The progressive blogosphere is ...

Much More Effective	36%
More Effective	36
About the Same	24
Less Effective	4
Much Less Effective	0

Real-World Community Building
The progressive blogosphere is ...

Much More Effective	36%
More Effective	28
About the Same	24
Less Effective	12
Much Less Effective	0

N = 25

interest-group liberalism. It would rest on extending to governance the open source model of campaigning exhibited by the Obama organization that balances the bottom-up advantages of Internet organizing with traditional command-and-control structures. As in previous periods of technological change, the new would accommodate rather than replace the old. The invention of the telephone didn't put an end to personal canvassing, and the invention of email didn't put an end to telephone canvassing.[2] There is no reason to believe the Internet will be different on this score.

But hybrid campaigning requires a monumental attitudinal shift on the part of candidates and a shift in power away from traditional consultant-driven campaigns. Neither of these things will be easy to accomplish and will require an unequivocal demonstration of the effectiveness of the approach in order to gain traction against the inertial forces of television-centered politics. This, in turn, requires campaigns to strike the right balance between decentralization and control: giving voters the tools to self-organize and the space to use them while maintaining the command over strategy and message discipline necessary to compete in a mass electorate.

The first sign of this shift took place when the Dean campaign demonstrated that the Internet could be used to tap into gushers of campaign cash if properly exploited. For all its other innovations, Dean for America could not have been viable without its ability to raise millions of dollars online. Thus on a summer day in 2003, when Dick Cheney was holding a $2,000-per-plate luncheon on behalf of Bush-Cheney '04, the Dean campaign countered with an Internet challenge to its supporters to match the vice president's take with small contributions. While the campaign impishly posted streaming video on its website of Governor Dean eating a turkey sandwich, it collected $500,000 from 9,700 people willing to virtually join him for his inexpensive lunch.[3] It was twice what Cheney brought in from his wealthy supporters, and the larger political world took notice.

It goes without saying that four years later, with broader appeal and a more deeply entrenched Internet, Barack Obama's campaign laid waste to all previous fund-raising totals, collecting a half-billion dollars online over twenty-one months from 3 million donors who made 6.5 million individual contributions. The average donation was $80.[4] But these staggering figures mask a more important point about the power of the Internet that was also evident in the Dean campaign. The idea for Dean's Cheney Challenge lunchtime fund-raiser originated online, from a citizen blogger. This fact demonstrates a deeper payoff from Internet politics: the ability to generate political activity from ordinary people who feel empowered to act on behalf of the campaign. Political insiders who quickly learned that it's possible to print money online had been slow to recognize this more essential lesson, as one might expect. Tapping new veins of cash to finance politics as usual is hardly threatening to the status quo. Surrendering control over campaign decisionmaking certainly is.

The first halting efforts at national online organizing beyond the Dean campaign occurred during the 2004 general election. Both the Bush and Kerry operations recognized the Internet's potential to empower supporters to engage in political action on behalf of their candidate, but neither was prepared to relinquish control over daily operations to the same extent as Dean. The result was a step forward in the use of the new technology to engage supporters in limited volunteer action and connect them to the campaign, but not nearly to the extent permitted by the Dean organization and far short of what is possible when the Internet is approached in genuine open source fashion, in which individuals are able to take action beyond campaign-imposed strictures.

Instead, the Bush and Kerry campaigns blended opportunities to engage in traditional one-way activities (giving money, registering to vote) with a select set of more complex organizational functions (recruiting campaign volunteers, sending email to undecided voters, organizing house parties on behalf of the candidate). The Kerry campaign created one Internet tool (Kerry Core) that enabled users to establish a personal webpage on the campaign site, and it maintained a blog with comment threads. The Bush blog did not permit comments, in keeping with a key difference between the right and left blogospheres.[5]

However, the Kerry campaign also shut down the MeetUp tool that the Dean campaign had used to devastating effect to build its network of supporters and multiply their potency. MeetUps create new opportunities for collective mobilization by altering the direction of authority from top-down to bottom-up and center-out.[6] People could click on a MeetUp icon on the Dean site, type in their ZIP code, and sign up to gather at a specified time and place with like-minded supporters to engage in collective action on behalf of the campaign. Headquarters would send materials to guide those efforts—addresses, for instance, of undecided voters in Iowa and New Hampshire to whom MeetUp participants might send letters urging them to vote for Dean—but ultimately decisions about what to do in the MeetUps were left to the participants.

Individuals were therefore empowered to decide on their own whether to attend a MeetUp, whether to recruit friends and neighbors to join them, and how to use their time and labor. The campaign exercised no control over original ideas that might come out of any individual gatherings, and supporters recognized they didn't need formal approval from the campaign to act in its name. Participants were subsequently invited to write about their experiences on Blog for America, where original ideas could be shared with distant supporters who might modify or replicate them if they were so inspired. Real-world activism meshed seamlessly with online activism as Dean's followers took his campaign into their hands. It is a textbook example of the power of many.

This is precisely what makes the Internet so threatening to practitioners of traditional top-down politics. Viewed from the perspective of message control, the prospect of countless amateurs, say, creating their own visibility events in the name of a candidate is a nightmare. It raises the possibility that someone with the best of intentions would create an event that was off message, embarrassing, or resulted in videotaped images that inadvertently made the candidate look bad and could not easily be explained—things that send campaign operatives into early retirement from politics.

It's safer and more familiar to use the Internet to instruct supporters to engage in limited individual action. But this, according to Dean's Internet champion, Joe Trippi, requires killing the golden goose. Speaking of his 2004 competitors, he writes:

> The other campaigns condescended to the people on the Internet. Like so many U.S. corporations do, in their tone and content, the other campaigns talked down to these people. They didn't engage them or listen to them or invite their opinions. And they made it abundantly clear that they didn't respect the power that these people had.... As I watched Bush and Kerry on television marching toward the November 2004 election as if it were still 1976, I was amazed that they still didn't seem to get it.[7]

What Bush and Kerry didn't get, Obama seemed to grasp instinctively. Governor Sarah Palin of Alaska mocked Obama's background as a community organizer during her vice-presidential acceptance speech at the Republican National Convention, but Obama's grasp of bottom-up organizing was reflected in a campaign structured to maintain control of daily operations while empowering millions of citizens to act on its behalf. This required balancing decentralization and control, then exhibiting willingness to take a chance that it's going to work. And it necessitated a paradigm shift on the part of campaign practitioners of the sort likely to occur only when the apparent benefits of empowering the base outweigh admittedly massive risks.

Obama took this chance. He succeeded where Dean had failed, counterbalancing decentralized campaign elements with robust traditional elements. Dean's effort came to be defined by, and ultimately held hostage to, its grassroots component because of his inability to build a durable infrastructure, leaving the campaign ill-equipped to manage the everyday demands of traditional campaigning in an age still dominated by television. Consequently, Dean lost control of his campaign.[8] But Obama found a way to make this delicate balance work, succumbing neither to Kerry's desire to control too much nor to Dean's inability to steady the beast he had created, appreciating instead the need to permit some power to flow in a controlled manner between the campaign center and its supporters at the periphery. As one British observer put it, "While Obama became the candidate of his party's most energized activists he never became their prisoner."[9]

At the top of the Obama hierarchy lived a close-knit group of advisers the likes of which you would find in any campaign organization. What set it apart, observed Joe Trippi, was how Obama maintained "command and control at the top while empowering the bottom to make a difference."[10] Thus where traditional campaigns depended on the top-down structure of local political organizations to help them compete in primaries and caucuses, Obama invested in local organizers—precinct captains and volunteer workers—to form the backbone of a bottom-up grassroots effort. The volunteers were given the tools they needed to succeed and were entrusted to do so.[11] Obama, like other candidates, sought endorsements and ran television ads, maintaining centralized control over these traditional elements of the campaign, but fieldwork was organized from the bottom up.

The same structure characterized Obama's get-out-the-vote machinery, traditionally a highly centralized and closely controlled operation. In the Obama campaign, as documented by the blog Fivethirtyeight.com, bottom-level volunteers shouldered the responsibility for success or failure:

> Neighborhood Team Leaders [are] volunteers who comprise the heart of Obama's volunteering infrastructure. The Obama campaign is doing something remarkable: rather than keeping their vote goals close to the vest and internal, they trust their NTLs with those numbers. [According to Obama's Ohio state director], "If we tell a team leader that the vote goal for this neighborhood is 100 votes, and we give them a list with 300 names of supporters and persuadable voters on it, they respond with, 'Wow, I can make this happen!'" Empower is not just an empty word emblazoned on Obama field office walls.
>
> Volunteers direct and train other volunteers, in turn directed by the coordinators under the NTL. The coordinators report numbers to the NTL, who in turn report to … the Community Directors, who in turn report to the field organizer. The field organizer reports to the deputy regional or regional field director, who reports to the state field director. The numbers are off the charts.… In the central Toledo field office this past [October] weekend, at least 2000 folks had streamed through to volunteer.[12]

None of these decentralized activities foreclosed having a television presence or succeeding in conventional strategic campaigning. But they did provide the foundation for the Internet portion of hybrid campaigns, which needs to be about the community that develops around the candidate, about their aspirations and goals. As long as the candidate presents himself similarly on television, his Internet presence need not conflict with his traditional campaign.

On this point, Obama is particularly interesting because of his ability to play so effectively in both the traditional and new media. Cool enough to project a compelling television presence but energetic enough to arouse passion on the Internet—his supporters, by their own account, were fired up and ready to go—Obama was the first national candidate to get it right. He could move with ease between both worlds, reaching less-engaged voters on television without undermining his large Internet base. And he was able to keep the two halves in balance. If supporters had less say over the intricate workings of his campaign than Dean's supporters had over his, this was by design. But it did not detract from their investment in the candidate, as evidenced by Obama's large and passionate online following.

The nexus for this online venture was the campaign website, a state-of-the-art vehicle that evoked the candidate's cool/hot personality and served as a virtual home for online supporters. Its objectives were quite conventional in that it was a vehicle for fund-raising, message dissemination, and voter mobilization. But the campaign's path to these traditional outcomes was revolutionary. One glance at the site's subdued blue hues told users they were someplace other than the typical red, white, and blue campaign page; political, yes, but understated and cool. A picture of Obama, his wife, Michelle, and their two young daughters greeted the user with an invitation to "join the movement." One click landed users on the homepage, the gateway to Obama's virtual presence, with the candidate's picture on a banner next to the inclusive words, "I'm asking you to believe. Not just in my ability to bring about real change in Washington . . . I'm asking you to believe in yours."

The page was a playground for activists yet meant for anybody. It overflowed with opportunities to take action on behalf of Obama, organized under clickable action-oriented headings like "Make a Difference" (with links to an event finder and a tool for making phone calls to voters in the state of your choice) and "Get Involved" (a signup for email updates from the campaign). If these were fairly mundane activities for a campaign website, there was also "Take Action Now," a tool for people to email positive impressions of Obama's faith and patriotism to their friends and acquaintances in order to virally generate a counternarrative to doubts raised about the candidate in the mainstream media. There was the "National Voter Protection Center" link that permitted users to report voting irregularities and "to empower yourself and others with the information you need to be sure you know the rules for your state on Election Day." The "Obama Mobile" feature made the website portable and allowed people to "join the movement" by signing up for regular text messages on the candidate's public events or policy pronouncements, and it included Obama ring tones and cell-phone wallpaper.

But it was the campaign's social networking features that best capitalized on the interactive potential of the Internet and made the Obama website stand out. By following a link to mybarackobama.com (or, as the campaign called it, MyBO—pronounced "my boh"), users could quickly establish a presence in the virtual Obama universe that was the campaign equivalent of Facebook (although, leaving nothing out, the site also had a link to Obama's actual Facebook page). With a few simple steps users could establish a profile and, if so inclined, a personal blog to compliment the heavily commented official campaign blog. At that point, users would be ready to network. The "My Neighborhood" link connected users with profiles of others within a ZIP code, entries from local bloggers to read and comment on, and a list of local Obama groups in the immediate vicinity. Users could maintain a friends list, search for other supporters, invite people to attend events, and establish their own Barack Obama group. By the Democratic National Convention in late August 2008, more than a million people had signed up on MyBO and had formed hundreds of groups: Environmentalists for Obama, Veterans for Obama, Women for Obama, and the like.[13] These groupings permitted people to identify and contact like-minded peers, enabling the Obama message to spread virally through cyberspace.

Like the community that developed around Blog for America, users could create their own campaign events and even engage in personal fund-raising (complete with their own testimonial about the candidate and a fund-raising thermometer to gauge progress). But whereas Dean's supporters would go off on their own or organize through MeetUp, at the Obama campaign users registered events with the organization so that the campaign could keep track of what people were doing. To facilitate planning—and maintain some control over what was being done in the candidate's name—the webpage featured categories of suggested events, like house parties, debate-watching parties, voter registration drives, and community service activities—which had been particularly popular on the Dean campaign and which helped position the Obama campaign as a movement. Unlike Dean's campaign, horizontal networking was tempered by centralized control. People were free to create, meet, persuade, and spread ideas virally through the Internet without causing chaos or undermining the campaign's mainstream objectives. If there was the same energy, there was also more structure. The Obama campaign found the balance that worked.

The organizational brainchild behind Obama's online tools was the group that came to be known as Triple O (Obama's Online Operation), headed by new media director Joe Rospars, who at twenty-seven was already a veteran of Howard Dean's campaign. Triple O had an innate sense of how to use the Internet as a social networking tool (one member had been a cofounder of Facebook), and their mission was to engage supporters through the Internet by leveraging a specific set of tools—text messages, video, blogs, personalized webpages—in a carefully controlled manner. It was, as Joe Trippi said, the Apollo project compared to the Dean campaign's Wright brothers operation.[14] As Washingtonpost.com reported, their goal was to take the campaign to the grassroots, then let the grassroots take the campaign to victory:

> If Triple O had a motto, it would be: "Meet the voters where they're at." Obama was the first candidate to have profiles on AsianAve.com, MiGente.com and BlackPlanet.com, social networking sites (a.k.a. socnets) targeting the Asian, Latino and black communities. His presence on BlackPlanet, which ranks behind MySpace and Facebook in terms of traffic, is so deep that he maintains 50 profiles, one for each state. On ALforObama, his Alabama page on BlackPlanet, for example, supporters can read an updated blog, watch YouTube videos and learn more about his text program. It's difficult to measure the value of these socnets in persuading voters to choose Obama. What's clear, however, is that online networking—how supporters communicate with one another within their online communities—has its advantages. A Facebook group called Students for Barack Obama, started in July 2006 by Bowdoin College student Meredith Segal, was so successful that it became an official part of the campaign. By the time Hans Riemer was brought on as Obama's youth-vote director in the spring of 2007, dozens of similar chapters were already up and running on campuses. "Some people only go to MySpace. It's where they're on all day. Some only go to LinkedIn. Our

goal is to make sure that each supporter online, regardless of where they are, has a connection with Obama," says Goodstein, who also is in charge of regularly updating Obama's profiles on these socnets. "Then, as much as we can, we try to drive everyone to our site."[15]

Nothing on this scale would have been possible in 2003, when the limits of the Digital Divide would have precluded a campaign from experiencing the reach of the Obama operation. Former Dean strategist Steve McMahon said, "It is what all of us hoped Dean for President would become.... Obama is Dean 2.0, dramatically updated to reflect the emergence of the grassroots."[16] But the point remains that no one else was willing to try it, or would have known how to pull it off had they been so inclined. Ari Berman, writing in the *Nation* before it was clear how the Democratic primary campaign would play out, called Hillary Clinton's campaign the "polar opposite" of the Obama effort: dominated by a sealed inner circle, closed to grassroots input, unfamiliar and uneasy with the Internet, uninterested in encouraging networking to expand the party base.[17] It would turn out to be her undoing. As Micah Sifry posted on Talking Points Memo at roughly the same point in the primary process, "If it were not for the Internet, and all the campaign- and voter-generated activism that it has enabled, Hillary Clinton would already be the Democratic Party's presumptive nominee, and Barack Obama or another reform-minded candidate would be trailing badly." He explained:

> On the Democratic side, we've seen the same pattern play out every time there has been an open field (i.e., no sitting president running for re-election). One candidate is the favorite of the party's establishment and its major sources of funding, and one tries to create a reform coalition to dislodge the establishment favorite. That, in broad strokes, is the story of Mondale vs. Hart in 1984, Dukakis vs. Jackson in 1988, Clinton vs. Brown in 1992, and Gore vs. Bradley in 2000. In 2004, something started to shift, and we saw a semi-outsider candidate powered mainly by small donations, Howard Dean, nearly steal the prize, but then the voters—and the establishment and the money—quickly solidified around John Kerry.[18]

It is not surprising that the first successful hybrid presidential efforts were run by candidates from outside the party establishment, who would be attracted to the potential of the Internet to serve as a force multiplier for a campaign that started from behind. The risks posed by decentralization are so great that no frontrunner, until they were proved effective, would want to take them. Howard Dean did not even set out to unleash an Internet army—more accurately, his supporters found him—but once they arrived via the Internet he had everything to gain by experimenting with decentralized campaigning because he began the campaign with virtually no resources, no name recognition, and no hope of winning. Ron Paul, the Republican congressman from Texas, had a small but intense Internet following in his 2008 presidential run that provided ready cash and a constant source of visibility. Even Obama, although a budding national figure with establishment ties when he announced his candidacy, was at a huge resource disadvantage running against the Democratic Party's biggest name.[19]

Equally unsurprising is that Obama and Paul, like Dean before them, naturally generated enthusiasm online, whereas other candidates with an Internet presence, like John Kerry, were not as fortunate. This is not coincidence. The common thread among these three is that their campaign messages and approaches, like Internet politics itself, deviated strongly from convention. Although stylistically and substantively the three were quite different, each positioned himself as a straight shooter who spoke directly to voters, in contrast to traditional candidates who speak in measured sound bites appropriate for television politics. Each projected an element of speaking truth to power that translated as honesty online. Unlike television, which requires good acting, the Internet rejects fakery and rewards straightforward talk.

Should hybrid politics take hold as a consequence of Obama's success, it would select out a new type of candidate with a different set of skills than what we saw during the television age. Before television, it was unnecessary for a presidential candidate to have a smooth, cool personality and easy body language that people would welcome into their homes. During the Internet age, successful candidates will need to be able to mass-market and microtarget both personality and message. They will need to marry a national advertising campaign to the words and actions of personal inclusion.

Note how Dean and Obama used inclusive language when they addressed their supporters, to speak in terms of "you" and "us" rather than the candidate-centered "I" of traditional television candidates (who, after all, are on display for the cameras). Dean was fond of telling his supporters, "*You* have the power to change this country." Obama would insist that his campaign was not about him but about "us" and "we"—that "we are the ones we've been waiting for," as he told his supporters following the Super Tuesday primaries. This is the language of Internet politics, the language of community.

And it is significant that Dean and Obama regarded their campaigns as social movements, something built around and dependent on the group that propelled it forward, bigger than the candidate himself. This mirrors the self-perceptions of netroots activists and captures the purpose of online activism while casting the mission of the campaign beyond and above the simple quest for power. Instead, it is the quest for power with a purpose, a perfect match for a medium that is about purposeful action.

Practitioners of traditional politics took notice. Donna Brazile, a veteran of Democratic presidential campaigns who served as Al Gore's campaign manager in 2000, noted that Obama "ignited a movement." Blogging at Huffingtonpost. com, Brazile observed, "He did what rarely is practiced in politics."

> Rather than build a traditional campaign where you have a campaign manager, a press secretary, a fundraiser and then a group of volunteers, he allowed people

to make a decision—where they live, where they work—to get involved in the process: to download their own bumper stickers, to download a list of the active party folks in their neighborhoods, to register new people into the process. He used every campaign event as an organizing meeting: to generate emails, to build a list of potential donors. And he followed up. And he created a buzz outside of the traditional campaign barriers that gave people the tools to get out there and start it by themselves.[20]

The other side of the aisle noticed as well. "Because of the Internet, Obama has built a movement," observed Republican consultant Alex Castellanos. "He's leading a cause. McCain's running on his resume. He's leading a campaign."[21]

Obama versus the netroots. Considering that Obama for America was regarded by Howard Dean's senior brain trust as the natural outgrowth of Dean for America, it may be surprising that relations between the Obama campaign and the netroots were not always smooth and natural. In fact the progressive blogosphere did not come quickly to the Obama movement, and even after they embraced it there were points of tension and conflict. Early in the campaign, Obama did not stand out as a consensus blogosphere choice. Although Obama had his supporters, so did John Edwards, and in the waning months of 2007 a fairly vocal online contingent was still holding out for Al Gore. Hillary Clinton had online support as well, although it would be hard to characterize her as a netroots favorite. And as the primary campaign narrowed to a Clinton-Obama contest, Clinton supporters and Obama supporters regularly engaged in heated and sometimes nasty online exchanges.

One of the chief reservations expressed by the netroots toward the Obama campaign was the perceived lack of outreach to the online progressive movement. Here was a campaign that engaged in precedent-setting efforts to empower supporters from the bottom up that, from the perspective of some prominent bloggers, maintained too much control when it came to coordinating with the netroots. "For the life of me," wondered MyDD's Jerome Armstrong, "I cannot figure out why he hasn't pursued a blog outreach strategy." The Obama campaign had leveraged a host of social networking sites "like none other," Armstrong acknowledged, but "they haven't replaced the partisan blogosphere, which has grown about 10X since 2004 in terms of bloggers and readership. And without the outreach, partisan Democratic bloggers are left on their own to pursue a decentralized strategy which has largely wandered in the desert looking for an attack angle on McCain."[22]

This sentiment extended to the sense that even though Obama engaged the netroots for fund-raising and to a degree for organizing, it was missing an opportunity to engage them in messaging. "Obama's team has really nailed down the field/finance side of what Internet tools and strategy can do," blogged Josh

Orton on MyDD. But in his judgment, the "communications/policy/research" side was lacking.[23]

From the standpoint of traditional campaign management, this may not have been an unreasonable approach for the Obama campaign. Because the blogosphere is far-flung, the risks of going off message are great, making message integration a risky venture. Having a controlled blog presence, as when the campaign hosts and maintains a blog, is one thing; having to anticipate defending yourself against a chorus of strong, independent online voices is quite different.

But this does raise the question of how much a hybrid campaign gives up by not fully embracing online activists. Is the greater degree of message control worth the loss of a powerful network of information-gatherers with a rapidly growing megaphone? As the netroots evolve, the calculus implied by this question will change, especially as the blogosphere is regarded in traditional circles as a more serious (read: mainstream) enterprise. This makes it possible, even likely, that the netroots' value as an online army that can go to battle with the candidate, offering a degree of defense and protection against the opposition campaign, will outweigh the risks of unwelcome comments the candidate would be forced to defend or condemn.

None of these hypotheticals were of use or interest to bloggers in 2008, however, so a degree of suspicion—perhaps it is best described as cautious distance—characterized some of the Obama-netroots relationship throughout the campaign. It was not uncommon to find diarists wondering aloud if Obama is in his heart a true progressive or, if he is a true progressive, whether he would sacrifice his principles to his ambition. Would his call for postpartisanship undermine the netroots' push for a partisan progressive agenda? It did not help matters that the campaign had strong insider roots. Obama himself was a senator (as opposed to governor of a small New England state), and his inner circle was filled with associates of former Senate Majority Leader Tom Daschle and former House Minority Leader Richard Gephardt (who, as a presidential candidate in 2004, was blamed by some blogosphere voices for going negative against Howard Dean before the Iowa caucus, forcing Dean to return fire in a mutually assured destruction pact that sunk both campaigns). Dana Goldstein and Ezra Klein explain the web of relationships, starting with Peter Rouse, Obama's campaign chief of staff who came from Daschle's office:

> His deputy campaign manager, Steve Hildebrand, managed Daschle's 2004 campaign. His director for battleground states, Jennifer O'Malley Dillon, and his director of communications, Dan Pfeiffer, were both deputy campaign managers for Daschle in 2004. Obama's foreign-policy director, Denis McDonough, was Daschle's foreign-policy adviser, and his finance director, Julianna Smoot, was head of Daschle's PAC. Many of those who didn't come from the Senate minority leader's office came from the House minority leader's office. Obama's campaign manager, David Plouffe, was Gephardt's deputy campaign manager in 2004. His head of

delegate operations, Jeff Berman, played the same role for Gephardt. His national press secretary, Bill Burton, was Gephardt's Iowa press secretary. Dozens of others come from related arms of the party, in particular the Democratic Congressional Campaign Committee.[24]

This is not exactly a who's who of outside-the-Beltway progressives, and if some bloggers were reticent about the Obama campaign, it gave them reason to be wary of the campaign's intentions. So it was that when Obama did take high-profile positions that were at odds with progressive goals, he heard about it from the netroots. Sometimes he heard about it loudly—as when the netroots turned his own social action tools against him.

In late June, when Obama was positioning himself for the fall contest against John McCain, word went out from the campaign that the senator would not filibuster an amendment to the Foreign Intelligence Surveillance Act, which would expand the president's spying powers while retroactively protecting telecommunication companies that may have participated in illegal spying activities.[25] Curtailing domestic spying and holding telecoms accountable for invasion of privacy rights are signature progressive positions, so a negative netroots reaction to Obama's move was to be expected. Less predictable was the nature of that reaction, which took the form of demonstrating against the campaign from within using its social networking tools.

On June 27, 2008, Mike Stark, who frequently blogs on Daily Kos, sent an email to friends suggesting that someone start a group on MyBO protesting the candidate's position and urging him to reconsider. Within a week the group had 17,000 members, making it the largest grassroots social action group on his website. From this vantage point, Stark and others urged Obama to reverse course and work with them to defeat the FISA amendment by having the campaign supply tools that would allow group members to contact voters and urge them to lobby their senators against the bill.[26] Essentially, they would oppose the politically sensitive measure at a time when Obama was trying to avoid making moves that could have been controversial come fall.

Observing that "Barack Obama does not seem like the type of person that surrounds himself with yes-men," Stark blogged about the logic behind his initiative on Daily Kos, noting that Obama himself was a community organizer, that he had pledged to use technology to boost political engagement, and that MyBO already provided the tools for action—so why not take advantage of it?[27] Not everyone agreed: Debates broke out in the comment threads of Stark's Daily Kos diaries over whether it was counterproductive to petition one's own candidate if it simply increased the likelihood of electing McCain, who, unlike Obama, was not philosophically opposed to telecom immunity under FISA.

Ultimately, the anti-FISA group failed to achieve its objective. But it did make waves, and it did get noticed. Jerome Armstrong called it "a moment that has been a long time in waiting, when the netroots would turn toward organizing effectively within the institutions around which they have campaigned for heavily."[28] Jeff Jarvis, writing at BuzzMachine, savored the irony of a grassroots campaign facing an internal grassroots revolt:

> When it's a grassroots organization that makes you—rather than a party—and you say you're beholden to them not to special interests and big money and lobbyists, well, then you really are beholden to them. If they rise up from within to tell you that they don't like what you're doing—when they use your own organizational tools to do that—then I'd say you ignore them at your peril.[29]

Jarvis felt the FISA revolt could be a harbinger of things to come in an Obama administration. "Will his supporters at MyBarackObama continue to use these tools to influence him and his government?" Jarvis asked. "And will he have to listen because he is beholden to them?"[30] Daily Kos contributing editor Mcjoan echoed this sentiment, saying that being a netroots supporter "doesn't mean setting aside your own beliefs and principles. We're not supposed to just shut up when we disagree—if we do, we're setting a very bad precedent for our role in a potential Obama presidency."[31]

Internet governance. So what exactly *is* the role of the netroots in an Obama presidency? What will Internet governance look like? As a policy matter, the promise of hybrid campaigns is hybrid governance: the candidate in office will respond to the interests of those who put him or her there, as opposed to responding automatically to well-financed organized groups, rekindling the connection between public and official that was badly damaged in the television age, when the need for large sums of money pulled candidates inexorably toward large interests. That there will be attention paid to traditional big-money concerns is to be expected, as is the expectation that Obama, like his predecessors, will continue to rely heavily on television. The hybrid campaign, after all, blends old with new. But it was more than a self-serving reference when Obama spoke of his movement as a form of campaign finance reform in which millions of people self-selected to donate their time and dollars to get him elected. The theory is that the candidate will subsequently represent some of their concerns, thereby reaching the same outcome as promised by public financing, albeit via a different route. It will be interesting to see how that works in practice.

There can be pitfalls: governing involves getting into details that can more easily be swept aside during campaigns. Disappointment is inevitable among those who, once removed from the sweeping rhetoric of the campaign season, inevitably disagree with some of the decisions of the newly minted president. Even with the emergence of Internet politics, traditional interests loom large. And what would President Obama do should the movement he created begin to lobby against his actions, as with the FISA uprising?

Still, the Obama administration knows what it created during the campaign and intends to leverage the power of the millions of people who gave money, wrote email, blogged, made phone calls, and networked on the president's behalf; he understands the netroots can be an ally in policymaking. Donna Brazile telegraphed as much just several days after Obama was elected: "This is not just a traditional, 'campaign's over with, let's fold the tent, everybody go back home.' No. There's another instrument that I'm sure is being created by the Obama people—because they are very strategic, ... [and] they are creating this other instrument to keep [online supporters] in the loop, to keep them energized throughout the next four years."[32]

Days later, the Obama transition team followed suit and reached out to the progressive blogosphere. During the initial stages of the presidential transition, Obama established the Internet Outreach Team, headed by Macon Phillips, who helped run Obama's online campaign operation, and Jesse Lee, who was tapped to run online communications after running Internet outreach for the Democratic Congressional Campaign Committee during the 2006 elections and for the Democratic National Committee in 2008.[33] Mike Lux, a Clinton White House veteran who blogs at Open Left, was chosen as the transition team's liaison to the progressive community.[34]

These appointments, which came swiftly after Election Day, were greeted with enthusiasm by high-profile bloggers. "Now *this* is a good sign," blogged Greg Sargent at Huffingtonpost.com.[35] John Aravosis at AmericaBlog was effusive: "Can't say enough good things about Jesse [Lee]. He knows the Netroots, knows politics, knows how to fight back."[36] Jonathan Singer of MyDD saw the moves as a signal of "real interest by the Obama transition team that they take the new media, and the netroots in particular, seriously."[37]

Obama has sent other organizational signals that have to please his online followers. Following his nomination, Obama maintained Howard Dean as DNC chair and pursued a national electoral strategy that dovetailed with Dean's fifty-state approach. This included sending paid operatives to states the campaign knew it was not going to win—like Texas—in order to help down-ballot Democrats secure seats in the state legislature, offering greater control over congressional redistricting following the 2010 census.[38] This type of long-term party-building, in addition to generating obvious electoral benefits, produces goodwill among the legions of Dean's online supporters—which potentially can be tapped should Obama decide to call on the netroots to help govern. One can imagine a twenty-first-century version of going public, with Obama employing the Internet for a messaging and persuasion campaign designed to win congressional votes the way bloggers once advocated in support of Obama's election and his online supporters once persuaded undecided voters.

These actions suggest the Obama organization appreciates the new media and the bonds it helps create between candidate and voter. The president's recognition of these bonds, forged as they were during a hard campaign, is an affirmation of democracy the likes of which we have not seen for some time, as they were so often taken for granted in the television age by officials who believed, often correctly, that if they could raise enough money and buy enough television time they could compensate for their failings with voters. In this regard, hybrid campaigning holds the promise of recalibrating the logic of representation, as officials elected with a strong base of netroots support remember who brought them to the dance.

Without question, now that the netroots have tasted electoral success, bloggers will be there to work for the president when he engages them in jointly shared progressive objectives. It is probably as certain that they will loudly express their disapproval when the candidate they helped to elect deviates from progressive goals. These are the two scenarios to look for as the new administration takes shape. If President Obama engages the Internet to help govern, and if he takes them seriously during moments of disagreement, then we'll know that the age of Internet politics has arrived.

Transforming Narratives: Blogging as Journalism

Open source politics is a natural companion to the open source journalism practiced on blogs. We have seen how the theory can be applied to reporting much as it can to campaigning: countless eyes and minds contribute research and shape narratives, documenting their claims with hyperlinks to original source material, correcting one another when necessary, and enhancing each other's work to produce thorough, well-researched stories, sometimes on topics that the mainstream press ignores. Talking Points Memo offers the clearest illustration in the progressive blogosphere of how open source journalism can work, as the editor, Josh Marshall, will periodically call upon his readers to contribute whatever leads and information they may have to help develop a story he and his small staff of reporters are investigating. As the *Columbia Journalism Review* noted in 2007, Marshall runs a shoestring operation. But he has gotten powerful results thanks in large part to the contributions of a committed elite readership:

> To get to the newsroom of Talking Points Media in lower Manhattan, you need to visit a pungent block of cut-flower wholesalers on Sixth Avenue, then climb a narrow stairway to an eight-hundred-square-foot suite that might once have been an accountant's office. This modest space is the home of a news organization that— among several other notches in its belt—was almost single-handedly responsible for bringing the story of the fired U.S. Attorneys to a boil. Not only were the major dailies slow to pick up on the controversy, but a Capitol Hill staffer says that the House Judiciary Committee itself would have missed the firings' significance if not for the barrage of reports from Talking Points. Other outlets, including The Wall Street Journal, noticed in January the sudden pattern of U.S. Attorney departures, but only Talking Points gave the matter sustained attention that month. When Alberto Gonzales, Kyle Sampson, and Monica Goodling testified before Congress this spring, they had the reporters in this obscure Flower District building to thank for the honor.... From the very early days of Talking Points Memo, [Marshall] has

(by accident or design) cultivated an intense relationship with a well-connected set of readers—lawyers, activists, policy wonks, and veterans of intelligence agencies. Those readers have offered an endless stream of tips, and they have occasionally been deployed en masse to plow through document dumps from the Department of Justice or to ask members of Congress to publicly clarify their positions on Social Security.[39]

These readers amplify the reporting of a skeletal staff supported on revenue from blog ads and periodic reader contributions, permitting Marshall's blog to cast a wide and sometimes influential presence. The distinguishing characteristic of Talking Points Memo is its professionalism, which sets it apart from the more free-form and chaotic blogging found on standard community blogs. Marshall regards his operation as a news outlet and sees himself as a twenty-first-century muckraking journalist. But this should not suggest that blogs set up for other means—like venting, community building, and political action—cannot contribute to newsmaking. Open source reporting is going on there, too, on full-fledged community blogs like Daily Kos, only in a more unstructured manner and with a less polished appearance. There, users will find a mixture of original information, commentary, and links to mainstream press coverage in what Markos Moulitsas described as "the aggregation of thousands [of minds] on behalf of a common cause."[40]

Of course, users also find misinformation, ill-sourced material, and poorly reasoned arguments glaringly at odds with conventional notions of professionalism, making it difficult to regard free-form blogging as anything close to journalism when viewed through conventional lenses. It can be taken seriously only when seen through the unconventional prism of open source, which contends these problematic contributions will come out in the wash. Argumentative diaries will quickly fall into the memory hole as sober readers disregard their content. Speculative postings that posit unfounded theories or dwell in conjecture will be shot down by other bloggers committed to rigorous argument. Incorrect information will swiftly be noticed by astute readers, updated, and corrected. Whereas conventional journalists would defend the integrity of their work by pointing to the correct application of widely accepted professional procedures, bloggers would ask to be judged on the product of their work rather than to dwell on process.

And they might add that the professional processes of traditional journalism have been insufficient to prevent misinformation, poor sourcing, and unsupported argument, only unlike blogs there is no corrective mechanism to prevent publication when this happens. We saw one such occasion in Chapter 5, when *Time* magazine lent its legitimacy to Joe Klein's questionable reporting on the FISA bill on the grounds that the process by which the story was developed permitted equal coverage to two sides in a political debate over the facts—even though the dispute itself was irrelevant because the facts were not in doubt. Defenders of traditional journalism might consider this to be an isolated incident, and it is difficult to assess whether flawed reporting is widespread, but they would not be in a position to judge traditional reporting procedures as necessarily superior to their open source counterpart. Each has its risks and potential flaws. They are simply two different ways of disseminating information, two forms of a reporting tradition that has assumed numerous shapes since the days when journalists were printers.

This is where the argument over whether bloggers are journalists loses meaning and misses the mark. Although this question may have great import to professionals interested in defending their turf from interlopers, in a larger sense it doesn't matter what bloggers are called because journalism itself has gone through so many iterations. And although their methods and values are different and often at odds, reporters and bloggers are engaged in uncovering information and shaping narratives. Some come to blogging with a background in journalism[41] or move on to journalism after a stint in blogging.[42] Apart from methodology, the two are not as different as skeptical journalists might have us think.

Furthermore, the strict barriers between information and commentary that may have been in place in an earlier time have long given way to reporters appearing on cable TV to espouse behind-the-scenes chatter and, more recently, sharing insider observations on their own blogs. Although many journalists take pains to appear nonpartisan in these venues in the best tradition of twentieth-century reporting, the convention of partisan reporting as practiced on blogs has storied roots as well, and critically acclaimed blogs like Talking Points Memo have shown it is possible to break news stories while openly advancing a political agenda.

In fact, the biggest objection that bloggers have to traditional journalists—that their methodology gets in the way of accurate reporting—mirrors the claim leveled by traditional journalists against blogs. The bloggers' case against objectivity as an appropriate value for reporting rests on the belief that objectivity itself is an artifact of a time when there was greater consensus in political debate, when Republicans and Democrats could operate in good faith more often than not despite different political objectives and goals. This was a day when the parties were not uniformly ideological, when "liberal Republican" wasn't an oxymoron and Southern Democrats were a major force in a party otherwise known for its leftward leanings. In that pre-Vietnam, pre-Watergate environment, with a cold war consensus operating in foreign policy and Republicans more inclined to accept than roll back the welfare state, news frames could reflect prevailing viewpoints without reporters having to worry about accusations of being stenographers for one side or the other.

As the pendulum slowly swung away from civility and broad consensus, it became increasingly difficult for reporters to keep their bearings and appear neutral. Frames shifted along with the political agenda. Democrats and Republicans began making different assumptions about government and policy, holding to sometimes starkly different worldviews. Republicans came to regard government as ineffectual and Democrats as weak. Democrats still saw government as good but viewed Republicans as ineffectual and sometimes dishonest stewards. The objectivity model, dependent as ever on balance to justify neutrality, required reporters to perform a juggling act between these perspectives without claiming that one was more valid than the other. But the frames became increasingly incompatible.

A common contention in the blogosphere is that Democrats, when Republicans were in power, succumbed to living under the GOP worldview and went on the defensive rather than speaking out for what bloggers consider principled progressive positions. Journalists followed suit by reporting news from within this perspective, which had the feel of objective reality and resolved the balance problem. This, the argument goes, gave Republicans greater license to move the center of gravity gradually to the right. Journalists, in the interest of balance, moved with them, and the mediated version of centrist opinion—that neutral sweet spot in traditional coverage—came to reflect these right-leaning elite narratives rather than real movement in public opinion. The result was a metanarrative about the country moving sharply to the right and a Democratic Party afraid to stand on principle for fear of appearing too far to the left. But in reality, bloggers will tell you, the country didn't move much at all.

Part of the impetus behind open source journalism is to correct this imbalance. Contending that partisan times call for partisan methods, netroots activists see open source reporting as a way of calling out Democrats who they feel are afraid or unable to see past the metanarrative as well as reporters who keep it locked in place. Some go farther, claiming that Republicans under Newt Gingrich and George W. Bush acted abusively toward the system and dishonestly with the public, knowing that even illegitimate actions and intentional falsehoods will win the blessings of legitimacy if they are uniformly offered to journalists as one side of an otherwise valid dispute. But even without delving into this tendentious territory, the case for open source journalism makes historical sense, as different political eras have produced their own distinctive forms of information dissemination. There is nothing sacrosanct about objectivity. It is simply what we know.

Thus anyone can see the threat posed to journalists from the Internet elite. So far the results have been mixed at best, with more success in promoting events episodically and locally and less success shaping thematic national narratives. But the blogosphere has been successful at establishing counternarratives that will receive greater attention as the netroots claim larger and broader political success. Like the aging generation of conservative insurgents, success in the political sphere will translate into greater influence over media coverage.

Some claimed to taste that success already during the 2008 general election campaign when, contrary to the often frustrated efforts at news agenda-setting (see Chapter 5), some in the blogosphere felt they had helped define how the McCain-Palin ticket was discussed by traditional reporters. Greg Sargent, blogging at Talking Points Memo, said there was "little question" that a "now robust infrastructure on the left" successfully pushed a narrative about Republican vice-presidential nominee Sarah Palin's "comical levels of incompetence and outright fraudulence, which fed the larger storyline about McCain's cynicism."[43] Todd

Beaton at MyDD agreed that the left had a far better media infrastructure in 2008 than in 2004, enabling it to drive countermessages about the McCain campaign and, as a consequence, "remarkably, we've seen facts and rationality win out over fear."[44] Markos Moulitsas, a firm advocate of attacking Palin against the advice of some bloggers and establishment party figures, claimed victory for his strategy:

> Republicans were busy trying to build a positive narrative about Palin—the "hockey mom" who was so folksy she could "field dress a moose" and had "said no to the Bridge to Nowhere and other government waste" and was overflowing with "small town values." McCain had shot up in the polls because of Palin. Common sense dictated it would be hard to knock him back down as long as she consolidated her popularity. So we set out to build the negative narratives about Palin … [and] her cratering popularity now hampers McCain's efforts to expand beyond [his] core base. All of this is happening because we did not relent on Palin, blocking Republican efforts to paint her in a positive light. The results are speaking for themselves.[45]

Moulitsas claimed the netroots were "successful beyond our wildest dreams" in counterbranding Palin, forcing McCain to use her only in controlled settings, and keeping her away from reporters as though she were in "Cheney's undisclosed location."[46] And he scolded "the likes of [Democratic political consultant] Paul Begala" and reluctant bloggers who contended that attacking Palin would be harmful to Obama's efforts to keep the focus on the top of the Republican ticket. "It wasn't," he wrote. "A popular Palin would've given us far less favorable dynamics in this race."[47]

It is difficult to disagree with Moulitsas's conclusion, although the wisdom and effectiveness of the netroots counternarrative strategy is best understood in the broader context of the campaign. Obama religiously avoided focusing on McCain's running mate so that the traditional media, following his cues, didn't turn the election into an Obama-versus-Palin contest. And as we have seen, the campaign did not enlist the blogosphere for help with messaging. But Obama did benefit tremendously from the unflattering Palin narratives that ultimately developed. In other words, the netroots were able to do some of the campaign's dirty work.

And to a degree perhaps not seen since the inception of the blogosphere, progressives had the wind at their backs. Governor Palin held high-profile interviews with Charles Gibson of ABC and Katie Couric of CBS shortly after her nomination, the results of which were widely regarded as catastrophic, and which, when coupled with a string of biting parodies on *Saturday Night Live,* cemented the popular culture portrayal of the governor as out of her league in national politics. Then when financial markets began melting down in mid-September 2008, the presidential contest turned deeply serious. Palin parodies were no longer laughing matters to a growing majority of voters in the middle of the political spectrum who doubted her readiness to take over in a crisis. Outside events were resonating with the counternarrative that the netroots were promoting.

So it is difficult to determine from the results of the 2008 campaign whether bloggers will effect a paradigm shift in journalism rather than simply continue to occupy a niche. But it is not ridiculous to speculate that they will. Progressive voices were beginning to make themselves heard more widely even before Obama's victory. In 2008 MSNBC handed its election desk to Keith Olbermann, a favorite of the left for his outspoken criticism of the Bush administration. There he and progressive-talk icon Rachel Maddow interacted with Tom Brokaw and Brian Williams, anchor-level standard-bearers of the traditional approach, as if the progressive hosts were just old-school journalists. Now, for the first time, the netroots will have the opportunity to play offense.

In the meantime, the media marketplace has fragmented. Young people are increasingly turning to the Internet to stay informed while abandoning newspapers and moving away from television. A recent Harvard study reports that less than half of young adults under age thirty read a newspaper at least once a week, whereas 51 percent of adults age eighteen to thirty and 58 percent of teenagers get Internet news at least that often. And while young adults are still watching television news, their rates of daily viewing are twenty-six points below people over thirty.[48] The millennial cohort will age as the Internet evolves, their news habits predisposed to changing with the technology.

This gives bloggers an opportunity. A young generation of political reporters that came of age during the turmoil of the 1960s and 1970s brought with them a narrative form of reporting that today's bloggers rail against. In today's turbulent times, bloggers offer a different genre. It may be difficult to picture someone blogging their way to a position of influence like that of David Broder and Joe Klein, but it is not impossible.

Transforming Politics:
The Self and the Community

In the quest to conquer the Democratic Party and reshape it as a vehicle for a progressive agenda, netroots activists have set their sights on nothing less than remaking the political process in their image of an extended network of grassroots activists. They seek to instill in our politics the morality of the Yearly Kos event where no one would think to steal from others and people voluntarily contributed for the greater good. It is their model both for progressive governance and the approach that would have them realize it, a balm for the cynical politics of the television age.

Framing guru George Lakoff, blogging at Huffingtonpost.com during the early weeks of the 2008 primary campaign, illustrates how these objectives divide Internet progressives, who at that point were just starting to coalesce around Barack Obama's candidacy, from establishment Democrats represented by Hillary Clinton. In a contest noteworthy for the lack of daylight between the two candidates' policy platforms, Lakoff identifies the fault lines that in the months following would define a bitter fight for the future of the Democratic Party:

> First, triangulation: moving to the right—adopting right-wing positions—to get more votes. Bill Clinton did it and Hillary believes in it. It is what she means by "bipartisanship." Obama means the opposite by "bipartisanship." To Obama, it is a recognition that central progressive moral principles are fundamental American principles. For him, bipartisanship means finding people who call themselves "conservatives" or "independents," but who share those central American values with progressives. Obama thus doesn't have to surrender or dilute his principles for the sake of "bipartisanship."
>
> The second is incrementalism: Hillary believes in getting lots of small carefully crafted policies through, one at a time, step by small step, real but almost unnoticed. Obama believes in bold moves and the building of a movement in which the bold moves are demanded by the people and celebrated when they happen. This is the reason why Hillary talks about "I," "I," "I" (the crafter of the policy) and Obama talks about "you" and "we" (the people who demand it and who jointly carry it out).
>
> The third is interest group politics: Hillary looks at politics through interests and interest groups, seeking policies that satisfy the interests of such groups. Obama's thinking emphasizes empathy over interest groups. He also sees empathy as central to the very idea of America. The result is a positive politics grounded in empathy and caring that is also patriotic and uplifting.
>
> For a great many Democrats, these are the real issues. These real differences between the candidates reflect real differences within the party. Whoever gets the nomination, these differences will remain.[49]

Notice how the three differences Lakoff addresses are about process, about how politics is done, and that process is understood in values terms. To those who practice triangulation, incrementalism, and interest group politics, they appear to be value-free strategies, pragmatic means to get what you want or at least to get as close as possible. To the netroots, they are essential moral characteristics: How you operate says everything about who you are. Who you represent says everything about how you will govern. These are not ideological differences in the traditional left-right sense, but they are defining differences.

In this regard, the netroots' struggle for open source governance would change what government does by changing the way the governed act. Common ground, as defined by a shared progressive morality, would serve as the point of departure for governing. Obama's seven-figure membership list backed by his equally large stable of small-dollar contributors would be Washington's primary interest group. Ordinary people, energized by the political process, would have their engagement rewarded by a responsive government attentive to their vital needs, in a clear rejection of the interest-group liberalism and sound-bite politics of the late twentieth century.

There is something decidedly retro about this. With its emphasis on social networks and collective engagement, netroots politics is a throwback to the communitarian politics prevalent during the early years of the republic, albeit espousing a different morality and a more progressive direction than the conservative anti-Federalists who lamented the loss of civic virtue. Contemporary communitarians, writes the constitutional theorist Beau Breslin, "seek to return a sense of community—a sense of connectedness if you will—to the current pluralist and largely ambiguous state composed of atomized individuals."[50] They do not reject liberal individualism so much as they seek greater balance from a society that they believe idealizes individualism while discouraging people from pursuing their best interests.[51] They hold that individual voices flourish with the replenishment of community ties, although their use of technology to facilitate network building stands in stark contrast to the unfulfilled dreams of a television-based plebiscitary democracy imagined by Ross Perot in the 1990s, in which millions would make policy decisions in collective isolation by casting votes using a device connected to their cable-TV boxes.[52] In Perot's America, technology facilitated autonomy; to the netroots, technology is all about connections.

Communitarian impulses historically come in different ideological hues, because people hold to different views of community (a term never comprehensively defined either by students of the subject or by blogger advocates), different ideas about virtue, and different remedies for problems that span the ideological spectrum.[53] People who share a communitarian bent can end up in different camps when the issue becomes specific policy options; some of the sharpest online exchanges occur over the policy means to a communal end (e.g., whether Hillary Clinton's health care proposal came closer than Obama's to the shared progressive ideal of universal coverage). This gives the term a bit of a catchall quality. For bloggers, it can perhaps best be understood as the marriage of the symbolic and functional elements of social structures with a moral imperative for social justice.

If blogs can be conceived as social networks, with their emphasis on community action and political participation,[54] then community can be defined in social networking terms using the language bloggers expressed when discussing the creation of social capital. This applies equally to virtual and real-world networks, because people can and do get social support from both.[55] From this vantage point, it is a communalism of process, built around the interactive benefits bloggers derive on the web and as a result of their activity on the web, and it is congruent both with a movement that sees process intertwined with outcomes and with a successful presidential campaign that believed the same thing. But it is also a communalism of results, where the end vision is a lasting center-left majority serving the needs of what its adherents firmly believe to be the dominant impulse in contemporary America. That they believe it has been the dominant impulse for many years, only to be strangled by television's politics of deception and distraction, is further testimony to how they view the communitarian impulses of their new medium to be the solution to the problems of the old political regime as well as the model for the new.

And it is a communalism of compassion. Perhaps the brand of politics that comes closest to that practiced online is captured by a secular version of the communitarian strain dating back centuries to the tradition of *tikkun olam*, the ancient Jewish mandate for social justice based on empathy and caring for others.[56] *Tikkun olam* speaks to the moral imperative of community, literally the imperative to repair the world by turning our attention to each other. Kid Oakland explains how this relates to netroots activism:

> On the one hand [establishment Democrats] have a political philosophy that is incremental, cautious, cynical of political opponents, and seeks the surety of its effectiveness by appealing to a politics of contrast that is inherently ideological and pits group against group. On the other hand, we [netroots activists] have a political philosophy whose fundamental contrast is methodological, historical and moral. It is, in essence, a politics of meaning. The contrast is with the failed policies of the past that have yielded us a divided public, a broken ecosystem, an economy with inequity in both opportunity and results, and a world that is less stable and less safe despite our enormous military expenditures and the pursuit of war in Iraq. To repair this world, to heal this nation, requires crafting majority positions founded on the pragmatism inherent in policies that have the broadest appeal because they bring the maximum number of people together to address the largest of our concerns.
>
> To subscribers of the first view, this movement calling for change might well seem frightening and without substance. What's important to understand here is that if you don't think it's possible to rebuild a zone of trust and common ground in this nation, then a movement calling for healing and repair, for a kind of renewal of hope in America, for *tikkun olam*, will necessarily seem dangerous and risky.
>
> To subscribers of the second view, *coming together to heal and repair the world is pragmatic common sense.* Faced with global warming, with the threat of terrorism from ideological splinter groups, with a global economy that is more inter-connected and inter-dependent every day, and with a nation where the two political parties have pitted one group against the other for forty long years of destructive politics, there is a thirst for a break from the failures of the past. To those who hold this viewpoint, it makes pragmatic sense to seek a fundamental common ground. The stakes are too high, the world is too broken, the perils of climate change and destabilization through a foreign policy that is unilateral and often done at the bidding of large corporations too great....
>
> Young people have voted for Barack Obama in overwhelming numbers. This new generation looking at a new century knows something, they understand *tikkun olam*, the moral imperative to heal our nation and repair our world.
>
> They can see, where some of us who are older can't, the utter futility of privileging the battles of the past, of a cautious approach that mistrusts, and even creates, enemies. They can see clearly how our politics have led our nation into this war in Iraq. Just because they are young does not mean they are not wise. Youth does not mean that they cannot see the wisdom and pragmatism of an appeal to unity, to a common moral ground, to hope. Sometimes those who are young can understand

the oldest and wisest words and apply them appropriately to our time: If I am not for myself, then who will be for me? And if I am only for myself, then what am I? And *if not now, when?*[57]

This is the hope and the promise of netroots activists: to forge a lasting majority coalition of progressives through the power of communities made possible by a new technology—communities that both model and facilitate the changes they seek, as they set out to end the rampant individualism they see as poisoning our polity and our politics. Ahead of the curve in understanding that the great potential of the Internet rests with empowering people laterally and from the bottom up, secure in their ability to relinquish the control necessary to make this happen, they would nudge television off center stage, replacing a politics of distraction with a politics of meaning. They are the group that figured out how to use the new technology well—this generation's Jackson, Lincoln, and FDR. They would openly embrace adding Obama to this list.

Theirs is not necessarily an egalitarian vision; they are an elite, and they would repair the world on their terms. Neither are they utopian; for all the soaring rhetoric, netroots activists are nothing if not pragmatic, regularly engaged in the minute, often mind-numbing requirements of social organizing. They do not doubt how difficult their task will be.

But their goals are lofty and audacious. They are challenging decades of convention about how to wage campaigns and attract voters with an approach that shows promise and has now claimed, in addition to some notable national and local successes, the biggest prize of all. They are powered by a medium that is still in the process of coming into its own, confronting a political establishment still largely wedded to another medium—television—that is safe, familiar, profitable, and easy to manipulate. And they are pushing hard against a political and media power structure composed of enormously wealthy interests that, like others before them in other transformational times, will tenaciously defend their ground until the ground beneath them is gone. Old elites do not yield readily to their replacements.

These obstacles are so formidable that it would be safe to assume they will not succeed, and in ordinary times that assumption would likely be correct. But in ordinary times a prohibitive presidential frontrunner with every establishment advantage would have quickly secured her party's presidential nomination over a newcomer to national politics running a different, unconventional type of campaign. In ordinary times a wave like the one that washed over Congress in 2006 would two years later carry vulnerable freshmen out to sea rather than continue to build behind a crescendo of angry voices expressing unprecedented disapproval of the nation's direction. In ordinary times people would remain apathetic to politics rather than flood campaigns with commitments of cash, time, and energy. In ordinary times an African American senator four years removed from serving in the Illinois State Senate would not have been elected president of the United States.

There have been moments like this in the past, and each time history was on the side of those who understood the advantages that moment presented. It is impossible to predict if they will succeed in establishing a lasting progressive majority, or if they ever will repair even a small portion of the world, but in the wake of the 2008 election it appears history is on the side of the bloggers.

If not now, when?

Appendix

This book incorporates data from a survey of bloggers and from seven metrics of netroots political effectiveness, the details of which are discussed below.

The blogger survey data derive from self-reports of the political and social effectiveness of the progressive blogosphere by progressive bloggers, measured through an online survey of regular contributors to a sample of national, state, and local progressive blogs. Because bloggers constitute a small but amorphous self-selected elite, it is difficult to define a universe of progressive bloggers from which to sample. Although a small number of bloggers achieve national reach and maintain a large readership, the blogosphere, by virtue of its decentralized structure, encompasses an ill-defined number of smaller progressive blogs. To address this problem, blogger distribution lists from progressive organizations were employed to identify those bloggers who maintain a high level of progressive political activity at the state and local levels. These lists, when coupled with a separate list of front-page contributors to national blogs, produce a cross-section of the progressive blogosphere from which to sample.

The national list includes twenty contributors to high-traffic blogs like Daily Kos and MyDD. It was constructed with input from blogger Chris Bowers of Open Left. The three distribution lists come from the organizations Blogs United, the Liberal Blog Advertising Network, and Fifty State Blogger. Blogs United has roughly 200–250 members and is an organization that describes itself as "a group by and for local and regional progressive political bloggers." The Liberal Blog Advertising network maintains a list of roughly 120 national bloggers whose blogs receive less traffic than the websites represented in the high traffic list. Fifty State Blogger reaches state bloggers who were funded in 2006 by the organization BlogPac. Collectively, these sources constitute a representative cross-section of the progressive blogosphere, consisting of high-profile national bloggers, low-profile national bloggers, state bloggers, and local/regional bloggers.

Allowing for a very high degree of overlap in the lists, there are approximately 250–300 bloggers in this population. Online surveys where participants self-select generally yield low response rates. In this instance, a response rate of 10 percent (generating approximately twenty-five to thirty responses) was expected. To boost response rates, Chris Bowers provided a "dear colleague" covering email to attest to the importance of the study and to inform the recipients how the survey responses would be used. The survey was in the field for a three-week period ending November 1, 2007. In total, forty-one bloggers completed the survey. The survey was brief (ten questions) and designed to be completed in twenty minutes or less.

* * *

Metrics of political effectiveness were developed to gauge how successful netroots activists were in achieving outcomes they deem important and desirable. In total, seven metrics were used to assess netroots political effectiveness following the 2006 election cycle. They are:

* Contesting every House seat (measured as the number of uncontested Republican House seats in 2004 and 2006)
* Building a large base of small donors (measured as the average contribution size and total donor base of the online activist organizations Moveon.org and Democracy for America)
* Online fund-raising effectiveness (measured as the winning percentage among online-funded House and Senate candidates)
* Degree of attention paid by congressional campaigns to Internet politics (measured with a scale of campaign web use that counts and weights the presence of interactive features on campaign websites, with greater weight assigned to more interactive features such as campaign blogs and hyperlinks)
* Degree of attention paid by bloggers to congressional campaigns (measured as the number of front-page and diary mentions of a campaign on Daily Kos during the period March 15 to November 6, 2006)
* Candidate convergence, or the degree of overlap in online fund-raising, web use, and blogger attention to congressional candidates
* Success of nonfederal candidates (measured as the winning percentage of candidates in statewide, state legislative, and local races endorsed by Democracy for America in 2004, 2005, and 2006).

Notes

Notes for Chapter 2

1. Douglas B. Craig, *Fireside Politics: Radio and Political Culture in the United States, 1920–1940* (Baltimore: Johns Hopkins University Press, 2000); F. Christopher Arterton, *Teledemocracy: Can Technology Protect Democracy?* (Beverly Hills, CA: Sage, 1987); Alvin Toffler, *The Third Wave* (New York: Bantam, 1980).

2. Craig, *Fireside Politics.*

3. Jeffrey B. Abramson, F. Christopher Arterton, and Gary R. Orren, *The Electronic Commonwealth: The Impact of New Technology on Democratic Politics* (New York: Basic, 1988).

4. Arterton, *Teledemocracy.*

5. Curiously, it would not be the last time that the son of a former president who failed to win the popular vote attained the White House as a consequence of the actions of another branch of the federal government.

6. Gerald J. Baldasty, *The Commercialization of News in the Nineteenth Century* (Madison: University of Wisconsin Press, 1992).

7. Culver G. Smith, *The Press, Politics, and Patronage* (Athens: University of Georgia Press, 1977).

8. Baldasty, *The Commercialization of News.*

9. Thomas C. Leonard, *News for All: America's Coming-of-Age with the Press* (New York: Oxford University Press, 1995).

10. Paul Starr, *The Creation of the Media: The Origins of Modern Communications* (New York: Basic, 2004).

11. Leonard, *News for All.*

12. Smith, *The Press, Politics, and Patronage.*

13. Donald Lewis Shaw, "At the Crossroads: Change and Continuity in American Press News, 1820–1860," *Journalism History* 8, no. 2 (Summer 1981): 38–50; Smith, *The Press, Politics, and Patronage;* Baldasty, *The Commercialization of News.*

14. Morton Keller, *America's Three Regimes: A New Political History* (New York: Oxford University Press, 2007).

15. Smith, *The Press, Politics, and Patronage.*

16. Keller, *America's Three Regimes.*

17. Richard P. McCormick, *The Second American Party System: Party Formation in the Jacksonian Era* (Chapel Hill: University of North Carolina Press, 1966).

18. Mark Wahlgren Summers, *The Press Gang: Newspapers and Politics, 1850–1878* (Chapel Hill: University of North Carolina Press, 1994).

19. Shaw, "At the Crossroads."

20. The name came from the practice of sending reporters to the harbor to gather news from Europe as it came in by ship.

21. George H. Douglas, *The Golden Age of the Newspaper* (Westport, CT: Greenwood, 1999); Summers, *The Press Gang.*

22. Smith, *The Press, Politics, and Patronage.*

23. Baldasty, *The Commercialization of News.*

24. Richard L. Kaplan, *Politics and the American Press: The Rise of Objectivity, 1865–1920* (New York: Cambridge University Press, 2002).

25. Summers, *The Press Gang.*

26. Tom Reilly, "Lincoln-Douglas Debates of 1858 Forced New Role on the Press," *Journalism Quarterly* 56, no. 4 (Winter 1979).

27. Summers, *The Press Gang.*

28. Lorman A. Ratner and Dwight L. Teeter Jr., *Fanatics and Fire-Eaters: Newspapers and the Coming of the Civil War* (Urbana: University of Illinois Press, 2003); Jeffrey B. Rutenbeck, "Newspaper Trends in the 1870s: Proliferation, Popularization, and Political Independence," *Journalism Quarterly* 72 (1995): 361–375.

29. Summers, *The Press Gang.*

30. Smith, *The Press, Politics, and Patronage.*

31. James H. Trietsch, *The Printer and the Prince: A Study of the Influence of Horace Greeley upon Abraham Lincoln as Candidate and President* (New York: Exposition, 1955).

32. Keller, *America's Three Regimes.*

33. Richard Carwardine, "Abraham Lincoln and the Fourth Estate: The White House and the Press during the American Civil War," *American Nineteenth-Century History* 7, no. 1 (March 2006): 1–27.

34. Ibid.

35. Ibid.

36. Summers, *The Press Gang*, 33.

37. Craig, *Fireside Politics.*

38. Ibid., 4.

39. C. M. Jansky Jr., "The Contribution of Herbert Hoover to Broadcasting," *Journal of Broadcasting* 3 (1957): 241–249.

40. Robert J. Brown, *Manipulating the Ether: The Power of Broadcast Radio in Thirties America* (Jefferson, NC: McFarland, 1998).

41. Brian Regal, *Radio: The Life Story of a Technology* (Westport, CT: Greenwood, 2005).

42. Craig, *Fireside Politics*; Brown, *Manipulating the Ether.*

43. Stephen Ponder, *Managing the Press: Origins of the Media Presidency, 1897–1933* (New York: St. Martin's, 1998).

44. Maybe because radio was still too small a medium to make much difference, Harding hedged against bad coverage by maintaining close ties to the reporters assigned to him so they would refrain from covering his womanizing, gambling, and illegal drinking (often with them) during Prohibition.

45. Joy Elizabeth Hayes, "Did Herbert Hoover Broadcast the First Fireside Chat? Rethinking the Origins of Roosevelt's Radio Genius," *Journal of Radio Studies* 7, no. 1

(2000): 76–92; Betty Houchin Winfield, *FDR and the News Media* (Urbana: University of Illinois Press, 1990); Ponder, *Managing the Press.*

46. Michael X. Delli Carpini, "Radio's Political Past," *Media Studies Journal* 7, no. 3 (1993): 23.

47. Ibid.

48. Jansky, "The Contribution of Herbert Hoover to Broadcasting."

49. Martin Carcasson, "Herbert Hoover and the Presidential Campaign of 1932: The Failure of Apologia," *Presidential Studies Quarterly* 28, no. 2 (Spring 1998): 349–365.

50. Delli Carpini, "Radio's Political Past."

51. Ibid., 26.

52. Hayes, "Did Herbert Hoover Broadcast the First Fireside Chat?"

53. David Michael Ryfe, "Franklin Roosevelt and the Fireside Chats," *Journal of Communication* 49, no. 4 (1999): 80–103; Louis Liebovich, *Bylines in Despair: Herbert Hoover, the Great Depression, and the U.S. News Media* (Westport, CT: Praeger, 1994).

54. Winfield, *FDR and the News Media.*

55. Ibid.

56. Richard W. Steele, *Propaganda in an Open Society: The Roosevelt Administration and the Media, 1933–1941* (Westport, CT: Greenwood, 1985); Brown, *Manipulating the Ether*; Ryfe, "Franklin Roosevelt and the Fireside Chats."

57. Ryfe, "Franklin Roosevelt and the Fireside Chats"; Steele, *Propaganda in an Open Society.*

58. Ryfe, "Franklin Roosevelt and the Fireside Chats."

59. Steele, *Propaganda in an Open Society.*

60. Brown, *Manipulating the Ether.*

61. Ibid.

62. Ibid.

63. Elmer E. Cornwell, *Presidential Leadership of Public Opinion* (Bloomington: Indiana University Press, 1965).

64. Ryfe, "Franklin Roosevelt and the Fireside Chats."

65. Davis W. Houck, *Rhetoric as Currency: Hoover, Roosevelt, and the Great Depression* (College Station: Texas A&M University Press, 2001).

66. Brown, *Manipulating the Ether.*

67. Hayes, "Did Herbert Hoover Broadcast the First Fireside Chat?"

68. Steele, *Propaganda in an Open Society.*

69. Robert J. Donovan and Ray Scherer, *Unsilent Revolution: Television News and American Public Life, 1948–1991* (New York: Cambridge University Press, 1992).

70. Abramson, Arterton, and Orren, *The Electronic Commonwealth*, 7.

71. Stephen C. Wood, "Television's First Political Spot Ad Campaign: Eisenhower Answers America," *Presidential Studies Quarterly* 20 (1990): 265–283; Noel L. Griese, "Rosser Reeves and the 1952 Eisenhower TV Spot Blitz," *Journal of Advertising* 4 (1975): 34–38.

72. Wood, "Television's First Political Spot Ad Campaign"; Mary Ann Watson, "The Kennedy-Television Alliance," in J. Richard Snyder, ed., *John F. Kennedy: Person, Policy, Presidency* (Wilmington, DE: Scholarly Resources, 1988), 45–54.

73. Wood, "Television's First Political Spot Ad Campaign."

74. Steve M. Barkin, "Eisenhower's Secret Strategy: Television Planning in the 1952 Campaign," *European Journal of Marketing* 20, no. 5 (June 1986): 18–28.

75. Barkin, "Eisenhower's Secret Strategy," 19.

76. Edwin Diamond and Stephen Bates, *The Spot: The Rise of Political Advertising on Television* (Cambridge, MA: MIT Press, 1988).

77. Wood, "Television's First Political Spot Ad Campaign," 277.

78. Griese, "Rosser Reeves and the 1952 Eisenhower TV Spot Blitz."

79. Diamond and Bates, *The Spot*.

80. Vito N. Silvestri, *Becoming JFK: A Profile in Communication* (Westport, CT: Praeger, 2000).

81. Craig Allen, *Eisenhower and the Mass Media: Peace, Prosperity, and Prime-Time TV* (Chapel Hill: University of North Carolina Press, 1993).

82. Donovan and Scherer, *Unsilent Revolution*.

83. Allen, *Eisenhower and the Mass Media*.

84. James N. Druckman, "The Power of Television Images: The First Kennedy-Nixon Debate Revisited," *Journal of Politics* 65, no. 2 (May 2003): 559–571; Alan Schroeder, *Presidential Debates: Forty Years of High-Risk TV* (New York: Columbia University Press, 2000); Watson, "The Kennedy-Television Alliance"; Donovan and Scherer, *Unsilent Revolution*.

85. Schroeder, *Presidential Debates*.

86. Silvestri, *Becoming JFK*.

87. Lori Cox Han, *Governing from Center Stage: White House Communication Strategies during the Television Age of Politics* (Cresskill, NJ: Hampton, 2001); Roderick P. Hart, *The Sound of Leadership: Presidential Communication in the Modern Age* (Chicago: University of Chicago Press, 1987); Silvestri, *Becoming JFK*; Donovan and Scherer, *Unsilent Revolution*.

88. Joseph P. Berry Jr., *John F. Kennedy and the Media: The First Television President* (Lanham, MD: University Press of America, 1987).

89. Donovan and Scherer, *Unsilent Revolution*, 110.

90. Joe McGinniss, *The Selling of the President 1968* (New York: Trident, 1969), 62.

91. Donovan and Scherer, *Unsilent Revolution*.

92. Robert E. Denton Jr., *The Primetime Presidency of Ronald Reagan: The Era of the Television Presidency* (Westport, CT: Praeger, 1988).

93. Charles H. Fant, "Televising Presidential Conventions, 1952–1980," *Journal of Communication* 30, no. 4 (1980): 130–139.

94. Donovan and Scherer, *Unsilent Revolution*.

95. McGinniss, *The Selling of the President 1968*.

96. Scott Keeter, "The Illusion of Intimacy: Television and the Role of Candidate Personal Qualities in Voter Choice," *Public Opinion Quarterly* 51, no. 3 (Autumn 1987): 344–358; Kurt Lang and Gladys Engel Lang, *Politics and Television* (Chicago: Quadrangle, 1968); Kurt Lang and Gladys Engel Lang, "The Television Personality in Politics: Some Considerations," *Public Opinion Quarterly* 20, no. 1 (Spring 1956): 103–112.

97. Han, *Governing from Center Stage*.

98. Cary R. Covington et al., "Shaping a Candidate's Image in the Press: Ronald Reagan and the 1980 Presidential Election," *Political Research Quarterly* 46, no. 4 (December 1993): 783–798; David L. Paletz and K. Kendall Guthriel, "Three Faces of Ronald

Reagan," *Journal of Communication* 37 (Autumn 1987): 7–23; Roberta Glaros and Bruce Miroff, "Watching Ronald Reagan: Viewers' Reactions to the President on Television," *Congress and the Presidency* 10 (1983): 25–46, 1983; Donovan and Scherer, *Unsilent Revolution.*

99. Lang and Lang, "The Television Personality in Politics," 112.

100. Dean Alger, "Television, Perceptions of Reality and the Presidential Election of '84," *Political Science* 20, no. 1 (Winter 1987): 49–57.

101. Denton, *The Primetime Presidency of Ronald Reagan.*

102. Seymour Martin Lipset, "The Elections, the Economy, and Public Opinion: 1984," *Political Science* 18, no. 1 (Winter 1985): 28–38.

103. Alger, "Television, Perceptions of Reality and the Presidential Election of '84."

104. Richard L. Rubin, "The Presidency in the Age of Television," *Proceedings of the Academy of Political Science* 34, no. 2 (1981): 138–152.

105. E. D. Dover, *The Presidential Election of 1996: Clinton's Incumbency and Television* (Westport, CT: Praeger, 1998); Jeffrey Tulis, *The Rhetorical Presidency* (Princeton, NJ: Princeton University Press, 1987); James Caesar et al., "The Rise of the Rhetorical Presidency," *Presidential Studies Quarterly* 11 (Spring 1981): 158–171.

106. Matthew Robert Kerbel, *Remote and Controlled: Media Politics in a Cynical Age* (Boulder, CO: Westview, 1999); Thomas E. Patterson, *Out of Order* (New York: Knopf, 1993); Darrell M. West, "Television and Presidential Popularity in America," *British Journal of Political Science* 21, no. 2 (April 1991): 199–214; Arterton, *Teledemocracy.*

107. Matthew A. Baum and Samuel Kernell, "Has Cable Eroded the Golden Age of Presidential Television?" *American Political Science Review* 93, no. 1 (March 1999): 99–114.

108. Abramson, Arterton, and Orren, *The Electronic Commonwealth.*

109. Political talk radio notwithstanding.

Notes for Chapter 3

1. Quoted in Zephyr Teachout and Thomas Streeter et al., *Mousepads, Shoe Leather, and Hope: Lessons from the Howard Dean Campaign for the Future of Internet Politics* (Boulder, CO: Paradigm, 2008), 233.

2. Matthew Robert Kerbel and Joel David Bloom, "Blog for America and Civic Involvement," *Harvard International Journal of Press/Politics* 10, no. 4 (Fall 2005): 3–27.

3. Teachout and Streeter, et al., *Mousepads, Shoe Leather, and Hope.*

4. Michael Keren, *Blogosphere: The New Political Arena* (Lanham, MD: Lexington, 2006); Jennifer Stromer-Galley and Andrea B. Baker, "Joy and Sorrow of Interactivity on the Campaign Trail: Blogs in the Primary Campaign of Howard Dean," in Andrew Paul Williams and John C. Tedesco, eds., *The Internet Election: Perspectives on the Web in Campaign 2004* (Lanham, MD: Rowman and Littlefield, 2006), 111–131.

5. Joe Trippi, *The Revolution Will Not Be Televised: Democracy, the Internet, and the Overthrow of Everything* (New York: Regan, 2004).

6. Boubacar Souley and Robert H. Wicks, "Tracking the 2004 Presidential Campaign Websites," *American Behavioral Scientist* 49, no. 4 (December 2005): 535–547;

Philip Paolino and Daron R. Shaw, "Can the Internet Help Outsider Candidates Win the Presidential Nomination?" *Political Science* 11, no. 2 (April 2003): 193–197.

7. Andrew Chadwick, *Internet Politics: States, Citizens, and New Communication Technologies* (New York: Oxford University Press, 2006).

8. Although it is also the case that some of these institutions and organizations now support weblogs on their websites.

9. Lada Adamic and Natalie Glance, "The Political Blogosphere and the 2004 U.S. Election: Divided They Blog" (2005), available at http://www.blogpulse.com/papers/2005/AdamicGlanceBlogWWW.pdf.

10. Susan C. Herring et al., "Conversations in the Blogosphere: An Analysis 'From the Bottom Up,'" paper presented at the International Conference on System Sciences, Waikoloa, Hawaii, January 2005.

11. Ibid.

12. Although it is true that cable television shattered the audience that was once dominated by the major commercial networks, the decentralization made possible by the introduction of hundreds of television channels created a top-down market for smaller pieces of a mass audience. In contrast, some bloggers are satisfied writing for an audience of one.

13. Jonathan Chait, "The Left's New Machine," *New Republic* (May 7, 2007): 18–26.

14. Chris Bowers and Matthew Stoller, "Emergence of the Progressive Blogosphere: A New Force in American Politics," New Politics Institute, August 10, 2005, available at http://www.newpolitics.net/node/87?full_report=1.

15. These figures understate the size of the progressive blogosphere by not including high-visibility sites like Talking Points Memo (excluded because it is primarily an online journalism blog), Raw Story, and Huffington Post (excluded because they are primarily news portals). On the conservative side, the widely read Drudge Report, also a news portal, is excluded from consideration.

16. Mark M. Blumenthal, "Toward an Open-Source Methodology: What We Can Learn from the Blogosphere," *Public Opinion Quarterly* 69, no. 5 (2005): 655–669; Thomas J. Johnson and Barbara K. Kaye, "Wag the Blog: How Reliance on Traditional Media and the Internet Influence Credibility Perceptions of Weblogs among Blog Users," *Journalism and Mass Communication Quarterly* 81, no. 3 (Autumn 2004): 622–642.

17. Trippi, *The Revolution Will Not Be Televised.*

18. David M. Anderson, "Cautious Optimism about Online Politics and Citizenship," in David M. Anderson and Michael Cornfield, eds., *The Civic Web: Online Politics and Democratic Values* (Lanham, MD: Rowman and Littlefield, 2003), 19–34.

19. Michael Cornfield, "Adding in the Net: Making Citizenship Count in the Digital Age," in David M. Anderson and Michael Cornfield, eds., *The Civic Web: Online Politics and Democratic Values* (Lanham, MD: Rowman and Littlefield, 2003), 97–112.

20. Eagle Publishing boasts a "full range of products and services" dedicated to "conservative, pro-American ideals." See http://www.eaglepub.com/about_us.html.

21. Bowers and Stoller, "Emergence of the Progressive Blogosphere."

22. See "Daily Kos Traffic through the Years," Daily Kos, December 30, 2007.

23. Kid Oakland, "Mavens, Persuaders, Connectors, and Us," Daily Kos, May 14, 2006.

24. Chris Bowers, "Why the Blogosphere and the Netroots Do Not Like Hillary Clinton," MyDD, January 14, 2006.

25. This is not to suggest that political blog traffic is inconsequential. Bowers and Stoller (2005) found that in 2003 the top 1,000 political blogs of the right and left received on average 500,000 unique visits per day. By 2006 that figure had climbed to 3 million.

26. See the 2007 Weblog Awards, at http://2007.weblogawards.org.

Notes for Chapter 4

1. Joseph Graf and Carol Darr, *Political Influentials Online in the 2004 Presidential Campaign* (Washington, DC: Institute for Politics, Democracy, and the Internet, George Washington University Graduate School of Political Management, 2004); David M. Anderson, "Cautious Optimism about Online Politics and Citizenship," in David M. Anderson and Michael Cornfield, eds., *The Civic Web: Online Politics and Democratic Values* (Lanham, MD: Rowman and Littlefield, 2003), 19–34; Lincoln Dahlberg, "Democracy via Cyberspace: Mapping the Rhetoric and Practices of Three Prominent Camps," *New Media and Society* 3, no. 2 (2001): 155–177.

2. Benjamin R. Barber, "The Uncertainty of Digital Politics: Democracy's Uneasy Relationship with Informational Technology," *Harvard International Review* 23, no. 1 (Spring 2001): 42–47; Cass Sunstein, *Republic.com* (Princeton, NJ: Princeton University Press, 2001).

3. Dan Drew and David Weaver, "Voter Learning in the 2004 Presidential Election: Did the Media Matter?" *Journalism and Mass Communication Quarterly* 83, no. 1 (Spring 2006): 25–42; Markus Prior, "News vs. Entertainment: How Increasing Media Choice Widens Gaps in Political Knowledge and Turnout," *American Journal of Political Science* 49, no. 3 (July 2005): 577–592.

4. Arthur Lupia and Tasha S. Philpot, "Views from Inside the Net: How Websites Affect Young Adults' Political Interest," *Journal of Politics* 67, no. 4 (November 2005): 1122–1142.

5. Kirsten A. Foot and Steven M. Schneider, "Online Action in Campaign 2000: An Exploratory Analysis of the U.S. Political Web Sphere," *Journal of Broadcasting and Electronic Media* 46, no. 2 (June 2002): 222–244.

6. Thomas J. Johnson and Barbara K. Kaye, "Wag the Blog: How Reliance on Traditional Media and the Internet Influence Credibility Perceptions of Weblogs among Blog Users," *Journalism and Mass Communication Quarterly* 81, no. 3 (Autumn 2004): 622–642.

7. Andrew Chadwick, *Internet Politics: States, Citizens, and New Communication Technologies* (New York: Oxford University Press, 2006); Eric M. Uslaner, "Trust, Civic Engagement, and the Internet," *Political Communication* 21, no. 2 (April–June 2004): 223–242; Norman Nie and Lutz Erbring, *Internet and Society: A Preliminary Report* (Palo Alto, CA: Stanford Institute for the Quantitative Study of Society, Stanford University, 2000).

8. John C. Tedesco, "Web Interactivity and Young Adult Political Efficacy," in Andrew Paul Williams and John C. Tedesco, eds., *The Internet Election: Perspectives on the Web in Campaign 2004* (Lanham, MD: Rowman and Littlefield, 2006), 187–202.

9. Chris Bowers, "Building a House Landslide, Part II," MyDD, February 7, 2006.

10. Ibid.

11. Jerome Armstrong, "DCCC and Challenging all 435 Seats in 2006," MyDD, August 1, 2005.

12. Chris Bowers, "Clueless Bloggers," MyDD, January 27, 2005. Originally quoted in Roll Call.

13. Shea-Porter ran a netroots campaign that tapped supporters through the Internet and encouraged them to advertise and organize in their communities. A Tier 5 candidate given no chance of winning by strategists in either party, Shea-Porter was ignored by national Democrats and operated with limited funds and without a formal campaign office, relying on volunteers to spread the campaign message by word of mouth. Her netroots strategy, born of necessity, culminated in an upset win over incumbent Republican Jeb Bradley. See Beverley Wang, "Carol Shea-Porter's Unusual Journey to U.S. Congress," *Boston Globe*, November 8, 2006, and Congresspedia at http://www.sourcewatch.org/index.php?title-Carol_Shea-Porter#Transparency.

14. Joe Trippi, *The Revolution Will Not Be Televised: Democracy, the Internet, and the Overthrow of Everything* (New York: Regan, 2004); Jennifer Stromer-Galley, "On-Line Interaction and Why Candidates Avoid It," *Journal of Communication* 50, no. 4 (Autumn 2000): 111–132.

15. The rankings used for this analysis come from the *Rothenberg Political Report* (May 18 and November 2, 2006), the *Cook Political Report* (April 28 and November 6, 2006), and Larry J. Sabato's *Crystal Ball* (June 29, July 13, and November 6, 2006).

16. Although the three analysts use slightly different terminology to classify congressional races, they all make the same distinctions about whether a race is a toss-up, leans slightly or heavily toward one party, or is safe for one party. When at least two of the three analysts agreed on a ranking, their judgment served as the basis for classifying the race into one of the five tiers. In rare cases where the three analysts disagreed, an average of the three rankings was used to classify the contest.

17. This sequence of events makes the Lamont candidacy difficult to categorize. The criteria employed in this study necessitate categorizing the Lamont effort as a loss because the candidate was not elected to the Senate. A less restrictive view of the Lamont campaign would consider his primary win over an entrenched incumbent a significant netroots victory, and a case can be made that Lamont, much like Howard Dean's presidential campaign, was a successful dark-horse insurgent who faltered after he achieved a notable level of mainstream success.

18. Kos, "Kos Dozen, Part I," Daily Kos, November 4, 2004.

19. Netroots candidates were endorsed by Daily Kos, MyDD, and Swing State Project and raised funds through ActBlue.

20. These figures include victorious Democrats. For instance, the seven "Lean Republican" races include five victorious Democrats and two Democrats who were defeated by four points or less.

21. Kaye D. Trammell, "Year of the Blog: Webstyle Analysis of the 2004 Presidential Candidate Blog Posts," presented at the National Communication Association Annual Meeting, Chicago, Illinois, November 2005.

22. Rebecca Verser and Robert H. Wicks, "Managing Voter Impressions: The Use of Images on Presidential Candidate Web Sites during the 2000 Campaign," *Journal of Communication* 56 (2006): 178–197; Michael A. Xenos and Kirsten A. Foot, "Politics as Usual, or Politics Unusual? Position Taking and Dialogue on Campaign Websites in the 2002 U.S.

Elections," *Journal of Communication* 55 (2005): 169–185; Sonia Puopolo, "The Web and U.S. Senatorial Campaigns 2000," *American Behavioral Scientist* 44, no. 12 (August 2001): 2030–2047; William L. Benoit and Pamela J. Benoit, "The Virtual Campaign: Presidential Primary Websites in Campaign 2000," *American Communication Journal* 3, no. 3 (2000); Dave D'Alessio, "Adoption of the World Wide Web by American Political Candidates, 1996–1998," *Journal of Broadcasting and Electronic Media* 44, no. 4 (2000): 556–568.

    23. Data were not available for fourteen House campaigns.

    24. Bluerevolt, "Off Your Ass and On Your Feet!" Daily Kos, October 20, 2006.

    25. Richard Cranium, "PA-07: Joe Sestak Update," Daily Kos, October 7, 2006.

    26. FleetAdmiralJ, "Candidate Websites—Good or Bad? (Part 2)," Daily Kos, September 6, 2006.

    27. Joe Sestak for Congress, "Sestak Outraises Weldon by $300k," Daily Kos, July 11, 2006.

    28. Kos, "Introducing the Orange to Blue List," Daily Kos, June 11, 2008.

    29. Ibid.

    30. See http://democracyforamerica.com/about.

Notes for Chapter 5

    1. C. W. Nevius, "Booby-Trapped: Politicians Get Caught on Candid Cameras," *San Francisco Chronicle*, August 24, 2006.

    2. Kos, "The YouTube Effect," Daily Kos, August 24, 2006.

    3. Kos, "VA-Sen: Allen and His Racist Hate Group Friends," Daily Kos, August 29, 2006. The blog post contains a link to the article in the *Nation*. See also Kos, "VA-Sen: More on Allen's Good Racist Friends," Daily Kos, August 30, 2006; Kos, "VA-Sen: Allen Thinks Virginians Are Racist," Daily Kos, August 31, 2006.

    4. Kos, "Building a Narrative," Daily Kos, September 12, 2006.

    5. Ibid.

    6. As the blogosphere has gained broader recognition and acceptance, some progressive bloggers have rejected the "mainstream" label and prefer to call long-established press operations "traditional" media so as not to denigrate the mainstream qualities of their own medium. Nonetheless, "MSM" is still a widely utilized term.

    7. TocqueDeville, "Not This Time," Daily Kos, March 23, 2008.

    8. Ibid.

    9. Kos, "The Best Book This Cycle," Daily Kos, September 19, 2004.

    10. Lakoff's choice for a progressive philosophy is a stronger America, broad prosperity, better future, effective government, and mutual responsibility. See George Lakoff, *Don't Think of an Elephant: Know Your Values and Frame the Debate* (White River Junction, VT: Chelsea Green, 2004); and George Lakoff, *Moral Politics: How Liberals and Conservatives Think* (Chicago: University of Chicago Press, 2002).

    11. Jeffrey Feldman, "Frameshop (Intro)," Daily Kos, November 19, 2004.

    12. Ibid.

    13. Jeffrey Feldman, "Frameshop: A Day in Iraq or Healthcare for Kids?" Daily Kos, September 26, 2007.

    14. Doolittle, "Frameshop: Why Republican Government Doesn't Work," Daily Kos, September 16, 2005.

15. BlueSpace, "Frameshop: Hating America," Daily Kos, March 25, 2005.

16. Kalil, "Frameshop: We're Paying for the Deficit NOW!" Daily Kos, October 6, 2005.

17. Jeffrey Feldman, "Frameshop: Immigration Has Two Borders," Daily Kos, March 29, 2006.

18. Jeffrey Feldman, "Frameshop: Bush, Alito Use Same Talking Point in 24 Hours," Daily Kos, January 10, 2006.

19. Media Advisory, "Tom Friedman's Flexible Deadlines: Iraq's 'Decisive' Six Months Have Lasted Two and a Half Years," http://www.fair.org, May 16, 2006.

20. Hunter, "Who's King of the Friedman Units?" Daily Kos, September 2, 2007.

21. Georgia10, "Will the Media Finally Report That the Surge Has Failed?" Daily Kos, March 26, 2008.

22. DemFromCT, "Public Rejects Iraq War Despite Surge," Daily Kos, December 2, 2007.

23. Matthew Robert Kerbel, *Edited for Television: CNN, ABC, and American Presidential Elections* (Boulder, CO: Westview, 1998); Marion Just et al., *Crosstalk: Citizens, Candidates, and the Media in a Presidential Campaign* (Chicago: University of Chicago Press, 1996); Thomas E. Patterson, *Out of Order* (New York: Knopf, 1993).

24. Hunter, "Seeking a Grand Unified Theory of Wankery: The Rise of the Booboisie," Daily Kos, March 27, 2007.

25. Ibid. Hunter adds: "By God, if there is any justice in the afterworld, each of you [mainstream journalists] can spend eternity in a warm, comfortable bar with George W. Bush, alone with nothing but you, a bowl of peanuts, two mugs, and that barren moonscape of a mind."

26. Hunter, "And the Sky Will Be Made of Candy," Daily Kos, December 4, 2006.

27. DemFromCT, "No One Wants to Be a Republican," Daily Kos, March 22, 2008.

28. David S. Broder, "Broder on Politics," http://www.washingtonpost.com, May 4, 2007.

29. Atrios, "More Broder," Eschaton, April 28, 2007.

30. Chris Andersen, "David Broder Gives His Definition of High Broderism," Daily Kos, May 4, 2007.

31. SusanG, "What Brownstein Gets Wrong: Just about Everything," Daily Kos, November 27, 2007.

32. Edward J. Epstein, *News from Nowhere: Television and the News* (New York: Vintage, 1973).

33. Gerald J. Baldasty, *The Commercialization of News in the Nineteenth Century* (Madison: University of Wisconsin Press, 1992), 25.

34. Ibid.

35. "More Americans Turning to Web for News," Reuters, February 29, 2008.

36. Neil Hickey, "Is Fox News Fair?" *Columbia Journalism Review* (March–April 1998): 30–35.

37. See http://www.brooklyn.liu.edu/polk/press/2007.html.

38. The post takes issue with Klein's characterization of Representatives Charlie Rangel and John Conyers as "embarrassments." See Armando, "Joe Klein Hates Black Members of Congress," Daily Kos, May 15, 2006.

39. The issue here was Klein's interpretation of the FISA bill that bloggers contended reflected spin from Republican sources rather than an accurate reading of the legislation. See Kos, "Joe Klein, Idiot Tool of the GOP," Daily Kos, November 25, 2007.

40. BooMan, "Joke Line Is Looking Foolish," Booman Tribune, May 25, 2007.

41. Kos, "Joe Klein Is a Moron, Part . . . Heck, I've Lost Count," Daily Kos, March 6, 2008.

42. Ibid.

43. Joe Klein, "The Tone-Deaf Democrats," http://www.time.com, November 21, 2007.

44. Joe Klein, "FISA Confusion and Correction," http://www.time.com, November 24, 2007.

45. Glenn Greenwald, "Time Magazine's FISA Fiasco Shows How Beltway Reporters Mislead the Country," http://www.salon.com, November 25, 2007, emphasis in original.

46. Ibid.

47. Joe Klein, "The Tone-Deaf Democrats," http://www.time.com, revised November 28, 2007.

48. Glenn Greenwald, "Everything That Is Rancid and Corrupt with Modern Journalism: The Nutshell," http://www.salon.com, November 27, 2007.

49. Joseph N. Cappella, "Cynicism and Social Trust in the New Media Environment," *Journal of Communication* (March 2002): 229–241.

50. See, for example, Ali Frick, "Fearful Conservatives Push New Talking Point: 'This Is a Center-Right Country,'" Think Progress, November 4, 2008. For an example of blogosphere pushback against the center-right frame, see DemFromCT, "Conservative Wishful Thinking," Daily Kos, November 9, 2008.

Notes for Chapter 6

1. Kos, "My YearlyKos Keynote Address," Daily Kos, August 4, 2007.

2. Kos, "We Mourn as a Community," Daily Kos, September 26, 2007.

3. Comments by bloggers posting under the screen names Road2DC, highfive, kredwyn, vets74, Dem in the heart of Texas, and adigal.

4. Matthew Robert Kerbel and Joel David Bloom, "Blog for America and Civic Involvement," *Harvard International Journal of Press/Politics* 10, no. 4 (Fall 2005): 3–27.

5. Michael Cornfield, "Adding in the Net: Making Citizenship Count in the Digital Age," in David M. Anderson and Michael Cornfield, eds., *The Civic Web: Online Politics and Democratic Values* (Lanham, MD: Rowman and Littlefield, 2003), 97–112.

6. Joseph N. Cappella, "Cynicism and Social Trust in the New Media Environment," *Journal of Communication* (March 2002): 229–241.

7. Michael J. Robinson, "Public Affairs Television and the Growth of Political Malaise: The Case of 'The Selling of the Pentagon,'" *American Political Science Review* 70, no. 2 (June 1976): 409–432.

8. Marion Just, Ann Crigler, and Tami Buhr, "Voice, Substance, and Cynicism in Presidential Campaign Media," *Political Communication* 16 (1999): 25–44.

9. William J. Schenck-Hamlin, David E. Procter, and Deborah J. Rumsey, "The

Influence of Negative Advertising Frames on Cynicism and Politician Accountability," *Human Communication Research* 26, no. 1 (January 2000): 53–74.

10. Joseph N. Cappella and Kathleen Hall Jamieson, *Spiral of Cynicism: The Press and the Public Good* (New York: Oxford University Press, 1997); Joseph N. Cappella and Kathleen Hall Jamieson, "New Frames, Political Cynicism, and Media Cynicism," *Annals of the American Academy of Political and Social Science* 546 (July 1996): 71–84; Cappella, "Cynicism and Social Trust."

11. Roderick P. Hart, *Seducing America: How Television Charms the Modern Voter* (Thousand Oaks, CA: Sage, 1999).

12. Kenneth Newton, "Mass Media Effects: Mobilization or Media Malaise?" *British Journal of Politics* 29 (1999): 577–599.

13. Lawrence Bowen, Keith Stamm, and Fiona Clark, "Television Reliance and Political Malaise: A Contingency Analysis," *Journal of Broadcasting and Electronic Media* 44, no. 1 (2000): 1–15.

14. Glenn Leshner and Michael L. McKean, "Using TV News for Political Information during an Off-Year Election: Effects on Political Knowledge and Cynicism," *Journalism and Mass Communication Quarterly* 74, no. 1 (Spring 1997): 69–83.

15. Karin Gwinn Wilkins, "The Role of Media in Public Disengagement from Political Life," *Journal of Broadcasting and Electronic Media* 44, no. 4 (2000): 569–580; Lynda Lee Kaid and Monica Postelnicu, "Political Advertising in the 2004 Election: Comparison of Traditional Television and Internet Messages," *American Behavioral Scientist* 49, no. 2 (October 2005): 265–278; Lynda Lee Kaid, "Effects of Political Information in the 2000 Presidential Campaign: Comparing Traditional Television and Internet Exposure," *American Behavioral Scientist* 46, no. 5 (January 2003): 677–691.

16. Robert D. Putnam, *Bowling Alone: The Collapse and Revival of American Community* (New York: Simon and Schuster, 2000).

17. Robert D. Putnam, "Tuning In, Tuning Out: The Strange Disappearance of Social Capital in America," *Political Science* 28, no. 4 (December 1995): 664–682; Putnam, *Bowling Alone.*

18. Putnam, "Tuning In, Tuning Out."

19. Andrew Chadwick, *Internet Politics: States, Citizens, and New Communication Technologies* (New York: Oxford University Press, 2006); Eric M. Uslaner, "Trust, Civic Engagement, and the Internet," *Political Communication* 21, no. 2 (April–June 2004): 223–242; Norman Nie and Lutz Erbring, *Internet and Society: A Preliminary Report* (Palo Alto, CA: Stanford Institute for the Quantitative Study of Society, Stanford University, 2000).

20. John C. Tedesco, "Web Interactivity and Young Adult Political Efficacy," in Andrew Paul Williams and John C. Tedesco, eds., *The Internet Election: Perspectives on the Web in Campaign 2004* (Lanham, MD: Rowman and Littlefield, 2006), 187–202.

21. Michael A. Xenos and Patricia Moy, "Direct and Differential Effects of the Internet on Political and Civic Engagement," *Journal of Communication* 57 (December 2007): 704–718; Dan Drew and David Weaver, "Voter Learning in the 2004 Presidential Election: Did the Media Matter?" *Journalism and Mass Communication Quarterly* 83, no. 1 (Spring 2006): 25–42; Caroline J. Tolbert and Ramona S. McNeal, "Unraveling the Effects of the Internet on Political Participation?" *Political Research Quarterly* 56, no. 2 (June 2003): 75–185; Cornfield, "Adding in the Net."

22. Matthew C. Nisbet and Dietram A. Scheufele, "Political Talk as a Catalyst for Online Citizenship," *Journalism and Mass Communication Quarterly* 81, no. 4 (Winter 2004): 877–896.

23. Barry Wellman and Milena Guila, "New Surfers Don't Ride Alone: Virtual Communities as Communities," in Barry Wellman, ed., *Networks in the Global Village* (Boulder, CO: Westview, 1999).

24. DrSteveB, "How Old Are You? Community Poll," Daily Kos, February 26, 2008.

25. DrSteveB, "What Is Your Sex/Gender? Community Poll," Daily Kos, March 4, 2008.

26. DrSteveB, "What's Your Household Income? Demographic Tuesday Community Poll," Daily Kos, April 15, 2008.

27. Jerome Armstrong, "The Power of Many," Daily Kos, October 12, 2004.

28. Andrew Orlowski, "Kerry Net Chief: Cool Software Doesn't Win Elections," *Register,* December 10, 2004, available at http://www.theregister.co.uk/2004/12/10/votesbitsbytes_kerry_chief_post_mortem.

29. Kos, "Fancy Tools and Communicating Online," Daily Kos, December 20, 2004.

30. Daily Kos, "About Daily Kos," available at http://dailykos.com/special/about2.

31. Ibid.

32. Kos, "A Brief History," Daily Kos, August 5, 2004.

33. DarkSyde, "Join Me in Welcoming New Members and Readers!" Daily Kos, January 23, 2006, emphasis in original.

34. Ibid.

35. Ibid.

36. Ibid.

37. Kos, "On Community," Daily Kos, October 3, 2004.

38. For a discussion of campaign surrogates posing as bloggers, see Adam B, "Paid Shills," Daily Kos, February 27, 2007.

39. Kos, "On Community."

40. Kos, "Changing of the Guard," Daily Kos, December 6, 2005.

41. Kos, "2008 Contributing Editors," Daily Kos, November 13, 2007.

42. Ibid.

43. Kos, "Announcing the dKosopedia," Daily Kos, May 28, 2004.

44. Ibid.

45. Ibid.

46. SusanG, "Cool Tools and Stuff for Political Peeps," Daily Kos, May 15, 2007.

47. Ibid.

48. Ibid., comments by timber, rwsab, and anotherdemocrat.

49. SusanG, "One of Our Own Declares Candidacy," Daily Kos, May 26, 2006.

50. Ibid., comments by nwprogressive, katiebird, Zwoof, bejammin075, and Historical Pessimist.

51. There were more than 1,800 diary references since 2003 on metasubjects, including discussions related to or about the blog.

52. Hunter, "Meta Kos," Daily Kos, March 3, 2005.

53. Ibid. These topics may also say something about the age and income demographics of participants.

54. Kos, "Josh Goes Scoop," Daily Kos, May 31, 2005.

55. Ibid.

56. Kos, "Daily Kos and Right Wing Bloggers," Daily Kos, April 14, 2004.

57. Netroots Nation homepage, available at http://yearlykosconvention.org.

58. Kos, "Yearly Kos," Daily Kos, May 23, 2005.

59. Pastordan, "Yearly Kos Convention Update," Daily Kos, November 24, 2004.

60. Ibid., comments by Percheronwoman, annrose, and cassandra m.

61. Ibid., comments by tilden and bestopheles.

62. Ibid., comments by onoekeh, tobysmom, WTC Survivor.

63. Gina, "Wrapping My Mind around Yearly Kos," Daily Kos, June 13, 2006.

64. Ibid.

Notes for Chapter 7

1. Joe Trippi, *The Revolution Will Not Be Televised: Democracy, the Internet, and the Overthrow of Everything* (New York: Regan, 2004), 100.

2. Kevin A. Hill and John E. Hughes, *Cyberpolitics: Citizen Activism in the Age of the Internet* (Lanham, MD: Rowman and Littlefield, 1998).

3. Trippi, *The Revolution Will Not Be Televised*.

4. Jose Antonio Vargas, "Obama Raised Half a Billion Online," http://www.washingtonpost.com, November 20, 2008.

5. Monica Postelnicu, Justin D. Martin, and Kristen D. Landreville, "The Role of Campaign Web Sites in Promoting Candidates and Attracting Campaign Resources," in Andrew Paul Williams and John C. Tedesco, eds., *The Internet Election: Perspectives on the Web in Campaign 2004* (Lanham, MD: Rowman and Littlefield, 2006), 99–110; and Kaye D. Trammel, "The Blogging of the President," in Williams and Tedesco, eds., *The Internet Election*, 133–146.

6. Zephyr Teachout and Thomas Streeter et al., *Mousepads, Shoe Leather, and Hope: Lessons from the Howard Dean Campaign for the Future of Internet Politics* (Boulder, CO: Paradigm, 2008).

7. Trippi, *The Revolution Will Not Be Televised*, 101.

8. Ibid.

9. Michael Grove, "Barack Obama's Campaign Makes UK Politics Look Antiquated," http://www. telegraph.co.uk, June 11, 2008.

10. Ari Berman, "The Dean Legacy," *Nation* (February 28, 2008).

11. Joe Trippi, "Rebooting Democracy," Daily Kos, March 11, 2008.

12. Sean Quinn, "On the Road: Toledo, OH," http://www.fivethirtyeight.com, October 14, 2008.

13. Joe Antonio Vargas, "Obama's Wide Web," http://www.washingtonpost.com, August 20, 2008.

14. Ibid.

15. Ibid.

16. Berman, "The Dean Legacy."

17. Ibid.

18. Micah Sifry, "Obama, the Internet, and the Decline of Big Money and Big Media," Talking Points Memo, February 6, 2008.

19. John McCain, in his prior presidential incarnation, also tapped into a vigorous Internet following, but in 2000 the medium was too primitive to support a presidential campaign.

20. Mark Green, "7 Days: Brazlie, Huffington, Reagan, and Green on Why Obama Won So Big," Huffington Post, November 8, 2008.

21. Vargas, "Obama's Wide Web," http://www.washingtonpost.com, August 20, 2008.

22. Jerome Armstrong, "Obama Operating," MyDD, August 20, 2008.

23. Josh Orton, "Firing on All Cylinders," MyDD, August 21, 2008.

24. Dana Goldstein and Ezra Klein, "It's His Party," *American Prospect* (August 18, 2008): 13–20.

25. See Ari Melber, "Obama Network Organizes and Revolts over Spying," *Nation* (June 30, 2008): 13–20.

26. Mike Stark, "Open Letter to Obama re: FISA (from 17,000 of His Biggest Fans)," Daily Kos, July 3, 2008.

27. Mike Stark, "The Last Two Days Have Been Unbelievable," Daily Kos, July 1, 2008.

28. Jerome Armstrong, "Obama's FISA Update," MyDD, July 2, 2008.

29. Jeff Jarvis, "When Organizers Organize You," BuzzMachine, June 30, 2008.

30. Ibid.

31. Mcjoan, "Obama Supporters Organize on FISA," Daily Kos, July 2, 2008.

32. Green, "7 Days."

33. Greg Sargent, "Obama Transition Team Staffs Up Internet Outreach Crew," Talking Points Memo, November 12, 2008.

34. "Obama Hires Progressive Liaison for Transition Team," Huffington Post, November 10, 2008.

35. Sargent, "Obama Transition Team Staffs Up."

36. John Aravosis, "Finally Some Good News," AmericaBlog, November 12, 2008.

37. Jonathan Singer, "Obama Transition Names Internet Team," MyDD, November 12, 2008.

38. Goldstein and Klein, "It's His Party."

39. David Glenn, "The (Josh) Marshall Plan," *Columbia Journalism Review* (September–October 2007): 22–27.

40. Kos, "The Rise of Open Source," Daily Kos, February 11, 2005.

41. Markos Moulitsas writes about his background as a journalist in "The Cult of the Professional," Daily Kos, October 30, 2007.

42. For instance, Justin Rood moved to ABC News from Talking Points Memo. See Glenn, "The (Josh) Marshall Plan."

43. Greg Sargent, "Why Did McCain Lose His Maverick Brand?" Talking Points Memo, October 7, 2008.

44. Todd Beaton, "The Last Throes of a Desperate Campaign," MyDD, October 5, 2008.

45. Kos, "Focusing on Palin Was the Smart Approach," Daily Kos, September 18, 2008.

46. Kos, "Palin Continues to Hurt McCain," Daily Kos, October 2, 2008.

47. Ibid.

48. Thomas E. Patterson, *Young People and News,* report by the Joan Shorenstein Center on the Press, Politics, and Public Policy, John F. Kennedy School of Government, Harvard University, July 2007.

49. George Lakoff, "What Counts as an 'Issue' in the Clinton-Obama Race?" Huffington Post, January 30, 2008.

50. Beau Breslin, *The Communitarian Constitution* (Baltimore: Johns Hopkins University Press, 2004), xiv.

51. William R. Lund, "Communitarian Politics and the Problem of Equality," *Political Research Quarterly* 46, no. 3 (September 1993): 577–600.

52. Lincoln Dahlberg, "Democracy via Cyberspace: Mapping the Rhetoric and Practices of Three Prominent Camps," *New Media and Society* 3, no. 2 (2001): 155–177.

53. Marc Stier, "How Much of Communitarianism Is Left (and Right)?" in Peter Augustine Lawler and Dale McConkey, eds., *Community and Political Thought Today* (Westport, CT: Praeger, 1998), 43–70.

54. Elizabeth Frazer, *The Problems of Communitarian Politics* (New York: Oxford University Press, 1999).

55. Barry Wellman and Milena Guila, "New Surfers Don't Ride Alone: Virtual Communities as Communities," in Barry Wellman, ed., *Networks in the Global Village* (Boulder, CO: Westview, 1999): 331–336.

56. Frazer, *The Problems of Communitarian Politics.*

57. Kid Oakland, "Tikkun Olam: To Repair the World," Daily Kos, March 1, 2008 (emphasis in original).

References

Abramson, Jeffrey B., F. Christopher Arterton, and Gary R. Orren. *The Electronic Commonwealth: The Impact of New Technology on Democratic Politics.* New York: Basic, 1988.

Adamic, Lada, and Natalie Glance. "The Political Blogosphere and the 2004 U.S. Election: Divided They Blog." (2005). www.blogpulse.com/papers/2005/AdamicGlanceBlogWWW.pdf.

Alger, Dean. "Television, Perceptions of Reality, and the Presidential Election of '84." *PS* 20:1 (Winter 1987): 49–57.

Allen, Craig. *Eisenhower and the Mass Media: Peace, Prosperity, and Prime-Time TV.* Chapel Hill: University of North Carolina Press, 1993.

Anderson, David M. "Cautious Optimism about Online Politics and Citizenship." In David M. Anderson and Michael Cornfield, eds., *The Civic Web: Online Politics and Democratic Values.* Lanham, MD: Rowman and Littlefield, 2003, 19–34.

Arterton, F. Christopher. *Teledemocracy: Can Technology Protect Democracy?* Beverly Hills, CA: Sage Publications, 1987.

Baldasty, Gerald J. *The Commercialization of News in the Nineteenth Century.* Madison: University of Wisconsin Press, 1992.

Barber, Benjamin R. "The Uncertainty of Digital Politics: Democracy's Uneasy Relationship with Informational Technology." *Harvard International Review* 23:1 (Spring 2001): 42–47.

Barkin, Steve M. "Eisenhower's Secret Strategy: Television Planning in the 1952 Campaign." *European Journal of Marketing* 20:5 (June 1986): 18–28.

Baum, Matthew A., and Samuel Kernell. "Has Cable Eroded the Golden Age of Presidential Television?" *American Political Science Review* 93:1 (March 1999): 99–114.

Benoit, William L., and Pamela J. Benoit. "The Virtual Campaign: Presidential Primary Websites in Campaign 2000." *American Communication Journal* 3:3 (2000).

Berry, Joseph P., Jr. *John F. Kennedy and the Media: The First Television President.* Lanham, MD: University Press of America, 1987.

Blumenthal, Mark M. "Toward an Open-Source Methodology: What We Can Learn from the Blogosphere." *Public Opinion Quarterly* 69:5 (2005): 655–669.

Bowen, Lawrence, Keith Stamm, and Fiona Clark. "Television Reliance and Political Malaise: A Contingency Analysis." *Journal of Broadcasting and Electronic Media* 44:1 (2000): 1–15.

Bowers, Chris, and Matthew Stoller. "Emergence of the Progressive Blogosphere: A New Force in American Politics." New Politics Institute, August 10, 2005. http://www.newpolitics.net/node/87?full_report=1.

Beslin, Beau. *The Communitarian Constitution*. Baltimore: Johns Hopkins University Press, 2004.

Brown, Robert J. *Manipulating the Ether: The Power of Broadcast Radio in Thirties America*. Jefferson, NC: McFarland, 1998.

Caesar, James, et al. "The Rise of the Rhetorical Presidency." *Presidential Studies Quarterly* 11 (Spring 1981): 158–171.

Cappella, Joseph N. "Cynicism and Social Trust in the New Media Environment." *Journal of Communication* (March 2002): 229–241.

Cappella, Joseph N., and Kathleen Hall Jamieson. "New Frames, Political Cynicism, and Media Cynicism." *Annals of the American Academy of Political and Social Science* 546 (July 1996): 71–84.

———. *Spiral of Cynicism: The Press and the Public Good*. New York: Oxford University Press, 1997.

Carcasson, Martin. "Herbert Hoover and the Presidential Campaign of 1932: The Failure of Apologia." *Presidential Studies Quarterly* 28:2 (Spring 1998): 349–365.

Carwardine, Richard. "Abraham Lincoln and the Fourth Estate: The White House and the Press during the American Civil War." *American Nineteenth Century History* 7:1 (March 2006): 1–27.

Chadwick, Andrew. *Internet Politics: States, Citizens, and New Communication Technologies*. New York: Oxford University Press, 2006.

Chait, Jonathan. "The Left's New Machine." *New Republic* (May 7, 2007): 18–26.

Cornfield, Michael. "Adding in the Net: Making Citizenship Count in the Digital Age." In David M. Anderson and Michael Cornfield, eds., *The Civic Web: Online Politics and Democratic Values*. Lanham, MD: Rowman and Littlefield, 2003, 97–112.

Cornwell, Elmer E. *Presidential Leadership of Public Opinion*. Bloomington: Indiana University Press, 1965.

Covington, Cary R., et al. "Shaping a Candidate's Image in the Press: Ronald Reagan and the 1980 Presidential Election." *Political Research Quarterly* 46:4 (December 1993): 783–798.

Craig, Douglas B. *Fireside Politics: Radio and Political Culture in the United States, 1920–1940*. Baltimore: Johns Hopkins University Press, 2000.

Dahlberg, Lincoln. "Democracy via Cyberspace: Mapping the Rhetoric and Practices of Three Prominent Camps." *New Media and Society* 3:2 (2001): 155–177.

D'Alessio, Dave. "Adoption of the World Wide Web by American Political Candidates, 1996–1998." *Journal of Broadcasting and Electronic Media* 44:4 (2000): 556–568.

Delli Carpini, Michael X. "Radio's Political Past." *Media Studies Journal* 7:3 (1993): 23–35.

Denton, Robert E., Jr. *The Primetime Presidency of Ronald Reagan: The Era of the Television Presidency*. New York: Praeger, 1988.

Diamond, Edwin, and Stephen Bates. *The Spot: The Rise of Political Advertising on Television*. Cambridge, MA: MIT Press, 1988.

Donovan, Robert J., and Ray Scherer. *Unsilent Revolution: Television News and American Public Life, 1948–1991*. New York: Cambridge University Press, 1992.

Douglas, George H. *The Golden Age of the Newspaper*. Westport, CT: Greenwood, 1999.

Dover, E. D. *The Presidential Election of 1996: Clinton's Incumbency and Television*. Westport, CT: Praeger, 1998.

Drew, Dan, and David Weaver. "Voter Learning in the 2004 Presidential Election: Did the Media Matter?" *Journalism and Mass Communication Quarterly* 83:1 (Spring 2006): 25–42.

Druckman, James N. "The Power of Television Images: The First Kennedy-Nixon Debate Revisited." *Journal of Politics* 65:2 (May 2003): 559–571.

Epstein, Edward J. *News from Nowhere: Television and the News.* New York: Vintage, 1973.

Fant, Charles H. "Televising Presidential Conventions, 1952–1980." *Journal of Communication* 30:4 (1980): 130–139.

Foot, Kirsten A., and Steven M. Schneider. "Online Action in Campaign 2000: An Exploratory Analysis of the U.S. Political Web Sphere." *Journal of Broadcasting and Electronic Media* 46:2 (June 2002): 222–244.

Frazer, Elizabeth. *The Problems of Communitarian Politics.* New York: Oxford University Press, 1999.

Glaros, Roberta, and Bruce Miroff. "Watching Ronald Reagan: Viewers' Reactions to the President on Television." *Congress and the Presidency* 10 (1983): 25–46.

Glenn, David. "The (Josh) Marshall Plan." *Columbia Journalism Review* (September–October 2007): 22–27.

Goldstein, Dana, and Ezra Klein. "It's His Party." *American Prospect* (August 18, 2008): 13–20.

Graf, Joseph, and Carol Darr. *Political Influentials Online in the 2004 Presidential Campaign.* Washington, DC: Institute for Politics, Democracy, and the Internet, George Washington University Graduate School of Political Management, 2004.

Griese, Noel L. "Rosser Reeves and the 1952 Eisenhower TV Spot Blitz." *Journal of Advertising* 4 (1975): 34–38.

Han, Lori Cox. *Governing from Center Stage: White House Communication Strategies During the Television Age of Politics.* Cresskill, NJ: Hampton, 2001.

Harper, Robert S. *Lincoln and the Press.* New York: McGraw-Hill, 1951.

Hart, Roderick P. *Seducing America: How Television Charms the Modern Voter.* Thousand Oaks, CA: Sage, 1999.

———. *The Sound of Leadership: Presidential Communication in the Modern Age.* Chicago: University of Chicago Press, 1987.

Hayes, Joy Elizabeth. "Did Herbert Hoover Broadcast the First Fireside Chat? Rethinking the Origins of Roosevelt's Radio Genius." *Journal of Radio Studies* 7:1 (2000): 76–92.

Herring, Susan C., et al. "Conversations in the Blogosphere: An Analysis 'From the Bottom Up.'" Paper presented at the International Conference on System Sciences, Waikoloa, Hawaii, January 2005.

Hickey, Neil. "Is Fox News Fair?" *Columbia Journalism Review* (March/April 1998): 30–35.

Hill, Kevin A., and John E. Hughes. *Cyberpolitics: Citizen Activism in the Age of the Internet.* Lanham, MD: Rowman and Littlefield, 1998.

Houck, Davis W. *Rhetoric as Currency: Hoover, Roosevelt, and the Great Depression.* College Station: Texas A&M University Press, 2001.

Jansky, C. M., Jr. "The Contribution of Herbert Hoover to Broadcasting." *Journal of Broadcasting* 3 (1957): 241–249.

Johnson, Thomas J., and Barbara K. Kaye. "Wag the Blog: How Reliance on Traditional Media and the Internet Influence Credibility Perceptions of Weblogs among

Blog Users." *Journalism and Mass Communication Quarterly* 81:3 (Autumn 2004): 622–642.

Just, Marion, Ann Crigler, and Tami Buhr. "Voice, Substance, and Cynicism in Presidential Campaign Media." *Political Communication* 16 (1999): 25–44.

Just, Marion, et al. *Crosstalk: Citizens, Candidates, and the Media in a Presidential Campaign.* Chicago: University of Chicago Press, 1996.

Kaid, Lynda Lee. "Effects of Political Information in the 2000 Presidential Campaign: Comparing Traditional Television and Internet Exposure." *American Behavioral Scientist* 46:5 (January 2003): 677–691.

Kaid, Lynda Lee, and Monica Postelnicu. "Political Advertising in the 2004 Election: Comparison of Traditional Television and Internet Messages." *American Behavioral Scientist* 49:2 (October 2005): 265–278.

Kaplan, Richard L. *Politics and the American Press: The Rise of Objectivity, 1865–1920.* New York: Cambridge University Press, 2002.

Keeter, Scott. "The Illusion of Intimacy: Television and the Role of Candidate Personal Qualities in Voter Choice." *Public Opinion Quarterly* 51:3 (Autumn 1987): 344–358.

Keller, Morton. *America's Three Regimes: A New Political History.* New York: Oxford University Press, 2007.

Kerbel, Matthew Robert. *Edited for Television: CNN, ABC, and American Presidential Elections.* Boulder, CO: Westview, 1998.

———. *Remote and Controlled: Media Politics in a Cynical Age.* Boulder, CO: Westview, 1999.

Kerbel, Matthew Robert, and Joel David Bloom. "Blog for America and Civic Involvement." *Harvard International Journal of Press/Politics* 10:4 (Fall 2005): 3–27.

Keren, Michael. *Blogosphere: The New Political Arena.* Lanham, MD: Lexington, 2006.

Lakoff, George. *Don't Think of an Elephant: Know Your Values and Frame the Debate.* White River Junction, VT: Chelsea Green, 2004.

———. *Moral Politics: How Liberals and Conservatives Think.* Chicago: University of Chicago Press, 2002.

Lang, Kurt, and Gladys Engel Lang. *Politics and Television.* Chicago: Quadrangle, 1968.

———. "The Television Personality in Politics: Some Considerations." *Public Opinion Quarterly* 20:1 (Spring 1956): 103–112.

Leonard, Thomas C. *News for All: America's Coming-of-Age with the Press.* New York: Oxford University Press, 1995.

Leshner, Glenn, and Michael L. McKean. "Using TV News for Political Information during an Off-Year Election: Effects on Political Knowledge and Cynicism." *Journalism and Mass Communication Quarterly* 74:1 (Spring 1997): 69–83.

Liebovich, Louis. *Bylines in Despair: Herbert Hoover, the Great Depression, and the U.S. News Media.* Westport, CT: Praeger, 1994.

Lipset, Seymour Martin. "The Elections, the Economy, and Public Opinion: 1984." *PS* 18:1 (Winter 1985): 28–38.

Lund, William R. "Communitarian Politics and the Problem of Equality." *Political Research Quarterly* 46:3 (September 1993): 577–600.

Lupia, Arthur, and Tasha S. Philpot. "Views from Inside the Net: How Websites Affect Young Adults' Political Interest." *Journal of Politics* 67:4 (November 2005): 1122–1142.

Maihafer, Harry J. *War of Words: Abraham Lincoln and the Civil War Press.* Washington, DC: Brassey's, 2001.

McCormick, Richard P. *The Second American Party System: Party Formation in the Jacksonian Era.* Chapel Hill: University of North Carolina Press, 1966.

McGinniss, Joe. *The Selling of the President 1968.* New York: Trident, 1969.

Melber, Ari. "Obama Network Organizes and Revolts over Spying." *Nation* (June 30, 2008).

Newton, Kenneth. "Mass Media Effects: Mobilization or Media Malaise?" *British Journal of Politics* 29 (1999): 577–599.

Nie, Norman, and Lutz Erbring. *Internet and Society: A Preliminary Report.* Palo Alto, CA: Stanford Institute for the Quantitative Study of Society, Stanford University, 2000.

Nisbet, Matthew C., and Dietram A. Scheufele. "Political Talk as a Catalyst for Online Citizenship." *Journalism and Mass Communication Quarterly* 81:4 (Winter 2004): 877–896.

Paletz, David L., and K. Kendall Guthriel. "Three Faces of Ronald Reagan." *Journal of Communication* 37 (Autumn 1987): 7–23.

Paolino, Philip, and Daron R. Shaw. "Can the Internet Help Outsider Candidates Win the Presidential Nomination?" *PS* 11:2 (April 2003): 193–197.

Patterson, Thomas E. *Out of Order.* New York: Alfred A. Knopf, 1993.

———. *Young People and News.* A report from the Joan Shorenstein Center on the Press, Politics, and Public Policy, John F. Kennedy School of Government, Harvard University, July 2007.

Ponder, Stephen. *Managing the Press: Origins of the Media Presidency, 1897–1933.* New York: St. Martin's, 1998.

Postelnicu, Monica, Justin D. Martin, and Kristen D. Landreville. "The Role of Campaign Web Sites in Promoting Candidates and Attracting Campaign Resources." In Andrew Paul Williams and John C. Tedesco, eds., *The Internet Election: Perspectives on the Web in Campaign 2004.* Lanham, MD: Rowman and Littlefield, 2006, 99–110.

Prior, Markus. "News vs. Entertainment: How Increasing Media Choice Widens Gaps in Political Knowledge and Turnout." *American Journal of Political Science* 49, no. 3 (July 2005): 577–592.

Puopolo, Sonia. "The Web and U.S. Senatorial Campaigns 2000." *American Behavioral Scientist* 44:12 (August 2001): 2030–2047.

Putnam, Robert D. *Bowling Alone: The Collapse and Revival of American Community.* New York: Simon and Schuster, 2000.

———. "Tuning In, Tuning Out: The Strange Disappearance of Social Capital in America." *PS* 28:4 (December 1995): 664–682.

Ratner, Lorman A., and Dwight L. Teeter Jr. *Fanatics and Fire-eaters: Newspapers and the Coming of the Civil War.* Urbana: University of Illinois Press, 2003.

Regal, Brian. *Radio: The Life Story of a Technology.* Westport, CT: Greenwood, 2005.

Reilly, Tom. "Lincoln-Douglas Debates of 1858 Forced New Role on the Press." *Journalism Quarterly* 56:4 (Winter 1979).

Robinson, Michael J. "Public Affairs Television and the Growth of Political Malaise: The Case of 'The Selling of the Pentagon.'" *American Political Science Review* 70:2 (June 1996): 409–432.

Rubin, Richard L. "The Presidency in the Age of Television." *Proceedings of the Academy of Political Science* 34:2 (1981): 138–152.

Rutenbeck, Jeffrey B. "Newspaper Trends in the 1870s: Proliferation, Popularization, and Political Independence." *Journalism Quarterly* 72 (1995): 361–375.

Ryfe, David Michael. "Franklin Roosevelt and the Fireside Chats." *Journal of Communication* 49:4 (1999): 80–103.

Schenck-Hamlin, William J., David E. Procter, and Deborah J. Rumsey. "The Influence of Negative Advertising Frames on Cynicism and Politician Accountability." *Human Communication Research* 26:1 (January 2000): 53–74.

Schroeder, Alan. *Presidential Debates: Forty Years of High-Risk TV.* New York: Columbia University Press, 2000.

Shaw, Donald Lewis. "At the Crossroads: Change and Continuity in American Press News, 1820–1860." *Journalism History* 8:2 (Summer 1981): 38–50.

Silvestri, Vito N. *Becoming JFK: A Profile in Communication.* Westport, CT: Praeger, 2000.

Smith, Culver G. *The Press, Politics, and Patronage.* Athens: University of Georgia Press, 1977.

Souley, Boubacar, and Robert H. Wicks. "Tracking the 2004 Presidential Campaign Websites." *American Behavioral Scientist* 49:4 (December 2005): 535–547.

Starr, Paul. *The Creation of the Media: The Origins of Modern Communications.* New York: Basic, 2004.

Steele, Richard W. *Propaganda in an Open Society: The Roosevelt Administration and the Media, 1933–1941.* Westport, CT: Greenwood, 1985.

Stier, Marc. "How Much of Communitarianism Is Left (and Right)?" In Peter Augustine Lawler and Dale McConkey, eds., *Community and Political Thought Today.* Westport, CT: Praeger, 1998, 43–70.

Stromer-Galley, Jennifer. "On-Line Interaction and Why Candidates Avoid It." *Journal of Communication* 50:4 (Autumn 2000): 111–132.

Stromer-Galley, Jennifer, and Andrea B. Baker. "Joy and Sorrow of Interactivity on the Campaign Trail: Blogs in the Primary Campaign of Howard Dean." In Andrew Paul Williams and John C. Tedesco, eds., *The Internet Election: Perspectives on the Web in Campaign 2004.* Lanham, MD: Rowman and Littlefield, 2006, 111–131.

Summers, Mark Wahlgren. *The Press Gang: Newspapers and Politics, 1850–1878.* Chapel Hill: University of North Carolina Press, 1994.

Sunstein, Cass. *Republic.com.* Princeton, NJ: Princeton University Press, 2001.

Teachout, Zephyr, and Thomas Streeter et al. *Mousepads, Shoe Leather, and Hope: Lessons from the Howard Dean Campaign for the Future of Internet Politics.* Boulder, CO: Paradigm, 2008.

Tedesco, John C. "Web Interactivity and Young Adult Political Efficacy." In Andrew Paul Williams and John C. Tedesco, eds., *The Internet Election: Perspectives on the Web in Campaign 2004.* Lanham, MD: Rowman and Littlefield, 2006, 187–202.

Toffler, Alvin. *The Third Wave.* New York: Bantam, 1980.

Tolbert, Caroline J., and Ramona S. McNeal. "Unraveling the Effects of the Internet on Political Participation?" *Political Research Quarterly* 56:2 (June 2003): 175–185.

Trammel, Kaye D. "The Blogging of the President." In Andrew Paul Williams, and John C. Tedesco, eds., *The Internet Election: Perspectives on the Web in Campaign 2004.* Lanham, MD: Rowman and Littlefield, 2006, 133–146.

———. "Year of the Blog: Webstyle Analysis of the 2004 Presidential Candidate Blog Posts." Presented at the National Communication Association Annual Meeting, Chicago, Illinois, November 2005.

Trietsch, James H. *The Printer and the Prince: A Study of the Influence of Horace Greeley upon Abraham Lincoln as Candidate and President.* New York: Exposition, 1955.

Trippi, Joe. *The Revolution Will Not Be Televised: Democracy, the Internet, and the Overthrow of Everything.* New York: Regan, 2004.

Tulis, Jeffrey. *The Rhetorical Presidency.* Princeton, NJ: Princeton University Press, 1987.

Uslaner, Eric M. "Trust, Civic Engagement, and the Internet." *Political Communication* 21:2 (April–June 2004): 223–242.

Verser, Rebecca, and Robert H. Wicks. "Managing Voter Impressions: The Use of Images on Presidential Candidate Web Sites During the 2000 Campaign." *Journal of Communication* 56 (2006): 178–197.

Watson, Mary Ann. "The Kennedy-Television Alliance." In J. Richard Snyder, ed., *John F. Kennedy: Person, Policy, Presidency.* Wilmington, DE: Scholarly Resources, 1988, 45–54.

Wellman, Barry, and Milena Guila. "Net Surfers Don't Ride Alone: Virtual Communities as Communities." In Barry Wellman, ed., *Networks in the Global Village.* Boulder, CO: Westview, 1999, 331–366.

West, Darrell M. "Television and Presidential Popularity in America." *British Journal of Political Science* 21:2 (April 1991): 199–214.

Wilkins, Karin Gwinn. "The Role of Media in Public Disengagement from Political Life." *Journal of Broadcasting and Electronic Media* 44:4 (2000): 569–580.

Winfield, Betty Houchin. *FDR and the News Media.* Urbana: University of Illinois Press, 1990.

Wood, Stephen C. "Television's First Political Spot Ad Campaign: Eisenhower Answers America." *Presidential Studies Quarterly* 20 (1990): 265–283.

Xenos, Michael A., and Kirsten A. Foot. "Politics as Usual, or Politics Unusual? Position Taking and Dialogue on Campaign Websites in the 2002 U.S. Elections." *Journal of Communication* 55 (2005): 169–185.

Xenos, Michael A., and Patricia Moy. "Direct and Differential Effects of the Internet on Political and Civic Engagement." *Journal of Communication* 57 (December 2007): 704–718.

Index

open source model of development,
4–6, 46–47; opposition to Democratic
establishment, 1–2, 3, 6–8, 11–12, 52;
opposition to mainstream journalists,
8, 9, 107–9; outcomes sought, 8–9;
politics of community, 11; power in
small numbers, 6; right blogosphere,
similarities with, 42–44; state and
local level, 10, 14, 37; transformational
potential, 3–4, 37–38. *See also* bloggers
neutrality, as unprincipled, 104–5
Newberry, Sterling (blogger), 96
New Deal, 16, 17, 29
New Direction (blogger), 113–14
New Republic, 44
newspaper readers, 116
newspapers, Jackson era, 16, 17–20, 103,
104–5; commercialism, rise of, 21–22;
editors as kingmakers, 22–23, 24, 29;
editors as party officials, 19–20; literacy
and, 18–19; management technique, 19,
23; patronage and, 18
news portals, 45
New York City Kossacks, 127
New York Times, 30, 97
New York Tribune, 22–23
Nixon, Richard, 4, 17, 32–36, 38, 131
Nixon-Kennedy debates, 32–36
nonfederal candidates, 64, 82–84
Nordhoff, Charles, 24

Obama, Barack, 2, 38, 110, 111, 132,
133; hybrid campaigning and, 137–48;
Internet operation, 4, 64; March 2008
speech on race relations, 94; online
fund-raising, 69, 135; postpartisanship
rhetoric, 12; victory engineered by
outsiders, 7
Obama campaign: campaign website,
138–40; on Facebook, 139, 140;
Internet governance and, 146–48; local
organizers and volunteer workers, 137–
38; mybarackobama.com (MyBO), 139,
145–46; netroots and, 143–46; social
networking, 139–40; unconventional
approaches, 142
Obama's Online Operation (Triple O), 140

objectivity model, 104, 150–51
officials, elected, 50, 51
Olbermann, Keith, 153
Open Left, 1, 58, 82, 147
open source model, 4–6, 46–47, 119,
135, 148–51; blogging as journalism,
148–49, 150; hybrid campaigning,
133–48; objectivity model and, 150–51
open thread, 120
opinion leaders, attacks on, 107–9
Orange to Blue list, 82
Orton, Josh, 143–44
Orvetti (blogger), 120

page views, 44–45, 49
Pajamas Media, 47–48
Palin, Sarah, 137, 151–52
participatory politics, 12, 20
party committees, 50, 51
Pastordan (blogger), 127–28
patronage, 17–18, 21
Paul, Ron, 69, 141
Perot, Ross, 155
Phillips, Macon, 147
policy, framing, 96–99
political action committees (PACs), 50
political culture, centered on television,
36–37
political figures, unelected, 50, 51
political interest, 61
political success, metrics of, 13–14
political websites, 42
Political Wire, 13, 45, 120
politics, centralized versus accessible, 5,
36–37
politics of community, 11
polls, 32
polls, online, 118
postal laws, Jackson era, 19–20
power, 103, 109; battle between bloggers
and establishment, 1–2, 3, 6–8, 11–12
powerlessness, television and, 115
PowerLine, 43, 45, 48
power of many, 119–20, 129
press conferences, 32
Primary Colors, 109
prime time, 28

About the Author

Matthew R. Kerbel is professor of political science at Villanova University. Over the past two decades he has written extensively about the relationship between television and politics, a subject that first caught his interest when he worked as a television newswriter for public broadcasting. His books on the subject include *Remote and Controlled: Media Politics in a Cynical Age* and *If It Bleeds, It Leads: An Anatomy of Television News,* which explore the impacts of television on the political process. In *Netroots,* his seventh book, Kerbel considers the possibility that Internet politics will rekindle the relationship between politicians and ordinary people that was largely lost in the television age. A graduate of the University of Michigan, he lives in Wayne, Pennsylvania, with his wife, Adrienne, and daughter, Gabrielle.

MEDIA_{and}POWER

David L. Paletz, Series Editor
Duke University